EVERYDAY
WHOLE GRAINS

EVERYDAY WHOLE GRAINS

175 NEW RECIPES
FROM AMARANTH TO WILD RICE

ANN TAYLOR PITTMAN, Executive Editor of CookingLight

FOREWORD BY HUGH ACHESON

Oxmoor
House.

Published by Oxmoor House, an imprint of Time Inc. Books
225 Liberty Street, New York, NY 10281

Senior Editor: Betty Wong
Contributing Writer: Mindy Hermann
Editorial Assistant: Nicole Fisher
Assistant Project Editor: Melissa Brown
Designers: Amy Bickell, Allison Chi
Executive Photography Director: Iain Bagwell
Photographer: Hélène Dujardin
Senior Photo Stylists: Kay E. Clarke, Mindi Shapiro Levine
Food Stylists: Nathan Carrabba, Victoria E. Cox
Test Kitchen Manager: Alyson Moreland Haynes
Senior Recipe Developer and Tester: Callie Nash
Recipe Testers: Julia Levy, Karen Rankin
Assistant Production Director: Sue Chodakiewicz
Senior Production Manager: Greg A. Amason
Copy Editors: Jacqueline Giovanelli, Dolores Hydock
Proofreader: Adrienne Davis
Indexer: Mary Ann Laurens
Fellows: Jessica Baude, Rishon Hanners, Olivia Pierce, Mallory Short

ISBN-13: 978-0-8487-4637-7
ISBN-10: 0-8487-4637-6
Library of Congress Control Number: 2015959277

First Edition 2016

Printed in the United States of America

10 9 8 7 6 5 4 3 2 1

To Patrick, Daniel, and Connor

CONTENTS

Grape and Olive
Spelt Focaccia,
page 276

FOREWORD

I REMEMBER BARLEY. That's about it. It was in canned oxtail soup and had a slightly chewy resilience that I loved. But other than that my exposure to grains growing up was pretty much the big three: wheat, corn, and rice. I remember Dad taking some risks with brown rice, and maybe we ate Kashi cereal for a week or two, but really we were like everyone else on our block, on our street, in our town: We didn't know squat about grains.

The age of convenience is something I talk about a lot in an attempt to encourage people to cook food from scratch again. From advances in food preservation to the emergence of the freezer aisle and the creation of highly processed foods laden with preservatives, convenience made strides quickly. These are amazing advances, but we are realizing that bad health and empty calories are part of the price paid for ease. We are at a crucial moment in how we feed ourselves, and it splits us into two camps. Some, let's call them "feeders," buy into the idea that sustenance should be supplied, ready to eat, whether from a box, a can, or a fast-food drive-thru. This is food eaten for the simple result of getting full. It has no connection to the soul, with no sign that it once grew out of the ground, coaxed from the land by a real person's hand. But some of us "nourishers" know that cooking is a pleasure like no other. It feeds us with knowledge, it makes us proud, it provides healthy sustenance to the ones we love, and it gives us a chance to connect with the land around us.

As her contribution to this uprising of nourishers, Ann Pittman has crafted an ode to whole and ancient grains. Grains were once currency, a revered and treasured crop. After a hundred years of refining and homogenizing them for the sake of convenience, we are finally looking outside of the basics of wheat and corn to diversify our diet.

Luckily, we have returned to a world where a variety of grains is readily available. Grains that seemed esoteric just a decade ago are gaining prominence again. Spelt, farro, Kamut®, barley, and millet are more popular than ever. Unfortunately, until now, we have forgotten one very important thing: how to cook them. In this book, Pittman casts away the mysteries and shifts whole grains back to the center of the plate. She shows why grains have been a staple for thousands of years and demonstrates their importance in all aspects of modern foodways.

How do we get ourselves healthy again? We get back in the kitchen, all of us. We learn to cook through the deep American larder, much of which is grains. Pittman shows us how to do just that, first by defining a variety of grains and second by incorporating those into recipes for breakfast, lunch, and dinner. Even such baked goods as whole-grain cookies and cakes shine with nutty goodness. She instructs the reader on various methods for cooking grains (including popping and frying), arming the home cook with tools typically reserved for the culinary trade. From porridges to breads, smoothies to desserts, casseroles to stews, *Everyday Whole Grains* clears a path to learn about a vast category of food in a whole new way. So go to your kitchen and make it grain.

—Hugh Acheson, chef and author

Tarragon Chicken
Salad with Pickled
Grains, page 192

INTRODUCTION

"WHOLE AND ANCIENT GRAINS, HUH? Why can't you be working on a meat book," my husband asked when I first told him about this project. I took his skepticism as a challenge and used it to set the bar for this book: Every recipe here should be so good, so *convincing*, that you *want* to work it into your everyday life.

Whole grains—many of which are also ancient grains—have been hot in the American food scene for several years now, with increasing availability at supermarkets through the dedicated work of a handful of companies. Chefs have rediscovered and embraced the beautiful textures and flavors that grains can bring to every course on the menu, from now-almost-ubiquitous farro salads to crunchy popcorn ice cream sundaes. Within months of each other, I enjoyed two amazing restaurant twists on steak tartare that blew my mind: speckled with chewy rye berries at Blackbird in Chicago, and mixed with crunchy fried ancient grains at Catbird Seat in Nashville. In both cases, the grains made the dish. Chefs are having fun with these grains, using their best qualities to provide real delight at the table; home cooks should, too.

There are compelling reasons to do so. The health halo around whole grains continues to blossom during a time when excessive consumption of refined grains (and added sugars) gets pointed at for our nation's health woes, including heart disease,

weight gain, and diabetes. In a way, whole grains are nature's original comfort food, nourishment straight from the earth in perfect balance of protein, fiber, complex carbohydrates, vitamins, and antioxidants, many of which get stripped away in the refining process. The goal for most Americans is to replace much of the refined grains in our diet with more whole grains. And it's easier (and tastier) than you might think.

As Executive Editor at *Cooking Light*, I spend every day working closely with an amazing team of food editors and test-kitchen cooks who keep their eye on trends while maintaining an in-depth understanding of current nutrition news. We are constantly experimenting and perfecting recipes in order to develop innovative, creative dishes that are deliciously healthy. I've been with the magazine for 17 years, and over that time have been thrilled to witness a real revolution in the way Americans eat and cook. Folks are using more whole foods and fewer processed ones, embracing more plants and consuming less meat. Whole grains are at the forefront of this new way of eating, providing far more satisfying heft and chew than refined grains and simple starches. We're seeing a real hunger for whole-grain recipes; quinoa is almost old hat, as cooks are asking to learn more about millet, sorghum, and amaranth.

The good news is that all these grains are easily within reach, and the recipes in this book will show you how best to cook them. This book is designed to take any home cook through the familiar dishes (pilafs and breads) and well beyond, helping you to avoid the mistakes that can lead to bland or mushy results. Whole grains can be nutty, crunchy, creamy, and chewy. In fact, what I found fascinating about these grains as I created recipes for this book is their incredible range. Quinoa, for example, shines as a pilaf, hot breakfast cereal (page 48), and—with the way the cooked grains pop between the teeth—a sort of play on tapioca in a creamy pudding (page 316). Along with flavorful, yet simple preparations, I wanted to showcase some new techniques to cook with grains, and I feel that I had some real breakthroughs: I discovered that grains can be smoked, pickled, fried, popped, and creamed to dazzling results. There are delicious ways to incorporate them into your everyday life, from weekday morning breakfasts to family weekend baking to special dazzle-the-guests dishes.

As the main cook in my house, I believe that making healthy food choices for my family is an act of love—and that's why I was excited to work on this book and why I was motivated to create the most appealing and satisfying dishes possible. The recipes here have all been tested out on my family—that meat-loving husband and our twin 10-year-old boys. I could not, would not, consider a recipe successful if I was the only one who liked it: That's not enough to move the needle toward more whole grains for anyone's family. I have to say, I've been inspired by my own household conversions. My kids told me to throw out all other brownie recipes and only make the teff ones (page 305) from now on, and they literally licked their bowls clean of the creamy tomato soup made with creamed brown rice (page 142). My husband learned that he loves freekeh in his frittatas (page 64), and that a layer cake made with whole-wheat pastry flour tastes more chocolaty than one made with all-purpose (page 335); it's become such a favorite that it's now his birthday cake.

My hope is that this book provides you and your family with the same joyful discoveries.

(From left) Me with my most important critics—my sons Daniel and Connor.

GRAIN BASICS

SO WHAT EXACTLY *IS* A WHOLE GRAIN? Whole grains are the seeds of a variety of different grasses. To qualify as a whole grain, all three parts of the seed—bran, endosperm, and germ—must be present. Refined grains have had their bran and the germ removed; without these parts, about 25% of a grain's protein is lost, and at least 17 key nutrients are greatly reduced—altogether that's about half to two-thirds of the nutrients naturally found in the whole grain.

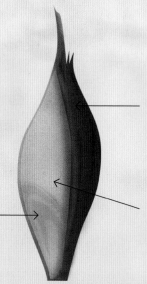

BRAN The outer coating of the grain, which protects the seed from damage and provides several nutrients—fiber being the most abundant—along with B vitamins and minerals. The unique combination of fiber, nutrients, and phytochemicals in grains is thought to help protect people from illnesses, such as heart disease, diabetes, metabolic syndrome, colon cancer, and from becoming overweight.

GERM The tiny germ is the inner embryo of the grain, meant to nourish the plant that grows from a whole grain seed. It is packed with antioxidants and other beneficial phytochemicals, vitamin E, B vitamins, and healthy unsaturated fats. Some people like to add wheat germ to their cereal, yogurt, and other foods for its nutty flavor and extra nutrition, but just note that wheat germ alone is not a true whole grain.

ENDOSPERM The carbohydrate-rich middle of the grain; this is the starchy part that is left after whole grains are milled to create refined grains, such as white flour and white rice.

Certain foods are always whole grain, such as corn (including popcorn), quinoa, and any non-white rice, while others are sometimes whole grain depending on how they've been processed. Whole grains are often processed to make them easier to use and digest. Oats, for example, are most commonly rolled or cut into small pieces for oatmeal and baking; all forms of oats—whether steel-cut or instant—are whole grain. Wheat berries can be cooked as is, coarsely ground into bulgur, or milled to make whole-wheat flour. Several whole grains, however, namely brown rice, wild rice, barley, corn, amaranth, quinoa, and teff, require little processing before they're eaten. Processed or not, a grain is a whole grain only if it contains all three parts of the seed—bran, endosperm, and germ.

Often breads, cereals, crackers, and other foods contain a mixture of whole and refined grains, as do some of the bread recipes in this book, to ensure you get just the right texture and structure. In the stores, a product is considered whole grain if it includes at least 51% whole-grain ingredients or 8 grams of whole grains per serving. A full serving is 16 grams of whole grains, which is the minimum amount you'll find in foods labeled 100% whole-grain or those that list whole wheat or another whole grain as the first ingredient.

The Dietary Guidelines for Americans recommend eating six servings of grains each day, and that at least half of those be whole—at least 48 grams of whole grain daily. Most of us eat only about one daily serving, leaving plenty of room for improvement! But it can be as simple as having a serving at breakfast, lunch, and either snack time or dinner.

WHAT ISN'T A WHOLE GRAIN

Walk through any supermarket and you'll find an array of grains. Here are foods that might seem to be whole grains—but really aren't:

Unbleached or Enriched Flour While both the unbleached and enriched aspects of flour are good qualities, they do not indicate a whole grain. I call for unbleached flour or all-purpose flour in some of the bread recipes in this book, but only in a mix with whole-grain flours.

Wheat Germ A great source of B vitamins, minerals, healthy fats, and protein, wheat germ isn't a true whole grain when the germ stands alone without the bran and endosperm. Use this product as a healthy addition to—but not a substitution for—whole-grain flour in breads, muffins, cakes, and cookies.

Wheat Bran or Oat Bran The bran stripped of the germ and endosperm can give your cereals a healthy high-fiber boost, but again, it's just one part of the grain and not a whole grain.

Pearled Barley Though extremely healthy and full of fiber, when barley is "pearled," most of the bran has been stripped from the grain. Same goes for pearled farro.

Degerminated or Degermed Cornmeal Degermination involves the removal of the oil-rich and vitamin-packed germ from the whole grain. It yields a more shelf-stable product, but one that isn't a whole grain. Look for products specifically labeled "whole-grain cornmeal" instead.

The Hominy Debate When dried corn is put through a process called nixtamalization—soaked in an alkaline solution (such as slaked lime or lye)—you end up with hominy, which is often made into masa flour for tortillas and tamales or used whole in recipes such as posole. Nixtamalization can result in the loss of some of the corn's bran, but when that loss is minimal, hominy and masa are considered whole grain. This is not universally agreed upon, however, and it's tricky if not impossible for consumers to decipher how much bran may have been lost. I have decided to include one hominy recipe in this book (page 168), but did not give hominy more coverage since it's not universally accepted as a whole grain.

WHAT IS AN ANCIENT GRAIN, ANYWAY?

Whole grains enjoy a long history. Wheat was one of the first crops to be domesticated over 10,000 years ago, most likely in Turkey and the Near East. Two types of wheat cultivated by our ancestors—einkorn and emmer—can now be found along with other specialty grains in the supermarket. The granaries of ancient Egyptians were filled with wheat and barley. Barley grains, possibly a symbol of resurrection, were also found in excavated tombs and used as necklaces decorating mummies. Some historians suggest that barley was even harvested by prehistoric humans. Rice, a staple in Asian countries, dates back to at least 2,500 BC in China. Corn is a New World crop that was domesticated in Mexico and traveled to Europe with Christopher Columbus. Amaranth was once a sacred food of the Aztecs, and the now-trendy quinoa was consumed 3,000 to 4,000 years ago by populations living in the Andes.

Given the long history of grains, in a certain sense you can say that most whole grains are ancient. But while there is no official definition of ancient grains, The Whole Grains Council, whose mission is to help people learn about and eat more whole grains, defines ancient grains as those that have remained largely unchanged over the last several hundred years. The common form of wheat that we eat today, for example, is not considered an ancient grain because it has undergone years of breeding to introduce desirable traits, including the ability to tolerate drought or high temperatures, resist insects and disease, and generate a larger crop. However, original types of wheat such as einkorn, emmer, farro, Kamut, and spelt are considered to be ancient grains. So is freekeh, a whole wheat that is harvested while still green and then roasted. Einkorn and farro

(emmer) may be the most ancient of all ancient grains, with use dating back to pre-Biblical days in the Fertile Crescent, the area between the Tigris and Euphrates Rivers, and what now includes parts of Iraq, Syria, Lebanon, Jordan, Israel, and Egypt.

The many heirloom varieties of common grains available today, including black or purple barley, red or black rice, and blue corn, qualify as ancient grains because their uniqueness has been preserved. So do grains such as teff, millet, quinoa in several colors, and amaranth. Bob's Red Mill, one of the top sources for whole grains, offers numerous ancient grains in its line of "Grains of Discovery"—amaranth, buckwheat, bulgur, farro, freekeh, Kamut®, millet, quinoa, sorghum, spelt, and teff.

Some of the allure of ancient grains no doubt stems from a vague mistrust of some aspects of our modern food supply, but ancient grains are not necessarily more nutritious than other whole grains like whole wheat, brown rice, and oats. For example, whole wheat berries and cracked wheat (bulgur) have more fiber per serving than any ancient grain. And nearly all whole grains (with the exception of brown rice and sorghum) are good sources of protein, meaning that one serving supplies 10-19% of the daily recommendation.

That said, ancient grains may have some additional benefits. As with any type of food, each variety of ancient grain has its own unique combination of essential nutrients and beneficial phytochemicals (plant compounds that are particularly abundant in grains whose husk is richly colored). Some studies have found that Kamut lowered cholesterol and cut inflammation markers better than modern wheat.

NUTRITIONAL BENEFITS OF WHOLE GRAINS

GRAIN	FIBER	PROTEIN	MAGNESIUM	FOLIC ACID
Amaranth	Good	Good	Excellent	
Barley	Excellent	Good	Good	
Brown rice			Good	
Buckwheat	Good	Good	Excellent	
Bulgur	Excellent	Good	Good	
Einkorn, Farro, Freekeh, Whole wheat berries	Excellent	Good	Good	
Kamut	Good	Good	Good	
Millet	Good	Good	Good	
Oats	Good	Good	Good	Excellent
Quinoa	Good	Good	Excellent	
Rye Berries	Excellent		Good	
Sorghum	Good		Good	
Spelt	Good	Good	Good	
Teff	Good	Good	Good	
Wild rice	Good	Good	Good	Good

WHAT ARE SPROUTED GRAINS?

Grains are seeds, so under the right conditions they can sprout and grow to form a new plant. Sprouted grains have intentionally been exposed to moisture and warmth to jumpstart the plant embryo. The growing process stimulates enzymes that boost the baby plant's access to nutrients and converts the starches into natural sugars. Advocates of sprouted grains say that they're easier to digest, richer in B vitamins and vitamin C, and taste better than nonsprouted whole grains. They can be mashed or dried and ground into flour. Still, it is still unclear if all those extra nutrients make it through the baking process. In this book, I have relied on "classic" whole grains and whole-grain flours since they are currently the most readily available nationwide; sprouted grains are still an emerging product category. If you have access to sprouted-grain products, do experiment with them and see what you like. You can look for them in the refrigerator case and on the shelf with other grains and flours, usually in specialty markets and health-oriented supermarkets.

cornmeal

millet

wheat berries

amaranth

oats

tricolor quinoa

buckwheat

brown rice

barley

KNOW YOUR GRAINS

AG Ancient Grains   **GF** Gluten Free

AMARANTH (AM-ah-ranth) has a slightly peppery, pronounced grassy flavor. The tiny grains are so small that they resemble farina or cornmeal when cooked. **AG** **GF**

WAYS TO ENJOY: When cooked, amaranth has a slightly viscous texture, like okra, so it works nicely as a breakfast porridge; you can also use it to thicken soups. Amaranth pops easily, creating fluffy, airy grains.

BARLEY is a hardy grain that is used frequently in cereals, breads, and soups. To ensure you're getting the whole-grain version, purchase hulled barley, not pearled. **AG**

WAYS TO ENJOY: With its neutral flavor and ability to readily absorb flavors, barley is a chameleon among grains. It can be treated like Arborio rice for risotto, added to soups and stews, or used as a base for pilafs or cold salads.

BROWN RICE has twice the fiber as white rice, along with a mild, nutty flavor and firm texture. Traditional brown rice can take 45 minutes to cook, but you can find quicker versions that are still whole grain (instant, boil-in-bag, and pouched precooked). **GF**

WAYS TO ENJOY: Reach for this whole-grain rice instead of white rice when making stir-fries, casseroles, soups, and salads.

BUCKWHEAT is a quick-cooking, gluten-free grain with a starchy interior and pronounced earthy flavor. You've probably enjoyed buckwheat flour in the form of Japanese soba noodles, French crepes, or Russian blini (pancakes). **AG** **GF**

WAYS TO ENJOY: Unless first coated with egg, (see Cheesy Buckwheat with Kale and Mushrooms, page 202) buckwheat groats cook up sticky, which makes them great for a hearty breakfast porridge. Buckwheat flour works well in pancakes and waffles, and soba noodles are delicious in soups and with stir-fries.

CORN, often classified as a vegetable rather than a grain, can be dried and ground to create cornmeal, grits, and polenta; just make sure the products you're buying aren't degermed/degerminated (see page 15). Folks often don't realize that good old corn on the cob also counts as a whole grain. **AG** **GF**

WAYS TO ENJOY: Fresh corn is tasty as is or tossed into salads, soups, or quiches. Ground corn products make for easy side dishes, such as polenta (page 232), and baked goods like corn bread (page 254). Popcorn is a whole grain, too!

MILLET is a small, round yellow whole grain that's a staple in many parts of Asia, Europe, and northern Africa. It is great in pilafs and casseroles, cooked as a cereal, and ground into flour for bread. **AG** **GF**

WAYS TO ENJOY: Toss toasted millet in salads and baked goods for a nutty crunch, or simmer and serve it with Parmesan and herbs as a side dish.

OATS are most widely available in rolled form, but steel-cut oats have become popular for their chewy texture. All forms are whole-grain, but due to differences in processing, double check the label if gluten free is desired. **AG** **GF**

WAYS TO ENJOY: A steaming bowl of oatmeal is a classic breakfast, but oats also can be added to baked goods. And the texture of steel-cut oats makes them a fine stand-in for rice in savory dishes (page 215).

QUINOA (KEEN-wah), tiny beige-, red- or black-colored seeds about the size of couscous, cook in only 10 to 20 minutes. Quinoa should be rinsed first to remove its bitter-flavored natural coating. **AG** **GF**

WAYS TO ENJOY: Quinoa is great for pilafs and salads. Also cook as a hot cereal, add to pancake and muffin batter, or stir into soups and casseroles.

RYE BERRIES are chewy, similar in texture to wheat berries, with a peppery, slightly tangy, nutty flavor. **AG**

WAYS TO ENJOY: Rye berries add a hearty flavor and texture to soups. Try them pickled as a savory and tasty addition to salads (page 139).

SORGHUM is mild and slightly sweet, like a chewier version of Israeli couscous when cooked. It requires 60 minutes or more to cook, so be patient. With the rise of all things gluten-free, sorghum flour has become more readily available. (AG) (GF)
WAYS TO ENJOY: Great to make in batches and freeze. Sorghum also can be popped like popcorn (page 31). Sorghum flour is slightly gritty and works well for hearty cookies (page 296).

....

TEFF, the world's tiniest grain, is believed to have originated in Ethiopia thousands of years ago. It contains more calcium than other grains and has a toasty, sweet-bitter (like molasses) flavor. (AG) (GF)
WAYS TO ENJOY: Whole teff can be cooked like polenta and used to thicken soups, stews, and casseroles. Teff flour becomes dense and slightly gelatinous when wet, making it good for certain baked goods that you want to be fudgy (page 305) or moist (page 294).

WHEAT VARIETIES

BULGUR is created from whole wheat berries that are cooked, dried, and cracked. It's available in different grinds for use in various types of dishes. Because bulgur is precooked, it takes only 10 minutes or so to prepare. (AG)
WAYS TO ENJOY: Choose finely ground for a creamier texture, medium for grain-veggie combos, and coarse to match the look and feel of ground meat. For the recipes in this book, I simplified by using only medium-ground bulgur.

....

EINKORN (rhymes with "nine corn"), the most ancient of all wheat varieties, has only two sets of chromosomes, just as it did thousands of years ago. Einkorn berries are considerably smaller than whole wheat berries and provide more protein. (AG)
WAYS TO ENJOY: Use as you would wheat berries in salads, soups, and side dishes. One of the most widely available einkorn flours (Jovial all-purpose einkorn flour) is 80% whole grain; you can find 100% whole-grain einkorn flour also by Jovial.

FARRO, also known as emmer, is an ancient wheat that was abandoned for other varieties with thinner outer husks. A lot of the farro you'll find at the supermarket is pearled (not whole-grain). (AG)
WAYS TO ENJOY: The firm texture of farro pairs beautifully with greens in salads and side dishes. Substitute farro for Arborio rice in a hearty risotto.

....

FREEKEH is wheat that's harvested while still green and then roasted, giving it a smoky flavor. Freekeh is sold either as an intact grain or cracked for faster cooking. (AG)
WAYS TO ENJOY: Like bulgur, freekeh is versatile enough to use in side dishes, soups, salads, and ground meat recipes.

....

KAMUT is an ancient Egyptian word for wheat and the trademarked name of Khorasan wheat. Its smooth texture and buttery flavor can be enjoyed by some people who can't tolerate modern strains of wheat. (AG)
WAYS TO ENJOY: Kamut flour offers a coarse texture that works well in homey cakes and cookies. The whole berries are good for salads and soups.

....

SPELT is thought to be a hybrid of farro and conventional wheat that originated in Europe. Spelt is called farro grande (big farro) in Italy. (AG)
WAYS TO ENJOY: Spelt flour lends a deep nutty flavor to baked goods. Try whole spelt paired with vegetables and fruit in a salad.

....

WHEAT BERRIES are wheat kernels that can be red or white, hard (higher protein) or soft (lower protein), and winter or spring, depending on when planted.
WAYS TO ENJOY: The firm texture of wheat berries works well in soups and casseroles, and also stands up well to dressing in make-ahead salads.

....

WILD RICE is a grass that grows around the Great Lakes and typically is cultivated and harvested by Native Americans. It has a strong, reedy flavor and firm texture. (GF)
WAYS TO ENJOY: Think traditional fall fare to partner with wild rice—poultry, squash, and stuffing.

wild rice

einkorn

spelt

Kamut

teff

rye berries

sorghum

freekeh

bulgur

farro

BUYING AND STORING

In the past you would have had to visit a health or specialty food store to buy whole and ancient grains, but now you'll find many of them at the supermarket. Several leading brands—Bob's Red Mill, Shiloh Farms, Lundberg Family Farms, Arrowhead Mills, Hodgson Mill, and Near East, to name just a few—maintain full displays in the rice, pasta, and flours aisle. Not all of their products are whole grain, so look for the word "whole" on the ingredient list—for example, whole wheat. Additionally, you may find the national Whole Grains Council's black and gold Whole Grain Stamp on some packaging to identify foods that are excellent or good sources of whole grain or 100% whole grain. (All pure whole grains, such as wheat berries, quinoa, and amaranth, are 100% whole grain.) Some packages also list the amount of whole grain in a single serving, although this is more common for breads and ready-to-eat cereals than for pure whole grains.

Whole grains contain naturally occurring oils, primarily in the germ. These oils can break down and become rancid if they are exposed to air, heat, moisture, and/or light for a period of time. Rancidity occurs more rapidly in whole grains that are rolled, cut, cracked, or milled into flour. (Grains should have a faint aroma or no detectable smell. A musty, oily, or off smell means that the product is rancid; these should not be purchased, and if you have any at home, should be thrown away.)

- For the freshest grains, shop from stores that appear to have quick turnover of their products and display grains away from windows and direct light.
- Look for the expiration date that is furthest into the future.
- Buy only what you plan to use within a few months.

Any grains being stored in a cupboard should be placed in a tightly sealed container. But if you have space, it's best to refrigerate or freeze whole grains, cracked whole grains, and whole-grain flours unless you plan to use them within a month or so. Sealable plastic and vacuum bags work particularly well for the refrigerator or freezer because you can get rid of as much air as possible before sealing. Label each bag with the name of the grain and the date so that you can use the oldest grains first. You still can't keep them forever. Use the smell test to check for freshness.

TERMS TO KNOW

Whole grains and groats Interchangeable terms for unrefined grains.

Cracked grains Grains ground into smaller pieces. Some cracked grains, such as bulgur and steel-cut oats, are derived from whole grains, others from refined grains.

Polished grains Grains that have been refined to remove the husk and most (or all) of the bran. Includes pearled barley.

Flakes Sliced whole grains or cracked grains that have been steamed and rolled.

Flour Grain that has been milled to a powder. Whole-wheat flour, for example, is the product of processing whole wheat berries.

Clear, airtight containers work well for pantry storage.

QUICK GUIDE TO COOKING WHOLE GRAINS

Whole grains may seem tricky and time consuming to cook, but in fact, they're easy to prepare, and there are plenty of quick alternatives, including grains that are done in less than 30 minutes (some as quick as 10 minutes). If you can boil water, you can cook whole grains. Add two more basic methods to your repertoire, and you have mastered how to cook any grain.

In general, I've found that longer-cooking, harder/chewier grains, such as wheat berries and spelt, do best when cooked like pasta—boiled in a large amount of water and then drained; you run the risk of the water boiling out and the grains scorching if you follow a pilaf-style method. But if you have a pressure cooker, you're in luck: It slashes the cook time of those harder grains by half or more; if you don't have one, no worries—a Dutch oven works just fine, too.

PASTA-STYLE METHOD

Most whole grains can be cooked just like pasta. Use a Dutch oven or a stockpot to allow room for the large amount of boiling water. Refer to the chart on pages 26-27 for the best ratio of grain to water and specific cook times.

1. Fill the pot with water, cover, and bring the water to a full rolling boil over high heat.

2. Add the grain; reduce heat, and simmer 25 to 75 minutes.

3. Drain the cooked grain through a fine-mesh sieve, and shake it well to remove the excess water.

PILAF-STYLE METHOD

This method uses only the amount of water the grains should absorb by the end of cooking. If grains cooked pilaf-style still have some unabsorbed liquid, drain them well in a sieve before serving. Use a medium saucepan with a tight-fitting lid.

1. Bring grain and liquid (see chart) to a boil; cover, reduce heat, and simmer 10 to 25 minutes.

2. Remove from heat; let stand, covered, 5 to 10 minutes. Uncover and fluff grains.

PORRIDGE-STYLE METHOD

Use a broad saucepan, deep skillet, or sauté pan with a snug-fitting lid.

1. Fill the pot with water (see chart), cover, and bring the water to a boil.

2. Stir in the grain; cover or leave uncovered (see chart), reduce heat, and simmer 20 to 30 minutes, stirring occasionally.

3. Remove pan from heat, and let stand, covered, 5 minutes. Uncover pan carefully.

These cook times are general guidelines; certain factors—such as the age of the grains and how they've been stored—can change the timing or rate of liquid absorption. As a general rule, check early: When the raw taste is cooked out but they're still chewy, they're done. Grains aren't delicate: Add more water during the cooking process, if necessary, or, if they're done before all liquid is absorbed, drain off the excess water.

HOW TO COOK A PERFECT POT OF GRAINS

GRAIN (1 cup)	PREFERRED COOKING METHOD	AMOUNT OF LIQUID (water or stock)	COOKING TIME
Amaranth	porridge-style	2½ cups	20 minutes
Barley, hulled	pasta-style	8 cups	45 to 60 minutes *Pressure cooker: Cook under pressure for 25 to 30 minutes. Release pressure; drain.
Brown Rice	pasta-style	8 cups	30 to 45 minutes
Buckwheat Groats	pilaf-style	1½ cups	10 to 15 minutes
Bulgur	pilaf-style	2 cups	12 minutes
Cornmeal, whole-grain (for polenta)	porridge-style	4 cups	5 minutes
Farro (emmer)	pasta-style	6 cups	25 to 60 minutes *Note: Whole-grain farro varies from producer to producer; some varieties are "scratched," which allow for shorter cook times. Much of the farro you'll see in grocery stores is pearled, which is not whole grain.*
Freekeh, cracked	pilaf-style	2¼ cups	20 to 25 minutes
Kamut Berries	pasta-style	8 cups	60 to 75 minutes *Pressure cooker: Cook under pressure for 25 to 30 minutes. Release pressure; drain.

Millet	pilaf-style	2 cups	20 minutes
Oats, old-fashioned	porridge-style	1½ to 2 cups	5 minutes
Quinoa, rinsed and drained	pilaf-style	1¼ cups	12 minutes
Rye Berries	pasta-style	8 cups	60 to 75 minutes *Pressure cooker: Cook under pressure for 25 to 30 minutes. Release pressure; drain.
Sorghum	pasta-style	8 cups	60 to 75 minutes *Pressure cooker: Cook under pressure for 25 to 30 minutes. Release pressure; drain.
Spelt	pasta-style	8 cups	60 to 75 minutes *Pressure cooker: Cook under pressure for 25 to 30 minutes. Release pressure; drain.
Teff	porridge-style	3 to 3½ cups (for creamier texture)	25 to 30 minutes
Wheat Berries	pasta-style	8 cups	50 to 60 minutes *Pressure cooker: Cook under pressure for 20 to 25 minutes. Release pressure; drain.
Wild Rice	pasta-style	6 cups	45 to 50 minutes *Pressure cooker: Cook under pressure for 20 to 25 minutes. Release pressure; drain.

HOW TO BAKE WITH WHOLE GRAINS

Whole-grain flours contain germ and bran, which soak up liquid during baking and add weight to the dough, creating a dense texture if you don't treat it properly. Learning the best way of incorporating them successfully into delicious baked recipes has been an exciting challenge. Many of the grains and seeds require higher amounts of hydration while at the same time need less mixing time, and sometimes combining whole-grain flours with all-purpose flour is the best way to get the crumb and texture you expect. I found this to be true with some of the bread recipes. Wherever possible, though, I've gone all in, all whole grain. I had great success with using all whole-grain flours in nearly all the desserts in this book.

In this cookbook, I've included recipes that use flours made from teff, millet, spelt, amaranth, sorghum, brown rice, buckwheat, Kamut, and einkorn. These recipes are designed to showcase the hearty texture and unique flavors of whole grains. But perhaps the easiest way to begin introducing whole grains into your everyday baking is to use white whole-wheat and whole-wheat pastry flours in place of the refined flours typically used in cookies, muffins, and breads. I favor an approach that's different from what you'll see almost anywhere else: I say go all in. Try it, at least, and know that as you stir, you might need to add a little more liquid to get the right consistency. At home, I will take any standard cake, pancake, waffle, or cookie recipe and make it using all whole-wheat pastry flour or white-wheat flour. I have always been pleased with the results, and no one in my family has batted an eye.

WHITE WHOLE-WHEAT FLOUR
This is milled from white, hard spring wheat so the color and flavor are lighter, but all the benefits from the whole grain are still there. White whole-wheat flour has a coarser texture than whole-wheat pastry flour, so if you're aiming for a delicate crumb, you should go with the latter.

WHOLE-WHEAT PASTRY FLOUR
Also known as graham flour, this is very finely milled from low-protein soft wheat and has a toasty-nutty flavor that yields tasty cookies, cakes, and pie crusts. It behaves most closely to all-purpose flour in baked goods.

Scones, cookies, quick breads, and other baking soda– or baking powder–leavened goods are fairly adaptable to whole-grain flour, and I've had good luck going all whole-grain with those. With yeast-leavened doughs, it's been trickier—just see my notes about the 10 tries it took to get my whole-wheat loaf bread where I wanted it (page 283). I advise adapting yeast bread recipes with 50% whole-grain flour and going up from there gradually if you find success; that is, try 75% whole-grain flour the next time.

ESSENTIAL TECHNIQUES AND BASIC RECIPES

AS I WORKED ON the recipes for this book, I did a lot of experimenting in my kitchen. I figured I should push some culinary boundaries, and boy did I have fun doing so. I fried cooked farro, and I fell so in love with the crunchy, nut-like grains that I started frying other cooked grains as well. They were all delicious, and it's no exaggeration to say that everyone who has tried them has fallen hard, too. (I've included lots of fried grain ideas in this cookbook.)

One day after frying a batch of leftover spelt, I thought, "What the hay," and I played around with dropping uncooked grains into the hot oil. Nearly all were disappointments, and as they were experiments, I was okay with that. But then I tried uncooked wild rice—what an incredible discovery! The uncooked grains puffed almost immediately, and when I scooped them out, I was left with a pile of light, fluffy, crunchy, slightly curved strands. They were so good that I just had to use them in a snack mix (page 102) and chocolate-coated sweet treat (page 301).

I also found creamed grains (intentionally overcooked brown rice or millet blended with milk) incredibly versatile, lending body to "cream" soups. Taking things a little further, I used this silky mixture to make a luscious ice cream (page 298) and a savory dip (page 85). I smoked grains—one of my favorite techniques—and whole-grain flour to add bold flavor without any calories. And I pickled rye berries and quinoa to make their chew that much more interesting.

Because these are new, more innovative techniques, I wanted to give ideas for how to use them across several recipes. And so the next few pages offer building-block recipes you can use for many great dishes.

POPPING GRAINS

Corn isn't the only grain that pops: Amaranth, quinoa, millet, and sorghum do, too— though I've focused on amaranth and sorghum in this book. With the smaller grains (amaranth and quinoa), popping in a dry pan works best; millet and sorghum work better with a little oil in the pan. Here's how it's done.

POPPED AMARANTH

HANDS-ON TIME: 5 MINUTES TOTAL TIME: 10 MINUTES

6½   tablespoons uncooked
      amaranth

1. Heat a large heavy Dutch oven over high heat at least 5 minutes. Spoon 1 tablespoon amaranth into pan, and check to see that seeds almost immediately start popping. If they don't, and they instead sit in the pan and burn, the pan isn't hot enough, and you'll need to start over. If they do, cover the pan (popped seeds will fly everywhere) and shake it back and forth on or just over the burner until you hear the seeds stop popping. Immediately pour popped amaranth into a bowl; repeat procedure with remaining amaranth, 1 tablespoon at a time.

MAKES ABOUT 2½ CUPS POPPED AMARANTH

Sorghum,
uncooked
and popped

POPPED SORGHUM

Unless you can find specifically labeled "popping sorghum," you need to go into this exercise with the right expectations. In my testing—using regular whole-grain sorghum—the best results I could get were about 50% of the grains popping. But it's worth it, if you just need a small amount as a crunchy garnish on a soup (see page 148). Why is it worth it? Because it's the cutest baby "popcorn" you'll ever see! And the crunch is heartier than popcorn, the flavor slightly toastier.

HANDS-ON TIME: 6 MINUTES TOTAL TIME: 6 MINUTES

2   teaspoons canola oil, divided

⅓   cup uncooked sorghum, divided

1. Heat a large Dutch oven over medium heat 2 minutes. Add 1 teaspoon oil; swirl to coat. Add half of sorghum; cook about 1 minute or until sorghum popping slows, stirring constantly.

2. Reduce heat to medium-low, and continue cooking 1 minute or until as much sorghum pops as possible, stirring constantly.

(If grains pop out of pan, cover pan and shake it frequently.)

3. Remove mixture from pan; repeat procedure with remaining oil and sorghum. Discard unpopped kernels, or reserve for another use (they're crunchy and delicious and, unlike unpopped popcorn, edible).

MAKES ABOUT 1 CUP POPPED SORGHUM

CRUNCHY FRIED GRAINS

This is my favorite discovery, my favorite technique in this book—and you'll see it used in several of the recipes. Yes, as the recipe title indicates, I am deep-frying whole grains. Why? First off, don't worry. If you keep the oil temperature as hot as specified, the grains don't absorb much oil: This does not take whole grains into unhealthy territory. More importantly, frying turns whole grains into the crunchiest, most wildly delicious little nuggets with amazing recipe versatility. They're great on creamy soups, in salads, on casseroles, and as breading. They're also a great substitute for nuts—good for folks with allergies.

Fried grains keep beautifully: up to a week in an airtight container at room temperature, or for 3 to 4 months in the freezer. I now always keep at least two types on hand (in the freezer)—one finer/smaller grain like quinoa, and a larger one like farro—and I'll sprinkle a little over yogurt, stir some into ice cream, top my mac and cheese with it, and use it anywhere else where I yearn for some crunch. The technique works best with quinoa, barley, farro, spelt, millet, and brown rice, and the frying time is the same for all.

HANDS-ON TIME: 30 MINUTES TOTAL TIME: 2 HOURS 40 MINUTES

3 cups cooked whole grains (see suggested grains above)

6 cups canola oil or peanut oil

1. Line a jelly-roll pan with several layers of paper towels. Spread cooked grains out into a thin layer on paper towels. Let stand 1 to 2 hours to dry out surface moisture, stirring grains occasionally.

2. Heat oil in a large Dutch oven until a thermometer submerged in oil registers 375°F. Do not use a smaller pot (moisture in the grains will cause the oil to bubble up vigorously). Add ½ cup cooked grains to oil; do not add more than this, or oil may bubble over. Cook 4 to 5 minutes or until grains are browned and crisp; do not allow temperature of oil to drop below 350°F. Remove fried grains from pan with a fine wire mesh ladle; drain on paper towels. Repeat procedure with remaining grains, ½ cup at a time.

MAKES ABOUT 3 CUPS

Barley
Uncooked barley (left) goes chewy when boiled (middle) and supremely crunchy when fried (right).

FRIED WILD RICE

One day, I started playing around with some hot oil, tossing in different uncooked grains to see what would happen. Most just burned, and a couple popped, dangerously sending hot oil airborne. However, something remarkable happened with the wild rice. It puffed up almost instantly and became super-crunchy; the fried grains were akin to canned crunchy chow mein noodles. You need to be sure your wild rice is on the fresh side; really old wild rice is so dried out that it won't puff. As with the Crunchy Fried Grains on page 32, these will keep up to a week in an airtight container at room temperature, or for 3 to 4 months in the freezer.

HANDS-ON TIME: 15 MINUTES TOTAL TIME: 15 MINUTES

4   cups canola oil
1   cup uncooked wild rice

1. Heat oil in a large Dutch oven until a thermometer submerged in oil registers 400°F. Add rice to oil; cook 10 seconds to 1 minute or until grains puff and float. Remove fried grains from pan with a slotted spoon or wire mesh ladle; drain on paper towels.

MAKES 3½ CUPS

PICKLED "HARD-SHELL" GRAINS

This technique works best with what I refer to as "hard-shell" grains—those with a chewy, closed texture such as wheat berries, rye berries, spelt, and Kamut. Grains with a more "open" texture such as farro or barley take on so much brine that they lose their own nutty flavor.

HANDS-ON TIME: 10 MINUTES TOTAL TIME: 2 HOURS 30 MINUTES

1½ cups cider or white wine vinegar
3 tablespoons sugar
1 teaspoon kosher salt
1 bay leaf, preferably Turkish
1 dried red chile (optional)
1 cup cooked rye berries, hard winter wheat berries, spelt, or Kamut

1. Combine first 5 ingredients in a small saucepan; bring to a boil. Cook 3 minutes, stirring to dissolve sugar.

2. Add cooked grains; simmer 2 minutes. Remove from heat; cool to room temperature. Let stand at least 1 hour before serving.

3. Store, in brine, in refrigerator for up to 2 weeks (flavor will intensify the longer it stands).

MAKES 1 CUP DRAINED GRAINS

MILLET OR BROWN RICE CREAM

Something wonderful happens when you puree intentionally overcooked, over-bloated millet or brown rice: You end up with a silky concoction that's wonderful for making "cream" soups without a lick of cream. The millet version makes a very thick mixture, the rice version a thinner cream.

HANDS-ON TIME: 7 MINUTES TOTAL TIME: 42 MINUTES

2 cups water
½ cup uncooked millet or instant brown rice
1 cup 2% reduced-fat milk

1. Bring water and millet or rice to a boil in a medium saucepan; cover, reduce heat, and simmer 30 minutes. Remove from heat; let stand 5 minutes. Pour mixture into a blender; add milk. Remove center piece of blender lid (to allow steam to escape); secure lid on blender. Place a clean towel over opening in blender (to avoid splatters). Blend until smooth (about 3 minutes).

MAKES 3 CUPS MILLET CREAM OR 2½ CUPS BROWN RICE CREAM

WHITE WHEAT PIZZA DOUGH

With this recipe, you get enough dough for two (13-inch) thin-crust pizzas. The vital wheat gluten is optional, but I do like including it because it gives the crust a little more chew; without it, the crust goes more cracker-like. Only making one pizza tonight? Stash the other piece of dough in the fridge and make another pizza tomorrow, or freeze for up to 2 months; thaw in the fridge overnight.

HANDS-ON TIME: 15 MINUTES TOTAL TIME: 1 HOUR 15 MINUTES

1 teaspoon sugar
1 package dry yeast
1 cup warm water (100 to 110°F)
1½ tablespoons olive oil
1 tablespoon white vinegar
12 ounces white whole-wheat flour (about 2½ cups)
1½ tablespoons vital wheat gluten (optional)
¾ teaspoon salt
Cooking spray

1. Dissolve sugar and yeast in 1 cup warm water in the bowl of a stand mixer; let stand 5 minutes or until foamy. Stir in oil and vinegar.

2. Weigh or lightly spoon flour into dry measuring cups; level with a knife. Combine flour, vital wheat gluten, if desired, and salt, stirring with a whisk. Add flour mixture to yeast mixture; mix on low speed using dough hook until just combined. Mix on medium-low speed for 5 minutes. Place dough in a large bowl coated with cooking spray, turning to coat top. Let stand in a warm place (85°F), free from drafts, 1 hour or until doubled in size.

3. Divide dough in half. Roll or pat each half into a 13-inch circle on a very lightly floured surface. Top as desired.

MAKES 2 CRUSTS

MORNING GRAINS

Front-load your energy bank each day with a serving of whole grains. It's easier to do than you might think! Here, you'll find recipes that get you off to a healthy start—everything from quick, workday porridge bowls to relaxing weekend dishes like frittatas, pancakes, and waffles. Whole grains make each dish hearty and filling, while fruits and veggies keep them feeling fresh and light.

Coconut-Caramel Oatmeal with Fresh Pineapple

Orange-Honey Oatmeal with Pistachios, Figs and Saffron Yogurt, page 42

Lemon-Blueberry Oatmeal with Mascarpone and Almonds

Oatmeal with Sunflower Seed Butter, Banana, and Dark Chocolate, page 42

OATMEAL BOWLS SIX WAYS

*No need to turn to packaged flavor mixes, which are surprisingly high in sodium.
Instead, whip up any one of these quick breakfasts with fresh fruit and indulgent sweet
touches. The amount of water here yields thick, hearty oatmeal; if you prefer yours
looser, use 1 cup water.*

COCONUT-CARAMEL OATMEAL WITH FRESH PINEAPPLE GF

HANDS-ON TIME: 10 MINUTES TOTAL TIME: 15 MINUTES

¾ cup water
½ cup old-fashioned rolled oats
Dash of salt
1½ tablespoons light coconut milk
1 teaspoon brown sugar
¼ cup fresh pineapple, cut into small pieces
1 tablespoon toasted flaked unsweetened coconut
1½ teaspoons prepared caramel sauce

1. Bring ¾ cup water to a boil in a medium saucepan. Stir in oats and dash of salt. Reduce heat and simmer 5 minutes, stirring occasionally. Remove pan from heat, and stir in coconut milk and brown sugar. Top oatmeal with pineapple and coconut flakes. Drizzle with caramel sauce.

> **MAKE IT FASTER**
>
> Toast a small amount of nuts (including coconut) quickly in the microwave. Place on a microwave-safe paper towel, and microwave at HIGH for 1½ to 2 minutes, checking every 30 seconds.

SERVES 1
CALORIES 266; **FAT** 8.2g (sat 5.1g, mono 1.1g, poly 1.1g); **PROTEIN** 6g; **CARB** 45g; **FIBER** 5g; **SUGARS** 13g (est. added sugars 8g); **CHOL** 3mg; **IRON** 2mg; **SODIUM** 170mg; **CALC** 11mg

LEMON-BLUEBERRY OATMEAL WITH MASCARPONE AND ALMONDS GF

HANDS-ON TIME: 10 MINUTES TOTAL TIME: 15 MINUTES

¾ cup water
½ cup old-fashioned rolled oats
Dash of salt
1 tablespoon prepared lemon curd
1 teaspoon sugar
3 tablespoons fresh blueberries
2 teaspoons mascarpone cheese
2 teaspoons sliced toasted almonds

1. Bring ¾ cup water to a boil in a medium saucepan. Stir in oats and salt. Reduce heat and simmer 5 minutes, stirring occasionally. Remove pan from heat; stir in lemon curd and sugar. Top with blueberries, cheese, and almonds.

SERVES 1
CALORIES 304; **FAT** 10.3g (sat 3.5g, mono 2.2g, poly 1.5g); **PROTEIN** 7g; **CARB** 47g; **FIBER** 7g; **SUGARS** 19g (est. added sugars 15g); **CHOL** 27mg; **IRON** 2mg; **SODIUM** 161mg; **CALC** 25mg

ORANGE-HONEY OATMEAL WITH PISTACHIOS, FIGS, AND SAFFRON YOGURT GF

HANDS-ON TIME: 10 MINUTES TOTAL TIME: 15 MINUTES

¾ cup water
½ cup old-fashioned rolled oats
Dash of salt
 1 tablespoon fresh orange juice
 2 teaspoons honey, divided
 2 tablespoons 2% reduced-fat Greek yogurt
 2 crumbled saffron threads
 1 tablespoon chopped unsalted pistachios
 1 tablespoon chopped dried figs

1. Bring ¾ cup water to a boil in a medium saucepan. Stir in oats and dash of salt. Reduce heat and simmer 5 minutes, stirring occasionally. Remove pan from heat, and stir in orange juice and 1 teaspoon honey.

2. Combine Greek yogurt and saffron threads in a small bowl, stirring with a whisk or spoon. Let sit, stirring occasionally, 5 minutes or until threads begin to "bloom" and yogurt turns yellow. Dollop yogurt on top of oatmeal; sprinkle with pistachios and figs. Drizzle with 1 teaspoon honey.

SERVES 1

CALORIES 284; **FAT** 7.2g (sat 1.3g, mono 2.8g, poly 2g); **PROTEIN** 9g; **CARB** 49g; **FIBER** 6g; **SUGARS** 20g (est. added sugars 12g); **CHOL** 2mg; **IRON** 2mg; **SODIUM** 159mg; **CALC** 47mg

OATMEAL WITH SUNFLOWER SEED BUTTER, BANANA, AND DARK CHOCOLATE GF

HANDS-ON TIME: 10 MINUTES TOTAL TIME: 15 MINUTES

¾ cup water
½ cup old-fashioned rolled oats
Dash of salt
½ large ripe banana
 1 tablespoon sunflower seed butter
 2 teaspoons brown sugar
 1 tablespoon shaved dark chocolate

1. Bring ¾ cup water to a boil in a medium saucepan. Stir in oats and dash of salt. Reduce heat and simmer 5 minutes, stirring occasionally. Remove pan from heat.

2. Slice banana into rounds. Mash one-third of banana slices with back of a fork in a small bowl. Stir sunflower seed butter, brown sugar, and mashed banana into warm oatmeal. Top with remaining banana slices and shaved chocolate.

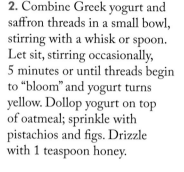

TIP

If you don't have sunflower seed butter on hand, try peanut butter or almond butter.

SERVES 1

CALORIES 362; **FAT** 14.4g (sat 2.7g, mono 7.3g, poly 2.6g); **PROTEIN** 9g; **CARB** 55g; **FIBER** 7g; **SUGARS** 20g (est. added sugars 10g); **CHOL** 1mg; **IRON** 3mg; **SODIUM** 201mg; **CALC** 19mg

CHAI SPICE AND PEAR OATMEAL (GF)

HANDS-ON TIME: 10 MINUTES TOTAL TIME: 15 MINUTES

¾ cup water

½ cup old-fashioned rolled oats

Dash of salt

Cooking spray

½ pear, thinly sliced

1 teaspoon honey

1 tablespoon low-fat sweetened
   condensed milk

⅛ teaspoon cinnamon

⅛ teaspoon cardamom

⅛ teaspoon ground ginger

⅛ teaspoon allspice

⅛ teaspoon vanilla extract

1 tablespoon toasted
   chopped walnuts

1. Bring ¾ cup water to a boil in a medium saucepan. Stir in oats and dash of salt. Reduce heat and simmer 5 minutes, stirring occasionally. Remove pan from heat.

2. Heat a small skillet over medium heat; coat pan with cooking spray. Add pear to pan; sauté 3 minutes. Stir in honey; cook 2 minutes or until tender. Stir sweetened condensed milk, cinnamon, cardamom, ginger, allspice, and vanilla into warm oatmeal. Top with sautéed pear slices. Sprinkle with walnuts.

SERVES 1
CALORIES 347; **FAT** 9.4g (sat 1.6g, mono 2.2g, poly 4.6g); **PROTEIN** 8g; **CARB** 60g; **FIBER** 8g; **SUGARS** 27g (est. added sugars 15g); **CHOL** 3mg; **IRON** 2mg; **SODIUM** 168mg; **CALC** 72mg

MAPLE-SWIRL OATMEAL WITH APPLE-BACON RELISH (GF)

HANDS-ON TIME: 10 MINUTES TOTAL TIME: 15 MINUTES

¾ cup water

½ cup old-fashioned rolled oats

Dash of salt

2 tablespoons diced peeled
   Fuji apple

1½ teaspoons chopped dried dates

¼ teaspoon brown sugar

1 center-cut bacon slice, cooked
   and crumbled

1½ teaspoons maple syrup

1. Bring ¾ cup water to a boil in a medium saucepan. Stir in oats and dash of salt. Reduce heat and simmer 5 minutes, stirring occasionally. Remove pan from heat.

2. Combine apple, dates, sugar, and crumbled bacon in a small bowl; toss to combine. Swirl maple syrup into warm oatmeal; top with relish.

SERVES 1
CALORIES 251; **FAT** 6.7g (sat 1.8g, mono 2.6g, poly 1.4g); **PROTEIN** 9g; **CARB** 41g; **FIBER** 5g; **SUGARS** 13g (est. added sugars 7g); **CHOL** 10mg; **IRON** 2mg; **SODIUM** 339mg; **CALC** 33mg

BAKED OATMEAL GF

Try baked oatmeal for an unexpected morning treat. It's a mix between an oatmeal bar and traditional creamy breakfast oatmeal, with an indulgent, bread pudding–like sweetness. For a less-sweet version, cut the sugar in half.

HANDS-ON TIME: 10 MINUTES TOTAL TIME: 35 MINUTES

2   cups uncooked
    quick-cooking oats
½   cup packed brown sugar
⅓   cup raisins
1   tablespoon chopped walnuts
1   teaspoon baking powder
1½ cups fat-free milk
½   cup applesauce
2   tablespoons butter, melted
1   large egg, beaten
Cooking spray

1. Preheat oven to 375°F.

2. Combine first 5 ingredients in a medium bowl. Combine milk, applesauce, butter, and egg. Add milk mixture to oat mixture; stir well.

3. Pour oat mixture into an 8-inch square glass or ceramic baking dish coated with cooking spray. Bake at 375°F for 20 minutes. Serve warm.

MAKE AHEAD

Bake the oatmeal, cool to room temperature, and store in the refrigerator up to 5 days; reheat in microwave 1 to 2 minutes. Or freeze individual servings in freezer-safe containers for up to 1 month; microwave 3 to 4 minutes to thaw and reheat.

SERVES 5 *(serving size: ⅔ cup)*
CALORIES 333; **FAT** 9.0g (sat 3.7g, mono 2.4g, poly 1.8g); **PROTEIN** 9g; **CARB** 58g; **FIBER** 4g; **SUGARS** 34g (est. added sugars 21g); **CHOL** 51mg; **IRON** 2mg; **SODIUM** 174mg; **CALC** 185mg

VANILLA AMARANTH WITH PEACH COMPOTE (GF)

Toasting the amaranth in butter takes the edge off its grassy flavor; this technique, plus the vanilla bean, lends light caramel notes.

HANDS-ON TIME: 10 MINUTES TOTAL TIME: 25 MINUTES

2   teaspoons butter
1   cup uncooked amaranth
2   cups 1% low-fat milk
Dash of salt
½   vanilla bean (split lengthwise)
¾   pound sliced peaches (fresh or frozen)
¼   cup water
2   tablespoons sugar
⅛   teaspoon cinnamon
Dash of ground ginger

1. Melt butter in a medium saucepan over medium heat. Add amaranth; cook 2 minutes. Stir in milk, dash of salt, and vanilla bean; bring to a boil. Cover, reduce heat, and simmer 20 minutes or until liquid is absorbed. Discard vanilla bean.

2. While amaranth cooks, combine peaches, ¼ cup water, sugar, cinnamon, and dash of ginger in a saucepan over medium-high heat; bring to a boil. Simmer 12 minutes or until peaches are tender and sauce thickens. Serve peaches over amaranth.

SERVES 4 *(serving size: ½ cup amaranth and ⅓ cup peaches)*
CALORIES 310; **FAT** 6.7g (sat 2.7g, mono 1.7g, poly 1.5g); **PROTEIN** 11g; **CARB** 53g; **FIBER** 5g; **SUGARS** 21g (est. added sugars 7g); **CHOL** 0mg; **IRON** 0mg; **SODIUM** 58mg; **CALC** 0mg

WEEKEND PORRIDGE WITH ROASTED GRAPES

This is the oatmeal you serve when you have weekend guests or when you want to treat your family to something a little special. I simply love the porridge's texture—creamy oats combined with chewy, toothsome farro.

HANDS-ON TIME: 10 MINUTES TOTAL TIME: 25 MINUTES

1 pound seedless red grapes
1 tablespoon extra-virgin olive oil
4 thyme sprigs
2½ cups water
1 cup 2% reduced-fat milk
1 cup uncooked quick-cooking steel-cut oats
¼ teaspoon kosher salt
¾ cup cooked whole-grain farro
3 tablespoons maple syrup
¼ cup plain 2% reduced-fat Greek yogurt

1. Preheat oven to 425°F.

2. Combine grapes, oil, and thyme on a jelly-roll pan. Bake at 425°F for 20 minutes or until grapes burst and start to caramelize.

3. While grapes roast, bring 2½ cups water and milk to a boil in a large saucepan; stir in oats and salt. Cover, reduce heat, and simmer 7 minutes or until thick, stirring occasionally. Stir in farro and syrup; simmer 7 to 10 minutes, until liquid is mostly absorbed and porridge is creamy. Top porridge with roasted grapes; dollop with yogurt.

> **CHANGE IT UP**
>
> The point of this recipe is to break up the oats' creaminess with a chewier grain. In place of farro, you can use leftover wheat berries, Kamut, spelt, barley, or rye berries.

SERVES 4 *(serving size: about 1 cup porridge, ¼ cup grapes, and 1 tablespoon yogurt)*
CALORIES 364; **FAT** 7.9g (sat 2g, mono 2.8g, poly 0.5g); **PROTEIN** 12g; **CARB** 71g; **FIBER** 6g; **SUGARS** 30g (est. added sugars 9g); **CHOL** 6mg; **IRON** 2mg; **SODIUM** 157mg; **CALC** 129mg

BREAKFAST QUINOA ⒼⒻ

You may not have thought to serve quinoa like oatmeal, but it's delicious as a warm breakfast cereal. Like most whole grains, quinoa is surprisingly filling; but if you need more for breakfast, serve with an egg on the side.

HANDS-ON TIME: 10 MINUTES TOTAL TIME: 22 MINUTES

½ cup uncooked quinoa
¾ cup light coconut milk
1 tablespoon brown sugar
2 tablespoons water
⅛ teaspoon salt
¼ cup flaked unsweetened coconut
1 cup sliced fresh strawberries
1 cup sliced banana

1. Preheat oven to 400°F.

2. Place quinoa in a fine sieve; place sieve in a large bowl. Cover quinoa with water. Using your hands, rub grains together 30 seconds; rinse and drain quinoa. Repeat procedure twice. Drain well. Combine quinoa, coconut milk, brown sugar, 2 tablespoons water, and salt in a medium saucepan, and bring to a boil. Reduce heat, and simmer 15 minutes or until liquid is absorbed, stirring occasionally. Stir mixture constantly during last 2 minutes of cooking.

3. While quinoa cooks, spread flaked coconut in a single layer on a baking sheet. Bake at 400°F for 5 minutes or until golden brown. Cool slightly.

4. Place about ½ cup quinoa mixture in each of 4 bowls. Top each serving with ¼ cup strawberry slices, ¼ cup banana slices, and 1 tablespoon toasted coconut. Serve warm.

SERVES 4
CALORIES 178; **FAT** 5.5g (sat 3.8g, mono 0.4g, poly 0.8g); **PROTEIN** 4g; **CARB** 30g; **FIBER:** 4g; **SUGARS** 12g (est. added sugars 3g); **CHOL** 0mg; **IRON** 2mg; **SODIUM** 89mg; **CALC** 22mg

CINNAMON-BANANA CRUNCH BOWL

If you've grown bored with your usual breakfast bowl, try toasty-nutty bulgur. Paired with meaty, crunchy walnuts, the result is a quick and easy breakfast of champions.

HANDS-ON TIME: 7 MINUTES TOTAL TIME: 7 MINUTES

¼ cup plain fat-free Greek yogurt
1 teaspoon honey
Dash of cinnamon
½ cup cooked bulgur
1 tablespoon chopped toasted walnuts
1 tablespoon brown sugar
⅓ cup sliced banana
Additional cinnamon (optional)

1. Combine yogurt, honey, and cinnamon in a small bowl. Toss bulgur with walnuts and brown sugar. Top with banana slices. Dollop yogurt mixture over bulgur mixture. Sprinkle with additional cinnamon, if desired.

SERVES 1
CALORIES 255; **FAT** 5g (sat 0.4g, mono 1.2g, poly 2.9g); **PROTEIN** 10g; **CARB** 46g; **FIBER** 6g; **SUGARS** 23g (est. added sugars 15g); **CHOL** 0mg; **IRON** 1mg; **SODIUM** 29mg; **CALC** 65mg

OVERNIGHT PEANUT BUTTER BULGUR WITH BERRIES

What could be better than a grain that works while you sleep and a no-cook cereal with a whopping 40g whole grains per serving? The soaked bulgur makes enough for three servings, but the topping amounts are for one; keep the bulgur in the fridge, and enjoy an easy breakfast two more days.

HANDS-ON TIME: 8 MINUTES TOTAL TIME: 8 HOURS 8 MINUTES

1½ cups 1% low-fat milk
1 cup uncooked bulgur
1 tablespoon peanut butter
⅓ cup fresh raspberries
1 tablespoon plain fat-free Greek yogurt
1 teaspoon chopped peanuts

1. Combine milk and uncooked bulgur in a small bowl. Cover and refrigerate overnight. Fluff mixture in the morning. Place ¾ cup soaked grains in a small microwave-safe bowl. Microwave at HIGH 1 minute. Stir in peanut butter. Top with raspberries, yogurt, and chopped peanuts.

SERVES 1
CALORIES 350; **FAT** 11.5g (sat 2.8g, mono 5g, poly 3.2g); **PROTEIN** 16g; **CARB** 51g; **FIBER** 12g; **SUGARS** 10g (est. added sugars 1g); **CHOL** 6mg; **IRON** 2mg; **SODIUM** 141mg; **CALC** 198mg

SAVORY BUCKWHEAT WITH TOMATO, CHEDDAR, AND BACON

Who says all porridge has to be sweet? A creamy bowl with bacon and cheese is a lovely way to start the day. This gluten-free, polenta-like cereal packs 41g whole grains into one serving.

HANDS-ON TIME: 10 MINUTES TOTAL TIME: 10 MINUTES

⅔ cup cooked creamy buckwheat hot cereal

1 center-cut bacon slice, cooked and crumbled

2 tablespoons reduced-fat shredded cheddar cheese

2 tablespoons chopped tomato

Slivered jalapeño pepper

1. Top cooked cereal with bacon, cheddar cheese, tomato, and desired amount of slivered jalapeño pepper. Serve warm.

CHANGE IT UP

Try the alluring bacon-tomato-cheddar-jalapeño topping on oatmeal; just cook the oats in water or milk without any sweetener.

SERVES 1
CALORIES 209; **FAT** 5.6g (sat 2.6g, mono 0.7g, poly 0.1g); **PROTEIN** 11g; **CARB** 31g; **FIBER** 3g; **SUGARS** 1g (est. added sugars 0g); **CHOL** 15mg; **IRON** 1mg; **SODIUM** 239mg; **CALC** 170mg

Mexicali
Grits Bowl

Grits with
Pesto, Cremini,
and Spinach,
page 54

Grits with Pancetta,
Fried Eggs, and
Red-Eye Gravy,
page 54

GRITS BOWLS SIX WAYS

Unlike the oatmeal bowls on pages 41-43, which are fast enough for busy weekday mornings, whole-grain grits take a little longer to cook and are better suited to weekends. These make enough for 4 servings.

MEXICALI GRITS BOWL (GF)

HANDS-ON TIME: 13 MINUTES TOTAL TIME: 48 MINUTES

3½ cups water
1 cup 2% reduced-fat milk
½ teaspoon kosher salt
1 cup whole-grain grits (such as McEwen & Sons)
½ cup refrigerated pico de gallo
2 teaspoons fresh lime juice
1 cubed peeled avocado
¼ cup crema Mexicana
Cilantro leaves (optional)

1. Bring 3½ cups water, milk, and salt to a boil in a large saucepan. Gradually stir in grits. Reduce heat, and cook, uncovered, 35 minutes or until thick, stirring frequently.

2. Combine pico de gallo, lime juice, and avocado. Spoon 1 cup grits into each of 4 bowls; top each serving with 1 tablespoon crema Mexicana and about ⅓ cup avocado mixture. Top with cilantro leaves, if desired.

SERVES 4
CALORIES 280; **FAT** 11.6g (sat 1.8g, mono 5.3g, poly 1g); **PROTEIN** 7g; **CARB** 37g; **FIBER** 5g; **SUGARS** 5g (est. added sugars 0g); **CHOL** 13mg; **IRON** 2mg; **SODIUM** 527mg; **CALC** 80mg

GREAT GRITS

If you've ever had instant grits and been disappointed, I understand. The flavor and texture are nowhere near the richness and, well, grit of whole-grain grits. They do take longer to cook, but they're absolutely worth it. (If you can't find whole-grain grits at your store, you can order them from McEwen & Sons or Anson Mills.) Here are tips for awesome grits:
- When adding grits to boiling liquid, add them gradually as you stir; don't dump the whole amount in at once. This is the best way to prevent lumps.
- As the grits cook, stir frequently. The liquid will try to separate to the top, resulting in lumps. If you do end up with this separation, stir the mixture with a whisk to reincorporate.

GRITS WITH PESTO, CREMINI, AND SPINACH (GF)

HANDS-ON TIME: 12 MINUTES TOTAL TIME: 47 MINUTES

3½ cups water

1 cup 2% reduced-fat milk

½ teaspoon kosher salt

1 cup whole-grain grits (such as McEwen & Sons)

1 tablespoon butter

8 ounces sliced cremini mushrooms

3 garlic cloves, minced

5 ounces fresh baby spinach

⅛ teaspoon kosher salt

¼ cup prepared refrigerated pesto

1. Bring 3½ cups water, milk, and ½ teaspoon salt to a boil in a large saucepan. Gradually stir in grits. Reduce heat, and cook, uncovered, 35 minutes or until thick, stirring frequently.

2. Melt butter in a large skillet over medium-high heat. Add mushrooms and garlic; sauté 6 minutes. Add spinach, tossing until spinach wilts. Stir in ⅛ teaspoon salt. Spoon 1 cup grits into each of 4 bowls; top each serving with 1 tablespoon pesto and ½ cup mushroom mixture.

SERVES 4

CALORIES 291; **FAT** 11.8g (sat 4.5g, mono 5.4g, poly 0.8g); **PROTEIN** 10g; **CARB** 38g; **FIBER** 5g; **SUGARS** 4g (est. added sugars 0g); **CHOL** 18mg; **IRON** 3mg; **SODIUM** 549mg; **CALC** 142mg

GRITS WITH PANCETTA, FRIED EGGS, AND RED-EYE GRAVY

HANDS-ON TIME: 22 MINUTES TOTAL TIME: 57 MINUTES

3½ cups water

1 cup 2% reduced-fat milk

½ teaspoon kosher salt

1 cup whole-grain grits (such as McEwen & Sons)

2 ounces diced pancetta

1½ tablespoons all-purpose flour

½ cup brewed black coffee

½ cup lower-sodium tomato-vegetable juice

4 large eggs

¼ teaspoon freshly ground black pepper

1. Bring 3½ cups water, milk, and salt to a boil in a large saucepan. Gradually stir in grits. Reduce heat, and cook, uncovered, 35 minutes or until thick, stirring frequently.

2. Cook pancetta in a medium skillet over medium heat until crisp, stirring occasionally. Remove pancetta from pan, reserving drippings. Stir flour into drippings. Add coffee and juice; cook 2 minutes or until thick. Heat a large nonstick skillet over medium heat. Crack eggs into pan; cover and cook 2 minutes or until desired degree of doneness. Spoon 1 cup grits into each of 4 bowls; top each serving with about 3 tablespoons gravy, 1 tablespoon pancetta, and 1 egg. Sprinkle with pepper.

SERVES 4

CALORIES 340; **FAT** 12.2g (sat 4.4g, mono 2.2g, poly 1.1g); **PROTEIN** 15g; **CARB** 40g; **FIBER** 3g; **SUGARS** 4g (est. added sugars0g); **CHOL** 204mg; **IRON** 3mg; **SODIUM** 569mg; **CALC** 108mg

GRITS WITH CHEDDAR, CHIVES, AND SCRAMBLED EGGS (GF)

HANDS-ON TIME: 11 MINUTES TOTAL TIME: 46 MINUTES

3½ cups water
1 cup 2% reduced-fat milk
½ teaspoon kosher salt
1 cup whole-grain grits (such as McEwen & Sons)
4 large eggs
2 tablespoons 2% reduced-fat milk
¼ teaspoon kosher salt
2 teaspoons canola oil
8 tablespoons shredded cheddar cheese
4 tablespoons sliced fresh chives

1. Bring 3½ cups water, milk, and salt to a boil in a large saucepan. Gradually stir in grits. Reduce heat, and cook, uncovered, 35 minutes or until thick, stirring frequently.

2. Heat a medium nonstick skillet over medium-low heat. Combine eggs, milk, and salt in a medium bowl, stirring well with a whisk.

3. Add oil to pan; swirl to coat. Add egg mixture; cook 1½ minutes or until desired degree of doneness, stirring constantly. Spoon 1 cup grits into each of 4 bowls; top each serving with 2 tablespoons shredded cheddar cheese, one-fourth of eggs, and 1 tablespoon sliced fresh chives.

SERVES 4
CALORIES 314; **FAT** 14g (sat 6g, mono 5g, poly 2g); **PROTEIN** 15g; **CARB** 31g; **FIBER** 2g; **SUGARS** 4g (est. added sugars 0g); **CHOL** 206mg; **IRON** 2mg; **SODIUM** 551mg; **CALC** 215mg

GRITS WITH BACON AND SEARED TOMATOES (GF)

HANDS-ON TIME: 15 MINUTES TOTAL TIME: 50 MINUTES

3½ cups water
1 cup 2% reduced-fat milk
½ teaspoon kosher salt
1 cup whole-grain grits (such as McEwen & Sons)
4 bacon slices
1½ cups halved red or yellow cherry tomatoes
1 cup lightly packed baby arugula
1 teaspoon fresh lemon juice

1. Bring 3½ cups water, milk, and salt to a boil in a large saucepan. Gradually stir in grits. Reduce heat, and cook, uncovered, 35 minutes or until thick, stirring frequently.

2. Cook bacon in a large cast-iron skillet over medium heat about 6 minutes or until crisp. Remove bacon from pan. Pour drippings into a small bowl (do not wipe pan clean). Increase heat to medium-high. Add tomatoes, cut sides down; cook 2 minutes or until seared. Place arugula in a medium bowl; drizzle with 2 teaspoons bacon drippings and juice. Discard remaining drippings. Spoon 1 cup grits into each of 4 bowls. Top each serving with about ¼ cup arugula mixture and ⅓ cup tomatoes. Crumble 1 bacon slice over each serving.

SERVES 4
CALORIES 235; **FAT** 7.3g (sat 2.7g, mono 2.8g, poly 0.7g); **PROTEIN** 9g; **CARB** 32g; **FIBER** 3g; **SUGARS** 5g (est. added sugars 0g); **CHOL** 16mg; **IRON** 2mg; **SODIUM** 461mg; **CALC** 88mg

SAUSAGE AND SWEET CORN GRITS BOWL GF

HANDS-ON TIME: 23 MINUTES TOTAL TIME: 58 MINUTES

3½ cups water
1 cup 2% reduced-fat milk
½ teaspoon kosher salt
1 cup whole-grain grits (such as McEwen & Sons)
6 ounces turkey breakfast sausage
2 cups fresh corn kernels
½ cup vertically sliced red onion

1. Bring 3½ cups water, milk, and salt to a boil in a large saucepan. Gradually stir in grits. Reduce heat, and cook, uncovered, 35 minutes or until thick, stirring frequently.

2. Heat a large nonstick skillet over medium-high heat. Add sausage; cook 5 minutes or until browned, stirring to crumble. Add corn and onion; cook 2 minutes, stirring frequently. Spoon 1 cup grits into each of 4 bowls; top each serving with about ½ cup sausage mixture.

SERVES 4
CALORIES 295; **FAT** 5.9g (sat 2.4g, mono 1.7g, poly 0.8g); **PROTEIN** 15g; **CARB** 46g; **FIBER** 4g; **SUGARS** 5g (est. added sugars 0g); **CHOL** 38mg; **IRON** 2mg; **SODIUM** 533mg; **CALC** 93mg

NUTTY WHOLE-GRAIN GRANOLA GF

There are two camps of granola lovers: those who like clusters and those who want things loose and separate. Luckily, both types are represented in this book. This granola offers robust clusters that are great for loading into breakfast parfaits or serving with milk.

HANDS-ON TIME: 10 MINUTES TOTAL TIME: 38 MINUTES

2 cups old-fashioned rolled oats
1 cup packed brown sugar
⅔ cup uncooked millet
⅔ cup dried cherries
¼ cup walnut halves
¼ cup roasted, salted almonds
¼ cup hazelnuts
¾ teaspoon kosher salt
3 tablespoons butter, melted
2 tablespoons light-colored corn syrup, honey, or agave nectar
1 large egg white
Cooking spray

1. Preheat oven to 400°F.

2. Combine first 8 ingredients. Combine butter, syrup, and egg white, stirring well. Drizzle butter mixture over oat mixture; toss well to coat. Spread in a single layer on a baking sheet lined with parchment paper coated with cooking spray. Bake at 400°F for 27 minutes or until golden, stirring twice. Store in an airtight container for up to a week.

SERVES 20 (serving size: ⅓ cup)
CALORIES 162; **FAT** 5.3g (sat 1.5g, mono 2g, poly 1.4g); **PROTEIN** 3g; **CARB** 27g; **FIBER** 2g; **SUGARS** 14g (est. added sugars 13g); **CHOL** 5mg; **IRON** 1mg; **SODIUM** 95mg; **CALC** 18mg

TOASTED BARLEY AND BERRY GRANOLA

Drier and more separate than the clustery granola on the previous page, this seed- and fruit-filled version is the style that's best sprinkled over Greek yogurt or fro-yo. While rolled barley flakes look nearly identical to rolled oats, they pack more fiber. Look for them in whole-food shops or supermarket bulk food bins.

HANDS-ON TIME: 15 MINUTES TOTAL TIME: 1 HOUR 30 MINUTES

¼ cup unsalted pumpkinseed kernels

¼ cup unsalted sunflower seed kernels

⅓ cup maple syrup

2 tablespoons brown sugar

2 tablespoons canola oil

1 teaspoon ground cinnamon

1½ teaspoons vanilla extract

¼ teaspoon salt

⅛ teaspoon ground cardamom

2 cups rolled barley flakes

¼ cup toasted wheat germ

⅓ cup dried blueberries

⅓ cup sweetened dried cranberries

1. Preheat oven to 325°F.

2. Place pumpkinseed kernels and sunflower seed kernels on a baking sheet lined with parchment paper. Bake at 325°F for 5 minutes. Cool seeds in pan on a wire rack.

3. Combine syrup and next 6 ingredients (through cardamom) in a medium bowl. Stir in toasted kernels, barley, and wheat germ.

4. Spread barley mixture in a single layer on a baking sheet lined with parchment paper. Bake at 325°F for 25 minutes or until lightly browned, stirring every 10 minutes.

5. Remove from oven; cool granola in pan on a wire rack. Stir in dried blueberries and dried cranberries. Store in an airtight container for up to a week.

SERVES 12 *(serving size: ⅓ cup)*
CALORIES 181; **FAT** 6.5g (sat 0.7g, mono 2.3g, poly 2.8g); **PROTEIN** 5g; **CARB** 27g; **FIBER** 4g; **SUGARS** 11g (est. added sugars 8g); **CHOL** 1mg; **IRON** 1mg; **SODIUM** 59mg; **CALC** 13mg

CITRUSY BANANA-OAT SMOOTHIE (GF)

Make morning prep even faster by freezing the banana and cooking and refrigerating the oatmeal the night before.

HANDS-ON TIME: 5 MINUTES TOTAL TIME: 30 MINUTES

⅔ cup fresh orange juice
½ cup prepared quick-cooking oats
½ cup plain 2% reduced-fat Greek yogurt
1 tablespoon flaxseed meal
1 tablespoon honey
½ teaspoon grated orange rind
1 large banana, sliced and frozen
1 cup ice cubes

1. Place first 7 ingredients in a blender; pulse to combine. Add ice; process until smooth.

SERVES 2 *(serving size: 1½ cups)*
CALORIES 228; **FAT** 3.9g (sat 1.2g, mono 0.8g, poly 1.4g); **PROTEIN** 3g; **CARB** 27g; **FIBER** 2g; **SUGARS** 26g (est. added sugars 9g); **CHOL** 5mg; **IRON** 1mg; **SODIUM** 95mg; **CALC** 18mg

◀ POPPED AMARANTH AND YOGURT PARFAITS (GF)

Here's a sweet and simple protein-rich breakfast for two. You can assemble these just before heading to work, and then enjoy at your desk. Don't make the parfaits too far ahead (like the night before) because the popped grains may get soggy. Use any fruits you like—in summertime, I go for peaches and blackberries.

HANDS-ON TIME: 10 MINUTES TOTAL TIME: 10 MINUTES

1 large pink or ruby red grapefruit
½ cup pomegranate arils
1 cup plain 2% reduced-fat Greek yogurt
1 tablespoon honey
1 cup Popped Amaranth (page 30)

1. Peel and section grapefruit. Combine grapefruit and pomegranate.

2. Combine yogurt and honey, stirring well. Spoon ¼ cup yogurt mixture in bottom of 2 (8-ounce) jars or glasses; top each serving with ¼ cup Popped Amaranth and one-fourth of grapefruit mixture. Repeat layers with yogurt mixture, Popped Amaranth, and grapefruit mixture.

SERVES 2 *(serving size: 1 parfait)*
CALORIES 268; **FAT** 4.3g (sat 1.9g, mono 0.4g, poly 0.6g); **PROTEIN** 14g; **CARB** 47g; **FIBER** 5g; **SUGARS** 31g (est. added sugars 9g); **CHOL** 8mg; **IRON** 2mg; **SODIUM** 40mg; **CALC** 131mg

QUICK EINKORN-STUFFED "BAKED" APPLES

If you have cooked einkorn berries on hand or in your freezer, this breakfast treat is weekday-doable. You can also use cooked wheat berries, spelt, rye berries, Kamut, or farro. Raise your hands and say hallelujah: The microwave turns what's usually a 1-hour cooking process into a no-sweat 5-minute walk in the park.

HANDS-ON TIME: 10 MINUTES TOTAL TIME: 17 MINUTES

4 medium Honeycrisp or Granny Smith apples (about 8 to 9 ounces each)

1 cup cooked einkorn berries

¼ cup packed dark brown sugar

¼ cup chopped dried cherries

¼ cup coarsely chopped walnuts, toasted

³/₈ teaspoon kosher salt

¼ cup water

4 teaspoons butter

1. Using a paring knife and/or melon baller, hollow out apples, cutting to but not through bottom end and leaving a ⅓-inch-thick shell.

2. Combine einkorn, sugar, cherries, walnuts, and salt in a small bowl. Divide mixture among apples, packing to fit. Place apples in a microwave-safe small, deep glass or ceramic baking dish. Pour ¼ cup water into bottom of dish. Top each apple with 1 teaspoon butter.

3. Cover baking dish tightly with plastic wrap; pierce twice with the tip of a knife to vent. Microwave at HIGH 5 minutes. Let stand 2 minutes before serving. Discard water.

MAKE AHEAD

Microwave-cook stuffed apples as directed, cover, and refrigerate. In the morning, heat each apple "to order" for 1 to 2 minutes in the microwave.

SERVES 4 *(serving size: 1 stuffed apple)*
CALORIES 299; **FAT** 9.1g (sat 3g, mono 1.7g, poly 3.8g); **PROTEIN** 4g; **CARB** 54g; **FIBER** 7g; **SUGARS** 35g (est. added sugars 13g); **CHOL** 10mg; **IRON** 1mg; **SODIUM** 221mg; **CALC** 39mg

FARRO AND POTATO HASH WITH POACHED EGGS

Leftover farro incorporates surprisingly well into a standard breakfast hash. The whole dish is a tasty way to use up bits of this and that, including a little piece of sausage or that one zucchini left in the fridge.

HANDS-ON TIME: 10 MINUTES TOTAL TIME: 38 MINUTES

1½ tablespoons canola oil
¾ cup chopped onion
2 garlic cloves, minced
12 ounces Dutch yellow baby potatoes or Yukon gold potatoes, cut into ½-inch cubes
½ cup water
1 cup (½-inch) cubed zucchini
4 ounces diced smoked sausage
1 cup cooked whole-grain farro
½ teaspoon kosher salt
4 large eggs
¼ cup chopped fresh chives
1 tablespoon thyme leaves
Freshly ground black pepper

1. Heat a large nonstick skillet over medium-high heat. Add oil to pan; swirl to coat. Add onion and garlic; sauté 3 minutes. Add potatoes and ½ cup water; cover and cook 10 minutes or until almost tender. Stir in zucchini and sausage; cook, uncovered, 5 minutes or until all liquid evaporates and potatoes begin to brown. Stir in farro and salt; cook 3 minutes or until thoroughly heated. Keep warm.

2. Add water to a large skillet, filling two-thirds full; bring to a boil. Reduce heat; simmer. Break each egg into a custard cup. Gently pour eggs into pan; cook 3 minutes or until desired degree of doneness. Carefully remove eggs from pan using a slotted spoon. Stir chives and thyme into hash; spoon about 1 cup hash onto each of 4 plates. Top each serving with 1 egg; sprinkle evenly with pepper.

CHANGE IT UP

The farro in this hash releases a little starch after it's combined with the potato mixture, which helps to bring everything together. You can get a similar result with cooked barley, freekeh, or buckwheat groats.

SERVES 4
CALORIES 355; **FAT** 19g (sat 5g, mono 8.9g, poly 3.4g); **PROTEIN** 15g; **CARB** 33g; **FIBER** 4g; **SUGARS** 2g (est. added sugars 0g); **CHOL** 206mg; **IRON** 2mg; **SODIUM** 523mg; **CALC** 58mg

SOFT-SCRAMBLED EGGS WITH HERBS AND CRUNCHY QUINOA (GF)

The secrets to perfect soft-scrambled eggs are to cook them over moderately low heat and to remove them from the heat shortly before they've reached the desired texture (because they will continue cooking in the pan). A touch of cream cheese in the eggs helps them stay creamy; the crunchy topping makes the perfect complement.

HANDS-ON TIME: 15 MINUTES TOTAL TIME: 15 MINUTES

½ cup Crunchy Fried Quinoa (page 32)

1 tablespoon finely chopped fresh flat-leaf parsley

⅜ teaspoon kosher salt, divided

⅛ teaspoon garlic powder (optional)

6 large eggs

1 tablespoon chopped fresh chives

2 teaspoons finely chopped fresh tarragon

2 tablespoons ⅓-less-fat cream cheese

Cooking spray

1. Combine Crunchy Fried Quinoa, parsley, ⅛ teaspoon salt, and garlic powder, if desired; set aside.

2. Combine eggs, chives, tarragon, and ¼ teaspoon salt, stirring well with a whisk.

3. Place cream cheese in a small microwave-safe bowl; microwave at HIGH 20 seconds or until very soft.

4. Heat a medium skillet over medium-low heat. Coat pan with cooking spray. Add egg mixture to pan; cook 1 to 2 minutes or until about halfway done, stirring constantly. Stir in cream cheese; cook 1 to 2 minutes or until eggs begin to set, stirring constantly to break up curds. Remove from heat; sprinkle with quinoa mixture.

SERVES 4 *(serving size: about ½ cup)*
CALORIES 192; **FAT** 12.8g (sat 3.6g, mono 5.5g, poly 2.8g); **PROTEIN** 12g; **CARB** 7g; **FIBER** 1g; **SUGARS** 1g (est. added sugars 0g); **CHOL** 284mg; **IRON** 2mg; **SODIUM** 311mg; **CALC** 59mg

KALE AND FREEKEH FRITTATA

We have frittata, which my kids call "egg pie," at least every other week at our house. It's such a versatile dish—you can toss in pretty much any whole grain or vegetable you like. The smoky taste of freekeh is fantastic here, matched perfectly with robust kale, loads of garlic, and a generous pinch of crushed red pepper. If you'd like an extra pop of color and flavor, top with wilted kale and seared cherry tomatoes.

HANDS-ON TIME: 20 MINUTES TOTAL TIME: 1 HOUR 5 MINUTES

1½ cups water
⅔ cup uncooked cracked freekeh
1½ tablespoons canola oil
½ cup chopped shallots
¼ teaspoon crushed red pepper
5 garlic cloves, thinly sliced
8 cups chopped stemmed kale, divided
½ cup water, divided
1 cup 2% evaporated milk
4 ounces sharp cheddar cheese, shredded (about 1 cup)
¾ teaspoon kosher salt
¼ teaspoon freshly ground black pepper
5 large eggs, lightly beaten

1. Bring 1½ cups water to a boil in a small saucepan; stir in freekeh. Cover, reduce heat, and simmer 20 minutes. Remove from heat; let stand 10 minutes. Drain any remaining liquid. Freekeh should be slightly al dente and a bit chewy.

2. Preheat oven to 375°F.

3. While freekeh cooks, heat a 10-inch cast-iron or other ovenproof skillet over medium heat. Add oil; swirl to coat. Add shallots, red pepper, and garlic; cook 5 minutes or until tender, stirring occasionally. Add half of kale and ¼ cup water; cover and cook 2 minutes or until kale wilts. Add remaining kale and ¼ cup water; cover and cook 6 minutes or until kale is tender. Stir in freekeh.

4. Combine milk and next 4 ingredients, stirring with a whisk. Pour evenly over freekeh mixture in pan without stirring; cook over medium heat 2 minutes or until egg mixture starts to set around edges. Place pan in oven. Bake at 375°F for 8 to 10 minutes or until almost set. Turn on broiler (do not remove pan from oven); broil 2 minutes or until top is lightly browned. Cool 5 minutes before cutting into wedges.

SERVES 6 *(serving size: 1 wedge)*
CALORIES 316; **FAT** 15.5g (sat 5.6g, mono 5.8g, poly 2.4g); **PROTEIN** 19g; **CARB** 29g; **FIBER** 4g; **SUGARS** 5g (est. added sugars 0g); **CHOL** 182mg; **IRON** 4mg; **SODIUM** 504mg; **CALC** 406mg

SWEET CORN AND ZUCCHINI QUICHE WITH CORNMEAL CRUST

This recipe provides a double hit of whole-grain corn with fresh kernels and whole-grain cornmeal. The crust is super easy—no rolling required: Simply pulse the ingredients in a food processor until crumbly, and pat into the pie plate.

HANDS-ON TIME: 18 MINUTES TOTAL TIME: 1 HOUR 23 MINUTES

1 tablespoon extra-virgin olive oil
2 cups (⅛-inch) sliced zucchini
⅓ cup chopped shallots
1¼ teaspoons kosher salt, divided
1 cup fresh corn kernels
1 tablespoon chopped fresh thyme
4.75 ounces white whole-wheat flour (about 1 cup)
½ cup whole-grain cornmeal
1 teaspoon freshly ground black pepper, divided
⅓ cup extra-virgin olive oil
¼ cup 2% reduced-fat milk
Cooking spray
3 ounces smoked Gouda cheese, shredded (about ¾ cup)
⅔ cup 2% reduced-fat milk
5 large eggs

1. Preheat oven to 400°F.

2. Heat a large nonstick skillet over medium-high heat. Add 1 tablespoon oil; swirl to coat. Add zucchini, shallots, and ¼ teaspoon salt; sauté 5 minutes or until tender and beginning to brown lightly. Add corn and thyme; sauté 1 minute. Remove from heat; cool slightly.

3. Weigh or lightly spoon flour into a dry measuring cup; level with a knife. Place flour, cornmeal, ½ teaspoon salt, and ¾ teaspoon pepper in a food processor; pulse 2 times to combine. Combine ⅓ cup oil and ¼ cup milk. With processor on, gradually add oil mixture through food chute; process until dough is crumbly. Sprinkle dough into a 9-inch pie plate coated with cooking spray; quickly press dough into an even layer in bottom and up sides of pan. Bake crust at 400°F for 15 minutes or until edges are lightly browned. Remove from oven.

4. Reduce oven temperature to 350°F.

5. Spoon zucchini mixture into warm crust; sprinkle evenly with cheese. Combine ⅔ cup milk, eggs, ½ teaspoon salt, and ¼ teaspoon pepper; stir well with a whisk. Pour egg mixture over filling in crust. Bake at 350°F for 40 to 45 minutes or until a knife inserted in center comes out clean and top is lightly browned. Cool 10 minutes on a wire rack before cutting into wedges.

SERVES 8 *(serving size: 1 wedge)*
CALORIES 306; **FAT** 18.1g (sat 4.8g, mono 10.1g, poly 2.1g); **PROTEIN** 11g; **CARB** 25g; **FIBER** 4g; **SUGARS** 4g (est. added sugars 0g); **CHOL** 131mg; **IRON** 2mg; **SODIUM** 453mg; **CALC** 136mg

WHOLE-WHEAT, BUTTERMILK, AND ORANGE PANCAKES

A gentle introduction to the wonderful world of whole grains, this starter recipe uses half all-purpose flour and half white whole-wheat flour. Once your family is on board, go for more white whole-wheat flour, gradually going all in. I make this recipe with all whole-grain flour, and everyone loves it. Allowing the batter to stand for a few minutes gives the leaveners a chance to work and is key to the light, fluffy texture.

HANDS-ON TIME: 25 MINUTES TOTAL TIME: 40 MINUTES

- 2 tablespoons butter, softened
- ¼ teaspoon grated orange rind
- ¾ teaspoon fresh orange juice
- 3.5 ounces white whole-wheat flour (about ¾ cup)
- 3.4 ounces all-purpose flour (about ¾ cup)
- 2 tablespoons sugar
- 1½ teaspoons baking powder
- ½ teaspoon baking soda
- 3/8 teaspoon salt
- 1½ cups low-fat buttermilk
- ¼ cup fresh orange juice
- 1 tablespoon canola oil
- 1 large egg
- 1 large egg white
- Cooking spray
- ¾ cup maple syrup

1. Combine first 3 ingredients in a small bowl.

2. Weigh or lightly spoon flours into dry measuring cups; level with a knife. Combine flours and next 4 ingredients (through salt) in a medium bowl, stirring with a whisk. Combine buttermilk, ¼ cup juice, oil, and 1 egg in a small bowl, stirring with a whisk. Add buttermilk mixture to flour mixture, stirring just until moist; let stand 15 minutes. Place egg white in a medium bowl; beat with a whisk until medium peaks form. Gently fold egg white into batter.

3. Preheat a griddle to medium heat. Coat pan with cooking spray. Spoon ¼ cup batter per pancake onto griddle. Cook 3 minutes or until edges begin to bubble and bottom is browned. Turn pancakes over; cook 3 minutes or until done. Serve with orange butter and syrup.

SERVES 6 *(serving size: 2 pancakes, 1 teaspoon butter, and 2 tablespoons syrup)*
CALORIES 336; **FAT** 8g (sat 3.2g, mono 3g, poly 1.1g); **PROTEIN** 7g; **CARB** 59g; **FIBER** 3g; **SUGARS** 32g (est. added sugars 28g); **CHOL** 44mg; **IRON** 2mg; **SODIUM** 477mg; **CALC** 182mg

CHOCOLATE-BUCKWHEAT WAFFLES WITH JUICY BERRIES (GF)

This recipe started out as straight-up buckwheat waffles. When my son Daniel walked through the kitchen and saw them, his face lit up: With their dark brown color, he thought they were chocolate waffles. I realized then that making these waffles chocolate-flavored would get the whole family to love them. With this new version, my other son, Connor, declared: "Rate of disgustingness: 0. Rate of deliciousness: 100." Best praise ever.

HANDS-ON TIME: 19 MINUTES TOTAL TIME: 35 MINUTES

4½ cups quartered fresh strawberries

9 tablespoons sugar, divided

½ cup plain fat-free Greek yogurt

¾ teaspoon vanilla extract, divided

4.5 ounces buckwheat flour (about 1 cup)

⅓ cup unsweetened cocoa

¾ teaspoon baking soda

⅛ teaspoon salt

1¼ cups nonfat buttermilk

¼ cup water

1 tablespoon canola oil

2 large egg yolks

3 large egg whites

Cooking spray

2 tablespoons sliced almonds, lightly toasted

1. Combine strawberries and 2 tablespoons sugar, tossing well to combine. Let stand at room temperature at least 30 minutes.

2. Place yogurt, 1 tablespoon sugar, and ¼ teaspoon vanilla in a small bowl, stirring well; chill until ready to serve.

3. Weigh or lightly spoon flour into a dry measuring cup; level with a knife. Combine flour, cocoa, baking soda, and salt in a large bowl, stirring with a whisk. Combine ½ teaspoon vanilla, buttermilk, and next 3 ingredients (through yolks) in a medium bowl, stirring with a whisk. Add buttermilk mixture to flour mixture; stir well to combine.

4. Preheat a Belgian waffle iron.

5. Place egg whites in a large bowl; beat with a mixer at high speed until foamy. Gradually add 6 tablespoons sugar, 1 tablespoon at a time, beating until stiff, glossy peaks form. Gently fold about one-fourth of egg white mixture into batter. Fold in remaining egg white mixture. Coat waffle iron with cooking spray. Spoon about ½ cup batter over each waffle plate, spreading to edges. Cook 4 minutes or until lightly browned and done; remove waffles from iron. Repeat procedure with cooking spray and remaining batter. Top waffles with strawberry mixture and yogurt mixture. Sprinkle with almonds.

MAKE AHEAD

Try cooking a double batch of waffles on the weekend and stash the extras in the freezer; cool completely after cooking, and freeze in a zip-top plastic freezer bag for up to 1 month. Pop waffles in the toaster to reheat.

SERVES 6 *(serving size: 2 waffles, about ⅔ cup strawberry mixture, about 4 teaspoons yogurt mixture, and 1 teaspoon almonds)*
CALORIES 267; **FAT** 6.3g (sat 1.2g, mono 3g, poly 1.3g); **PROTEIN** 11g; **CARB** 45g; **FIBER** 7g; **SUGARS** 26g (est. added sugars 19g); **CHOL** 62mg; **IRON** 2mg; **SODIUM** 296mg; **CALC** 113mg

BEST-EVER FRENCH TOAST WITH MAPLE APPLES

OK, if I call something "best-ever," bourbon has to be involved. Here, just a splash adds smoky richness and sweet depth. The 2% evaporated milk is the key to the custard; it has a similar richness to cream at a fraction of the fat. Make sure the bread fully soaks up the custard; that's what gives this French toast its creamy center.

HANDS-ON TIME: 30 MINUTES TOTAL TIME: 30 MINUTES

1   cup 2% evaporated milk

¼   cup maple syrup, divided

1   tablespoon bourbon (80 to 90 proof)

½   teaspoon vanilla extract

⅛   teaspoon salt

4   large eggs, beaten

8   (1-ounce) slices whole-wheat or whole-grain French bread (not baguette, but a larger loaf)

1½   tablespoons butter, divided

2   medium Honeycrisp apples, cored and thinly sliced

½   teaspoon ground cinnamon

1. Combine milk, 3 tablespoons syrup, bourbon, vanilla, salt, and eggs in a 13 x 9–inch glass or ceramic baking dish, stirring with a whisk. Add bread in a single layer; let stand 10 minutes or until liquid is absorbed, turning bread over after 5 minutes.

2. Heat a large nonstick skillet over medium heat. Add ½ tablespoon butter; swirl until butter melts. Add apples; sprinkle evenly with cinnamon. Cook 10 minutes or until apples are tender, stirring occasionally. Remove from heat; stir in 1 tablespoon syrup. Keep warm.

3. Heat a large griddle or nonstick skillet over medium heat. Add 1½ teaspoons butter; spread melted butter over surface with a spatula. Add 4 bread slices; cook 3 minutes on each side or until browned and done. Remove from pan. Repeat procedure with 1½ teaspoons butter and 4 bread slices. Top French toast with apple mixture.

SERVES 4 *(serving size: 2 French toast slices and about ½ cup apple mixture)*
CALORIES 401; **FAT** 12.2g (sat 5.2g, mono 3.3g, poly 1.2g); **PROTEIN** 15g; **CARB** 55g; **FIBER** 3g; **SUGARS** 29g (est. added sugars 12g); **CHOL** 211mg; **IRON** 2mg; **SODIUM** 561mg; **CALC** 214mg

PANCETTA AND EGG BREAKFAST PIZZA WITH PARMESAN GRAVY

What a fun twist on the standard toast or biscuits with gravy and eggs! Pancetta is wonderful here; it's salty with a nutty sweetness, plus, it's leaner than bacon. But if you'd rather use bacon, go for it—just discard all but about 1½ teaspoons of the drippings.

HANDS-ON TIME: 15 MINUTES TOTAL TIME: 30 MINUTES

2 ounces diced pancetta

1 garlic clove, minced

2 tablespoons white whole-wheat flour

1 cup 1% low-fat milk

1 ounce Parmigiano-Reggiano cheese, grated (about ¼ cup)

1 portion White Wheat Pizza Dough (page 37)

4 large eggs

⅛ teaspoon kosher salt

2 tablespoons coarsely chopped fresh flat-leaf parsley

1. Place a pizza stone or heavy baking sheet in oven. Preheat oven to 500°F (leave stone in oven as it heats).

2. Cook pancetta in a medium nonstick skillet over medium heat 5 minutes or until crisp, stirring occasionally. Remove pancetta from pan with a slotted spoon, reserving drippings. Add garlic to drippings in pan; cook 1 minute, stirring constantly. Add flour; cook 30 seconds, stirring constantly. Gradually add milk, stirring constantly with a whisk; cook 2 minutes or until thick, stirring frequently. Remove from heat; add cheese, stirring until cheese melts.

3. Roll White Wheat Pizza Dough into a 13-inch circle on a lightly floured sheet of parchment paper, shaking occasionally to make sure dough does not stick. Spread gravy over dough, leaving a ½-inch border. Place parchment paper and dough on preheated stone. Bake at 500°F for 7 minutes or until bottom of crust hardens. While crust bakes, crack each egg into a ramekin or custard cup. Once bottom has crisped, pull oven rack out so pizza is easily accessible. Pour each egg onto pizza. Return to oven, and bake an additional 6 minutes (set whites, runny yolks), or until desired degree of doneness. Sprinkle eggs evenly with salt. Sprinkle pizza with pancetta and parsley. Cut into 8 wedges.

SERVES 4 *(serving size: 2 wedges)*
CALORIES 350; **FAT** 12.9g (sat 4.6g, mono 4.4g, poly 1.3g); **PROTEIN** 20g; **CARB** 35g; **FIBER** 5g; **SUGARS** 4g (est. added sugars 0g); **CHOL** 199mg; **IRON** 4mg; **SODIUM** 607mg; **CALC** 227mg

SNACKS AND BITES

What I love most about these appetizers and snacks is the element of surprise. Many take inspiration from global classics and old-school American favorites, yet they're elevated with a modern, healthy, whole-grain spin. Imagine the delight you'll bring to your next party when you serve a creamy dip made from millet, a supremely crunchy wild rice snack mix, or oysters topped with pickled quinoa "caviar."

QUINOA, FETA, AND SPINACH—STUFFED MUSHROOMS (GF)

Give the staid stuffed mushroom hors d'oeuvre a fun makeover by ditching the breadcrumb filling and using quinoa instead. Dill, feta, and spinach give the perfect party bites a little bit of Greek flair. Add the cheese while the other filling ingredients are still warm so that it softens and helps bind the filling.

HANDS-ON TIME: 30 MINUTES TOTAL TIME: 1 HOUR

½ cup plus 1 tablespoon water

⅓ cup uncooked quinoa, rinsed and drained

1 tablespoon extra-virgin olive oil

¼ cup minced shallots

4 garlic cloves, minced

5 ounces fresh baby spinach, coarsely chopped

3 ounces feta cheese, crumbled (about ¾ cup)

2 tablespoons chopped fresh dill

¼ teaspoon kosher salt

¼ teaspoon freshly ground black pepper

36 large cremini mushrooms, stems removed

1. Bring ½ cup plus 1 tablespoon water to a boil. Add quinoa; cover, reduce heat, and simmer 20 minutes or until quinoa is tender and liquid is absorbed. Fluff quinoa with a fork.

2. Preheat oven to 350°F.

3. Heat a medium skillet over medium heat. Add oil to pan; swirl to coat. Add shallots and garlic; cook 5 minutes or until tender, stirring occasionally. Gradually add spinach, tossing constantly until spinach wilts. Remove from heat. Stir in quinoa, cheese, dill, salt, and pepper. Spoon mixture evenly into mushroom caps (about 1½ teaspoons each). Arrange mushrooms on a foil-lined jelly-roll pan. Bake at 350°F for 25 minutes or until mushrooms are tender.

MAKE AHEAD

You can stuff the mushroom caps up to a day in advance; refrigerate in a single layer. Bake as directed, adding up to 5 minutes to the cook time to ensure the filling is thoroughly heated.

SERVES 12 *(serving size: 3 stuffed mushrooms)*
CALORIES 68; **FAT** 3g (sat 1.3g, mono 1.2g, poly 0.4g); **PROTEIN** 4g; **CARB** 8g; **FIBER** 1g; **SUGARS** 2g (est. added sugars 0g); **CHOL** 6mg; **IRON** 1mg; **SODIUM** 142mg; **CALC** 60mg

CHEESY SAUSAGE BALLS GF

Five simple ingredients make for a crowd-pleasing appetizer. Traditional recipes call for boxed baking mix—a combination of refined white flour, leavening, salt, and shortening (a known source of trans fats). This recipe uses quinoa instead, and less cheese and leaner sausage to shave off half the calories, fat, and sodium of the original version. Not to worry: All the great flavor and appeal are still there.

HANDS-ON TIME: 10 MINUTES TOTAL TIME: 30 MINUTES

1 cup cooked quinoa, chilled

4 ounces reduced-fat sharp cheddar cheese, shredded (about 1 cup)

1 pound reduced-fat pork sausage (such as Jimmy Dean)

1 tablespoon cornstarch

¼ teaspoon freshly ground black pepper

Cooking spray

1. Preheat oven to 375°F.

2. Combine first 5 ingredients in a bowl. Shape mixture into 40 (1½-inch) balls. Place balls on a foil-lined baking sheet coated with cooking spray. Bake at 375°F for 18 minutes or until lightly browned and done.

MAKE AHEAD

Cover and refrigerate unbaked balls up to 24 hours; or place in a heavy-duty zip-top plastic bag, and freeze unbaked balls up to 1 month. Bake frozen balls at 375°F for 22 to 25 minutes or until done.

SERVES 20 *(serving size: 2 sausage balls)*
CALORIES 85; **FAT** 5.3g (sat 2.1g, mono 2.1g, poly 0.5g); **PROTEIN** 6g; **CARB** 3g; **FIBER** 0g; **SUGARS** 0g (est. added sugars 0g); **CHOL** 17mg; **IRON** 0mg; **SODIUM** 175mg; **CALC** 53mg

MILLET "ARANCINI" CROQUETTES

Traditional arancini is made with rice that's combined with cheese and other fillings; then it's breaded and fried. This version uses millet that's cooked in extra water so that it's soft and sticky, and combines it with two kinds of cheese and buttery-garlicky wilted spinach. You can cook the croquettes ahead and refrigerate until shortly before serving; warm them in a 350°F oven for 15 minutes or until thoroughly heated.

HANDS-ON TIME: 34 MINUTES   TOTAL TIME: 1 HOUR 14 MINUTES

2   cups water
⅔   cup uncooked millet
1   tablespoon butter
3   garlic cloves, minced
5   ounces fresh baby spinach
2   ounces part-skim mozzarella cheese, shredded (about ½ cup)
1   ounce Parmigiano-Reggiano cheese, grated (about ¼ cup)
⅝   teaspoon kosher salt
¼   teaspoon freshly ground black pepper
2   large egg whites
1   large egg
1   cup whole-wheat panko (Japanese breadcrumbs)
3   tablespoons canola oil

1. Combine 2 cups water and millet in a small saucepan; bring to a boil. Cover, reduce heat, and simmer 25 minutes. Remove from heat; let stand 10 minutes. Fluff millet with a fork. Place in a large bowl; cool slightly.

2. Heat a medium skillet over medium heat. Add butter; swirl until butter melts. Add garlic; cook 2 minutes, stirring frequently. Add spinach; cook 1 minute or until spinach wilts, tossing constantly. Add spinach mixture to millet. Stir in cheeses and next 4 ingredients (through whole egg).

3. Place panko in a shallow dish. Divide millet mixture into 24 equal portions, shaping each into a ball. Lightly dredge balls in panko, flattening each slightly into a 2-inch patty.

4. Heat a large nonstick skillet over medium heat. Add 1½ tablespoons oil to pan; swirl to coat. Add 12 patties to pan; cook 3 minutes on each side or until browned and thoroughly heated. Repeat procedure with 1½ tablespoons oil and 12 patties.

CHANGE IT UP

If you don't have millet on hand, you can make the croquettes with 3 cups cooked brown rice. If possible, overcook the rice a bit so that it's soft and slightly sticky.

SERVES 12 *(serving size: 2 croquettes)*
CALORIES 139; **FAT** 6.9g (sat 2g, mono 3.1g, poly 1.4g); **PROTEIN** 6g; **CARB** 14g; **FIBER** 2g; **SUGARS** 1g (est. added sugars 0g); **CHOL** 23mg; **IRON** 1mg; **SODIUM** 208mg; **CALC** 82mg

MILLET CREAM TARATOR DIP ⒼⒻ

Hugh Fearnley-Whittingstall's River Cottage Veg cookbook introduced me to Turkish tarator dip. I was smitten with the creamy combo of walnuts, breadcrumbs, garlic, and olive oil. In place of bread, I use Millet Cream, which works fantastically. Be sure to show this dip some respect by serving it with interesting crudités (I have a thing about boring crudités). Try any combo of multicolored radishes and baby carrots, baby cucumbers, blanched sugar snap peas, golden beet slices, and fennel strips.

HANDS-ON TIME: 10 MINUTES TOTAL TIME: 10 MINUTES

¾ cup coarsely chopped walnuts, toasted
2 garlic cloves
1 cup Millet Cream (page 36)
2 tablespoons fresh lemon juice
¾ teaspoon kosher salt
⅓ cup extra-virgin olive oil, divided
½ teaspoon smoked paprika

1. Place walnuts and garlic in a food processor; pulse until finely chopped. Add Millet Cream, juice, and salt; process until smooth. Reserve 1½ teaspoons oil.

2. With food processor on, drizzle remaining oil through food chute. Spoon dip into a bowl; drizzle with reserved 1½ teaspoons oil. Sprinkle with paprika.

SERVES 10 (serving size: about 3 tablespoons)
CALORIES 143; **FAT** 13g (sat 1.7g, mono 6.1g, poly 5g); **PROTEIN** 2g; **CARB** 5g; **FIBER** 1g; **SUGARS** 1g (est. added sugars 0g); **CHOL** 1mg;
IRON 0mg; **SODIUM** 149mg; **CALC** 22mg

POLENTA TOASTS WITH BALSAMIC ONIONS, ROASTED PEPPERS, FETA, AND THYME (GF)

Polenta is surprisingly adaptable, morphing from a creamy porridge to firm, sear-able "toasts" after a little time in the fridge. This is a good technique to have in your back pocket for those times when you'll be feeding gluten-free guests; anything you would have served as bruschetta can become topped polenta toasts.

HANDS-ON TIME: 1 HOUR TOTAL TIME: 3 HOURS

3   cups water
¾   teaspoon salt, divided
1   cup dry whole-grain polenta
2   tablespoons olive oil, divided
2   tablespoons butter, divided
Cooking spray
1   teaspoon minced fresh garlic
2   cups vertically sliced onion
1   thyme sprig
1   tablespoon balsamic vinegar
¼   cup chopped bottled roasted red bell pepper
2   ounces feta cheese, crumbled (about ¼ cup)
2   teaspoons thyme leaves

1. Bring 3 cups water and ½ teaspoon salt to a boil in a medium saucepan. Gradually add polenta, stirring constantly with a whisk. Reduce heat to low, and cook 20 minutes, stirring frequently. Stir in 1 tablespoon oil and 1 tablespoon butter. Spoon polenta into an 8-inch square glass or ceramic baking dish coated with cooking spray. Press plastic wrap onto surface of polenta; chill 2 hours or until firm.

2. Heat a large skillet over medium-high heat. Add 1 tablespoon oil and 1 tablespoon butter; swirl to coat. Add garlic; sauté 15 seconds. Add ¼ teaspoon salt, onion, and thyme sprig; sauté 3 minutes or until onion begins to soften. Reduce heat to low; cook 30 minutes or until onion is very tender, stirring frequently. Add vinegar; cook 5 minutes, stirring frequently. Discard thyme sprig.

3. Invert polenta onto a cutting board; cut into 16 squares. Cut each square in half diagonally. Heat a skillet over medium heat. Lightly coat polenta triangles with cooking spray. Add 16 triangles to pan; cook 5 minutes on each side or until lightly browned. Repeat procedure with remaining triangles.

4. Divide onion mixture, bell pepper, and feta evenly among triangles. Sprinkle evenly with thyme leaves.

MAKE AHEAD

You can prepare the polenta and onions a few days in advance. Proceed with step 3 shortly before your party.

SERVES 16 *(serving size: 2 triangles)*
CALORIES 77; **FAT** 4g (sat 1.7g, mono 1.8g, poly 0.3g); **PROTEIN** 2g; **CARB** 9g; **FIBER** 1g; **SUGARS** 1g (est. added sugars 0g); **CHOL** 7mg; **IRON** 1mg; **SODIUM** 172mg; **CALC** 22mg

CRISPY GREEN BEANS WITH SRIRACHA MAYO

Toasted panko makes these veggie sticks supremely, addictively crunchy. No leftover green beans? Sub in a bag of microwaved steamed beans.

HANDS-ON TIME: 15 MINUTES TOTAL TIME: 30 MINUTES

¼ cup canola mayonnaise

¼ cup low-fat buttermilk

2 teaspoons Sriracha (hot chile sauce, such as Huy Fong)

1 tablespoon fresh lime juice

2½ cups whole-wheat panko (Japanese breadcrumbs)

2 teaspoons thyme leaves

1 teaspoon garlic powder

½ teaspoon ground red pepper

⅛ teaspoon kosher salt

½ cup all-purpose flour

4 large egg whites, beaten

1 pound leftover steamed green beans

1. Preheat oven to 375°F.

2. Combine mayonnaise, buttermilk, Sriracha, and lime juice in a small bowl; cover and chill.

3. Place panko in an even layer on a baking sheet. Bake at 375°F for 4 minutes or until golden. Transfer panko to a shallow dish; cool completely. Add thyme, garlic powder, pepper, and salt; toss well. Place flour in a shallow dish. Place egg whites in another shallow dish. Dredge half of green beans in flour. Dip in egg whites; dredge in panko mixture. Place beans on a baking sheet. Repeat procedure with remaining beans, flour, egg whites, and panko mixture. Place remaining coated beans on another baking sheet. Bake green beans at 375°F for 8 minutes or until crisp. Serve with Sriracha mayo.

SERVES 8 *(serving size: about ¾ cup beans and 1 tablespoon dip)*
CALORIES 151; **FAT** 2.8g (sat 0.1g, mono 1.2g, poly 0.8g); **PROTEIN** 7g; **CARB** 24g; **FIBER** 3g; **SUGARS** 2g (est. added sugars 0g); **CHOL** 0 mg; **IRON** 1mg; **SODIUM** 198mg; **CALC** 38mg

POPPED AMARANTH CHAAT (GF)

Bhel puri *is one of India's most popular* chaats, *or street snacks; the classic version is made with puffed rice, chutney, boiled potatoes, and other mix-ins. I thought it would be fun to try it with Popped Amaranth, with its toasty flavor and soft crunch. Mix up single servings at a time, and serve immediately. You'll make more of the cilantro-mint chutney than you need, but it's nearly impossible to make less using a regular blender. If you have a mini-blender, it's perfect for this job. Stir leftover chutney into rice, drizzle over pizza or grilled meat, or make more bhel puri.*

HANDS-ON TIME: 18 MINUTES TOTAL TIME: 33 MINUTES

½ cup (¼-inch) diced peeled Yukon gold potato

1 cup lightly packed mint leaves

1 cup lightly packed cilantro leaves and stems

¼ cup water

1 tablespoon fresh lemon juice

1 teaspoon grated peeled fresh ginger

¼ teaspoon kosher salt

1 serrano pepper (stem removed), coarsely chopped

2 cups Popped Amaranth (page 30)

½ cup diced seeded tomato

8 teaspoons Major Grey chutney (such as Patak's)

2 tablespoons minced red onion

Cilantro leaves

1. Place potato in a small saucepan; cover with water. Bring to a boil. Reduce heat, and simmer 10 minutes or until tender; drain and set aside.

2. Place mint, cilantro, ¼ cup water, juice, ginger, salt, and serrano in a mini blender; process until completely pureed and sludgy-looking, scraping sides as needed. This should yield about ½ cup; you'll use only ¼ cup for this recipe.

3. Place ½ cup Popped Amaranth into each of 4 bowls. Top each serving with 1 tablespoon mint-cilantro chutney, 2 tablespoons potato, 2 tablespoons tomato, 2 teaspoons Major Grey chutney, and 1½ teaspoons onion; toss well to combine. Top with cilantro leaves.

SERVES 4 *(serving size: about ¾ cup)*
CALORIES 139; **FAT** 1.5g (sat 0.3g, mono 0.3g, poly 0.6g); **PROTEIN** 4g; **CARB** 28g; **FIBER** 2g; **SUGARS** 7g (est. added sugars 5g); **CHOL** 0mg; **IRON** 2mg; **SODIUM** 178mg; **CALC** 43mg

POPPED AMARANTH AND SESAME CANDIES (GF)

This is a fun, ancient-grain spin on a traditional candy you see in Asian, Greek, and Middle Eastern cuisines. I'm basing this on a Korean version made with all sesame seeds, but here I've replaced half the seeds with Popped Amaranth. The texture is crunchy-chewy, and the flavor is absolute toasty goodness.

HANDS-ON TIME: 12 MINUTES TOTAL TIME: 54 MINUTES

½ cup packed dark brown sugar
½ cup honey
⅜ teaspoon salt
½ cup sesame seeds, toasted
½ cup black sesame seeds, toasted
1⅓ cups Popped Amaranth (page 30)
   Cooking spray

1. Combine first 3 ingredients in a medium, heavy saucepan; bring to a boil over medium-high heat. Reduce heat to medium, and cook 2 minutes. Remove from heat; stir in sesame seeds and Popped Amaranth; toss well to combine. Spoon mixture into a 9-inch square metal baking pan coated with cooking spray; press into an even layer. Cool 15 minutes.

2. Invert warm sesame mixture onto a large cutting board. Cut mixture into 4 (9 x 2¼–inch) strips; cut each strip into 10 pieces to yield 40 (2¼ x about ¾–inch) pieces. Cool completely. Store in an airtight container.

SERVES 20 *(serving size: 2 pieces)*
CALORIES 91; **FAT** 3.2g (sat 0.5g, mono 1.2g, poly 1.4g); **PROTEIN** 1g; **CARB** 15g; **FIBER** 1g; **SUGARS** 12g (est. added sugars 12g); **CHOL** 0mg; **IRON** 1mg; **SODIUM** 49mg; **CALC** 17mg

OYSTERS WITH PICKLED QUINOA MIGNONETTE (GF)

Set out a tray of these oysters on the half shell, and you'll be talked about (in a good way!) for weeks. Quinoa soaks in red wine vinegar and gets tossed with shallots, black pepper, and dill—taking on the flavor of classic mignonette sauce—with the added fun pop on the palate similar to that of caviar. The puckery quinoa mixture would also be fantastic on or in deviled eggs.

HANDS-ON TIME: 20 MINUTES TOTAL TIME: 2 HOURS

2/3 cup red wine vinegar

½ teaspoon kosher salt

1 bay leaf

½ cup cooked quinoa

2 tablespoons minced shallots

1 tablespoon chopped fresh dill

½ teaspoon freshly ground black pepper

24 shucked oysters

Dill sprigs (optional)

1. Bring first 3 ingredients to a boil in a small saucepan; cook 1 minute. Add quinoa; remove from heat. Let stand at room temperature 1 hour; drain and discard bay leaf. Place pickled quinoa in a bowl; add shallots, chopped dill, and pepper, tossing to coat. Spoon about 1 teaspoon quinoa mixture on each oyster; garnish with dill sprigs, if desired.

SERVES 8 *(serving size: 3 topped oysters)*
CALORIES 42; **FAT** 0.9g (sat 0.2g, mono 0.1g, poly 0.3g); **PROTEIN** 3g; **CARB** 5g; **FIBER** 0g; **SUGARS** 0g (est. added sugars 0g); **CHOL** 11mg; **IRON** 3mg; **SODIUM** 106mg; **CALC** 22mg

KOREAN ROASTED BARLEY TEA

This is a common Korean drink called bori cha, *often served hot at the table or as a surprisingly refreshing chilled beverage. I think of it as a happy by-product of something I'm already making—because it's the cooking liquid most people discard. In Korean markets, you'll find packages of pre-toasted, browned barley, but it's easy to just toast it yourself.*

HANDS-ON TIME: 11 MINUTES TOTAL TIME: 41 MINUTES

1 cup uncooked hulled barley

8 cups water

1. Heat a Dutch oven over medium heat. Add barley to pan; cook 10 minutes or until evenly toasty-brown and fragrant, stirring frequently. Add 8 cups water to pan. Increase heat to high, and bring to a boil. Reduce heat, and simmer 30 minutes, uncovered. Strain through a cheesecloth-lined sieve into a heatproof pitcher.* Serve hot, or allow to cool to room temperature and chill.

* Note: The barley likely won't be done at this point, but you can return it to the pan, cover with fresh water, and continue cooking for another 15 minutes or so or until tender; then it's ready to use in recipes.

SERVES 6 *(serving size: ½ cup)*
CALORIES 8; **FAT** 0.1g (sat 0g, mono 0g, poly 0g); **PROTEIN** 0g; **CARB** 2g; **FIBER** 0g; **SUGARS** 0g (est. added sugars 0g); **CHOL** 0mg; **IRON** 0mg; **SODIUM** 0mg; **CALC** 1mg

BROWN RICE SUSHI WITH SMOKED SALMON AND QUICK-PICKLED CARROT (GF)

Sushi-making isn't hard, but it sure does seem to impress. I like to make inside-out rolls, where the rice is on the outside. If you want to get really fancy, you can lay slivers of avocado on the outside of the rolls, and wrap in plastic wrap to shape. Chill that way for 30 minutes, and then slice into rolls. Serve with wasabi and lower-sodium soy sauce for dipping. (Note: Not all soy sauces are gluten-free. Make sure to check the label.)

HANDS-ON TIME: 25 MINUTES TOTAL TIME: 1 HOUR 50 MINUTES

Rice:
- 3 cups water
- 1½ cups uncooked short-grain brown rice
- 3 tablespoons seasoned rice vinegar

Carrot:
- ¼ cup seasoned rice vinegar
- ¼ cup water
- 1 large carrot, peeled and cut into 4-inch-long matchstick strips

Remaining ingredients:
- 1 English cucumber
- 4 nori sheets (seaweed)
- 4 ounces thinly sliced cold-smoked salmon
- 1 tablespoon toasted sesame seeds

1. To prepare rice, bring 3 cups water and rice to a boil in a medium saucepan; cover, reduce heat, and simmer 45 minutes. Remove from heat; let stand, covered, 10 minutes. Uncover; drizzle with 3 tablespoons vinegar, tossing well to combine. Spread rice out onto a jelly-roll pan to cool. Cool to room temperature.

2. To prepare carrot, bring ¼ cup vinegar and ¼ cup water to a boil in a small saucepan. Add carrot; cook 2 minutes. Let cool in saucepan 5 minutes. Drain and pat dry.

3. Cut a 4-inch-long chunk of cucumber. Cut in half lengthwise; cut each half lengthwise into 4 pieces.

4. Wrap a sushi mat entirely in plastic wrap. Arrange 1 nori sheet on mat, rough side up; using damp hands, pat about 1¼ cups rice over nori. Flip nori over, rice side down. Arrange 1 ounce salmon, 2 cucumber pieces, and one-fourth of carrot along edge of nori closest to you. Roll up nori tightly using mat. Place roll, seam side down, on a cutting board. Repeat procedure with remaining nori, rice, salmon, cucumber, and carrot. Sprinkle rolls with sesame seeds, pressing gently to adhere. Cut each roll into 9 pieces.

MAKE IT FASTER

You can save about an hour if you use precooked brown sticky rice, found in Asian markets and in the Asian section of large grocery stores. You'll need 5 cups.

SERVES 12 (serving size: 3 pieces)
CALORIES 114; **FAT** 1.3g (sat 0.1g, mono 0.3g, poly 0.3g); **PROTEIN** 4g; **CARB** 21g; **FIBER** 1g; **SUGARS** 2g (est. added sugars 0g); **CHOL** 2mg; **IRON** 1mg; **SODIUM** 134mg; **CALC** 23mg

BROWN RICE—CHEESE CRACKERS (GF)

Gluten-free, whole-grain, crunchy, and savory-good—what could be better? Super-simple prep, that's what. A quick stir-together dough rolls out easily and bakes off perfectly. The crackers keep well, too, up to a week or two in an airtight container.

HANDS-ON TIME: 15 MINUTES TOTAL TIME: 1 HOUR 10 MINUTES

6.63 ounces brown rice flour (about 1½ cups)

3 ounces extra-sharp cheddar cheese, shredded (about ¾ cup)

¼ cup cornstarch

½ ounce Parmigiano-Reggiano cheese, finely grated (about 2 tablespoons)

1 teaspoon garlic powder

½ teaspoon baking powder

⅜ teaspoon salt

¼ teaspoon ground red pepper

¼ cup canola oil

¼ cup water

1 large egg, lightly beaten

1. Preheat oven to 375°F.

2. Weigh or lightly spoon flour into dry measuring cups; level with a knife. Combine flour and next 7 ingredients (through red pepper) in a large bowl. Combine oil, ¼ cup water, and egg, stirring with a whisk. Add oil mixture to flour mixture; stir well. Knead in bowl until a soft dough forms.

3. Turn dough out onto a large sheet of parchment paper; cover with a large sheet of plastic wrap. Roll dough to a 14 x 11–inch rectangle; discard plastic wrap. Cut dough with a pizza wheel or sharp knife into 1¼-inch squares; do not separate dough pieces. Pierce each dough square once with a fork. Slide dough, on parchment paper, onto a large baking sheet. Bake at 375°F for 25 minutes or until lightly browned around edges. Cool crackers (as 1 large piece) on a wire rack. When cool, break into individual crackers.

SERVES 12 *(serving size: about 8 crackers)*
CALORIES 156; **FAT** 8.4g (sat 2.3g, mono 3.1g, poly 1.6g); **PROTEIN** 4g; **CARB** 16g; **FIBER** 1g; **SUGARS** 0g (est. added sugars 0g); **CHOL** 24mg; **IRON** 0mg; **SODIUM** 163mg; **CALC** 79mg

CRUNCHY CHOCOLATE-ALMOND ENERGY BITES GF

Pop a couple of these little snacks to satisfy sweet-tooth cravings. Bonus: You'll get a wholesome whole-grain punch and a good bit of protein.

HANDS-ON TIME: 15 MINUTES TOTAL TIME: 1 HOUR 25 MINUTES

½ cup uncooked amaranth

½ cup agave nectar or honey

½ cup unsalted creamy almond butter (such as Justin's)

¼ cup unsweetened cocoa

1 teaspoon vanilla extract

⅜ teaspoon kosher salt

1½ cups Crunchy Fried Sorghum (page 32)

1. Heat a large skillet over medium-high heat. Add amaranth; cook 1½ minutes or until toasty-fragrant, shaking pan frequently (do not pop grains). Pour amaranth into a bowl; cool to room temperature.

2. Place agave and almond butter in a large microwave-safe bowl; microwave at HIGH 20 seconds (just to loosen almond butter). Stir with a whisk until smooth. Stir in cocoa, vanilla, and salt. Add amaranth and Crunchy Fried Sorghum; stir well to combine.

3. Scoop mixture by level tablespoonfuls, and roll into 32 balls. Place on a platter lined with wax or parchment paper. Refrigerate 1 hour or until firm.

SERVES 16 *(serving size: 2 balls)*
CALORIES 153; **FAT** 7.6g (sat 0.8g, mono 4.3g, poly 2g); **PROTEIN** 4g; **CARB** 20g; **FIBER** 2g; **SUGARS** 9g (est. added sugars 8g); **CHOL** 0mg; **IRON** 1mg; **SODIUM** 63mg; **CALCIUM** 41mg

CRANBERRY-PISTACHIO ENERGY BARS ⓖⒻ

These DIY snack bars are so easy to make, you may never buy a boxed version again. Think of this recipe as a template, and vary the bars to suit your taste—try different nut or seed butters, any other dried fruit, and whatever nuts you have on hand. The bars fit snugly into snack-sized zip-top plastic bags but also divide easily into squares.

HANDS-ON TIME: 10 MINUTES TOTAL TIME: 35 MINUTES

1 cup uncooked old-fashioned rolled oats

¾ cup uncooked quinoa, rinsed and drained

¾ cup sweetened dried cranberries, coarsely chopped

¾ cup salted, dry-roasted pistachios, chopped

⅓ cup flaked unsweetened coconut

2 tablespoons flaxseed meal

1 ounce bittersweet chocolate, finely chopped

½ cup unsalted creamy almond butter (such as Justin's)

6 tablespoons agave nectar

1 tablespoon canola oil

¼ teaspoon salt

Cooking spray

1. Preheat oven to 350°F.

2. Spread oats and quinoa on a baking sheet. Bake at 350°F for 8 minutes or until lightly browned. Cool. Place oat mixture in a large bowl, and stir in cranberries, pistachios, coconut, flaxseed meal, and chocolate.

3. Combine almond butter, agave nectar, oil, and salt in a small saucepan over medium heat; bring to a boil. Cook 1 minute, stirring constantly. Pour almond butter mixture over oat mixture; toss well to coat. Press mixture into an 8-inch square glass or ceramic baking dish coated with cooking spray. Bake at 350°F for 13 minutes or until lightly browned. Cool completely in dish. Cut into 16 (1 x 4–inch) bars.

MAKE AHEAD

Store bars in an airtight container up to 3 days, or freeze in a heavy-duty freezer bag for up to 1 month.

SERVES 16 *(serving size: 1 bar)*
CALORIES 193; **FAT** 10g (sat 2.1g, mono 4.6g, poly 2.6g); **PROTEIN** 5g; **CARB** 23g; **FIBER** 3g; **SUGARS** 12g (est. added sugars 9g); **CHOL** 0mg; **IRON** 1mg; **SODIUM** 72mg; **CALC** 43mg

EVERYTHING AMARANTH CRACKERS (GF)

The popular everything bagel topping makes delicious savory flavoring for these whole-grain bites. Toasting the amaranth flour removes some of its bitterness and strong grassy flavor, resulting in a nutty-tasting cracker with a light, crisp texture.

HANDS-ON TIME: 15 MINUTES TOTAL TIME: 45 MINUTES

4 ounces amaranth flour (about 1 cup plus 2 tablespoons)
3 tablespoons cornstarch
1 teaspoon garlic powder
1 teaspoon onion powder
½ teaspoon baking powder
½ teaspoon kosher salt
¼ cup extra-virgin olive oil
5 to 6 tablespoons ice water
1 large egg yolk, lightly beaten
2 teaspoons sesame seeds
1½ teaspoons poppy seeds or black sesame seeds
⅜ teaspoon cracked black pepper

1. Preheat oven to 350°F.

2. Weigh or lightly spoon flour into a dry measuring cup; level with a knife. Spread flour out in an ovenproof skillet or jelly-roll pan. Bake at 350°F for 15 minutes or until lightly browned and flour smells nutty and not grassy, stirring every 5 minutes. Cool flour.

3. Increase oven temperature to 375°F.

4. Place flour, cornstarch, and next 4 ingredients (through salt) in a food processor; pulse 3 times to combine. Drizzle flour mixture with oil; pulse to combine. Drizzle 5 to 6 tablespoons ice water through food chute while pulsing mixture, just until a dough forms. Remove dough from processor.

5. Roll dough to ⅛-inch thickness between sheets of plastic wrap. Cut with a 2-inch round cutter to form 32 rounds, rerolling scraps. Arrange dough rounds on a large baking sheet lined with parchment paper. Brush egg yolk over dough. Combine sesame seeds, poppy seeds, and pepper; sprinkle over dough, pressing gently to adhere. Bake at 375°F for 15 to 16 minutes or until lightly browned. Place crackers on wire racks; cool completely.

SERVES 8 *(serving size: 4 crackers)*
CALORIES 156; **FAT** 9.1g (sat 1.5g, mono 5.4g, poly 1.1g); **PROTEIN** 3g; **CARB** 16g; **FIBER** 2g; **SUGARS** 0g (est. added sugars 0g); **CHOL** 23mg; **IRON** 2mg; **SODIUM** 158mg; **CALC** 58mg

Crunchy Wild Rice
Snack Mix,
page 102

CRUNCHY WILD RICE SNACK MIX (GF)

Ever find yourself seriously loving the crunchy-salty bowl of yum at the bar, even to the point that you'd choose it over the drink? This is that kind of snack.

HANDS-ON TIME: 3 MINUTES TOTAL TIME: 45 MINUTES

2 tablespoons honey
1½ tablespoons butter
½ teaspoon kosher salt
½ teaspoon ground cinnamon
½ teaspoon ground cumin
¼ teaspoon ground red pepper
2 cups Fried Wild Rice (page 34)
½ cup pecan halves
½ cup salted dry-roasted cashews
Cooking spray

1. Preheat oven to 325°F.

2. Place honey and butter in a large microwave-safe bowl. Microwave at HIGH 40 seconds or until butter melts. Stir in salt, cinnamon, cumin, and pepper. Add Fried Wild Rice, pecans, and cashews; toss well to coat. Spread mixture onto a foil-lined jelly-roll pan coated with cooking spray. Bake at 325°F for 15 to 17 minutes, stirring after 8 minutes. Cool completely; break up any large clumps.

SERVES 10 *(serving size: about ⅓ cup)*
CALORIES 150; **FAT** 10.7g (sat 2.2g, mono 5.7g, poly 2.3g); **PROTEIN** 3g; **CARB** 13g; **FIBER** 1g; **SUGARS** 4g (est. added sugars 3g); **CHOL** 5mg; **IRON** 1mg; **SODIUM** 156mg; **CALC** 11mg

POPCORN SIX WAYS

Folks often forget that popcorn is a great whole-grain snack, and a hefty serving size has a modest calorie count. Here, six delicious and quick ways to snazz up your bowl.

KOREAN SWEET-SALTY POPCORN

HANDS-ON TIME: 10 MINUTES TOTAL TIME: 15 MINUTES

1½ tablespoons brown sugar

4 teaspoons lower-sodium soy sauce

2 tablespoons dark sesame oil, divided

1 garlic clove, grated

⅓ cup unpopped popcorn

1. Combine brown sugar, soy sauce, 1 tablespoon oil, and garlic in a small jar; cover and shake until emulsified and sugar dissolves. Heat a Dutch oven over medium-high heat. Add 1 tablespoon oil; swirl to coat. Add popcorn; cover and cook 3 minutes or until kernels pop, shaking pan frequently. When popping slows down, remove pan from heat. Let stand 1 minute or until popping stops. Drizzle with sugar mixture; toss well to combine. Serve immediately.

SERVES 4 *(serving size: about 2⅔ cups)*
CALORIES 147; **FAT** 7.7g (sat 1g, mono 3g, poly 3g); **PROTEIN** 2g; **CARB** 18g; **FIBER** 2g; **SUGARS** 7g (est. added sugars 7g); **CHOL** 0mg; **IRON** 0mg; **SODIUM** 194mg; **CALC** 7mg

TRUFFLE AND PARMESAN POPCORN GF

HANDS-ON TIME: 10 MINUTES TOTAL TIME: 15 MINUTES

1 tablespoon canola oil

⅓ cup unpopped popcorn

1 tablespoon white or black truffle oil

Cooking spray

1 ounce finely grated Parmigiano-Reggiano cheese (about ¼ cup)

2 tablespoons chopped fresh chives

⅛ teaspoon salt

1. Heat a Dutch oven over medium-high heat. Add canola oil; swirl to coat. Add popcorn; cover and cook 3 minutes or until kernels pop, shaking pan frequently. When popping slows down, remove pan from heat. Let stand 1 minute or until popping stops. Drizzle with truffle oil; toss well. Lightly coat popcorn with cooking spray. Add cheese, chives, and salt; toss well.

SERVES 4 *(serving size: about 2⅔ cups)*
CALORIES 144; **FAT** 9.5g (sat 1.9g, mono 5g, poly 1.5g); **PROTEIN** 4g; **CARB** 11g; **FIBER** 2g; **SUGARS** 0g (est. added sugars 0g); **CHOL** 5mg; **IRON** 0mg; **SODIUM** 187mg; **CALC** 85mg

CHIMICHURRI POPCORN GF

HANDS-ON TIME: 10 MINUTES TOTAL TIME: 15 MINUTES

3 tablespoons extra-virgin olive oil, divided

⅓ cup unpopped popcorn

1 teaspoon grated lime rind

½ teaspoon dried oregano

⅓ teaspoon kosher salt

¼ teaspoon crushed red pepper

1 garlic clove, grated

¼ cup chopped fresh flat-leaf parsley

¼ cup chopped fresh cilantro

1. Heat a Dutch oven over medium-high heat. Add 1 tablespoon oil; swirl to coat. Add popcorn; cover and cook 3 minutes or until kernels pop, shaking pan frequently. When popping slows down, remove pan from heat. Let stand 1 minute or until popping stops.

2. Combine 2 tablespoons oil, lime rind, oregano, salt, red pepper, and 1 grated garlic clove in a microwave-safe bowl; microwave at HIGH 45 seconds. Drizzle oil mixture over popcorn; toss well to coat. Toss in parsley and cilantro. Serve immediately.

SERVES 4 (serving size: about 2⅔ cups)
CALORIES 150; **FAT** 10.9g (sat 1.4g, mono 7.4g, poly 1.1g); **PROTEIN** 2g; **CARB** 12g; **FIBER** 3g; **SUGARS** 0g (est. added sugars 0g); **CHOL** 0mg; **IRON** 1mg; **SODIUM** 183mg; **CALC** 10mg

CINNAMON TOAST POPCORN GF

HANDS-ON TIME: 10 MINUTES TOTAL TIME: 15 MINUTES

1 tablespoon plus 1½ teaspoons canola oil, divided

⅓ cup unpopped popcorn

1 tablespoon butter

¼ teaspoon kosher salt

¼ teaspoon vanilla extract

¼ cup powdered sugar

¾ teaspoon ground cinnamon

1. Heat a Dutch oven over medium-high heat. Add 1 tablespoon oil; swirl to coat. Add popcorn; cover and cook 3 minutes or until kernels pop, shaking pan frequently. When popping slows down, remove pan from heat. Let stand 1 minute or until popping stops.

2. Cook butter in a small skillet over medium heat 3 minutes or until browned and fragrant; stir in 1½ teaspoons oil, salt, and vanilla extract. Drizzle mixture over popcorn; toss well to coat. Combine sugar and cinnamon; sprinkle over popcorn, and toss well.

SERVES 4 (serving size: about 2⅔ cups)
CALORIES 158; **FAT** 8.8g (sat 2.2g, mono 3.8g, poly 1.6g); **PROTEIN** 2g; **CARB** 19g; **FIBER** 3g; **SUGARS** 8g (est. added sugars 7g); **CHOL** 8mg; **IRON** 0mg; **SODIUM** 146mg; **CALC** 6mg

CHOCOLATE MALT POPCORN (GF)

HANDS-ON TIME: 10 MINUTES TOTAL TIME: 15 MINUTES

1 tablespoon canola oil

⅓ cup unpopped popcorn

2 tablespoons powdered sugar

2 tablespoons malted milk powder

1 tablespoon unsweetened cocoa

⅛ teaspoon salt

Cooking spray

1. Heat a Dutch oven over medium-high heat. Add oil; swirl to coat. Add popcorn; cover and cook 3 minutes or until kernels pop, shaking pan frequently. When popping slows down, remove pan from heat. Let stand 1 minute or until popping stops.

2. Combine sugar, malted milk powder, cocoa, and salt. Lightly coat popcorn with cooking spray. Sprinkle with sugar mixture, and toss well.

SERVES 4 (serving size: about 2⅔ cups)
CALORIES 150; **FAT** 5.5g (sat 0.8g, mono 2.4g, poly 1.2g); **PROTEIN** 3g; **CARB** 23g; **FIBER** 3g; **SUGARS** 9g (est. added sugars 6g); **CHOL** 3mg; **IRON** 1mg; **SODIUM** 116mg; **CALC** 31mg

HIPSTER BAIT POPCORN (POPCORN WITH KALE AND SRIRACHA BUTTER) (GF)

HANDS-ON TIME: 10 MINUTES TOTAL TIME: 15 MINUTES

3 ounces stemmed, torn, patted-dry curly kale

2 tablespoons canola oil, divided

⅓ cup unpopped popcorn

2 teaspoons butter

2 teaspoons Sriracha (hot chile sauce, such as Huy Fong)

¼ teaspoon kosher salt

1. Combine kale and 1½ teaspoons oil, tossing well; arrange half of kale on microwave-safe paper towels. Microwave at HIGH 4 minutes or until crisp, checking every 20 seconds after 2½ minutes. Repeat with remaining kale. Heat a Dutch oven over medium-high heat. Add 1 tablespoon oil; swirl to coat. Add popcorn; cover and cook 3 minutes or until kernels pop, shaking pan frequently. When popping slows down, remove pan from heat. Let stand 1 minute or until popping stops.

2. Combine butter, Sriracha, 1½ teaspoons oil, and salt in a microwave-safe bowl; microwave at HIGH 30 seconds. Drizzle butter mixture over popcorn; toss well to coat. Toss with kale chips. Serve immediately.

SERVES 4 (serving size: about 2⅔ cups)
CALORIES 147; **FAT** 9.7g (sat 1.7g, mono 4.5g, poly 2.1g); **PROTEIN** 2g; **CARB** 14g; **FIBER** 3g; **SUGARS** 0g (est. added sugars 0g); **CHOL** 5mg; **IRON** 1mg; **SODIUM** 196mg; **CALC** 29mg

SALADS

A good salad is more than just a set formula of greens and dressing: It should be beautiful—not difficult with the glorious and varied produce available everywhere—and should involve an interplay of interesting textures. This is where whole grains are the salad builder's best friend, lending their unique bite to bowls of tender, crisp, and juicy produce. Now, get creative.

SMOKED BARLEY, BEET, AND GRAPEFRUIT SALAD

The Cooking Light *Test Kitchen perfected a stovetop smoking technique (which works on gas and electric stovetops) that has changed my life. I now keep wood chips and disposable aluminum foil pans on hand because you never know when you might want to smoke something... like barley! A sweet vinaigrette, earthy beets, and the bright citrus twang of grapefruit balance the robust smoky hit of the grains for a truly memorable salad. You can certainly make the salad without smoking the barley—just adjust the honey down to suit the milder flavor.*

HANDS-ON TIME: 25 MINUTES TOTAL TIME: 25 MINUTES

Cooking spray
⅓ cup cherry or apple wood chips
1 cup cooked hulled barley
3 medium beets with greens
2½ tablespoons extra-virgin olive oil
1½ tablespoons champagne vinegar or white wine vinegar
2 teaspoons honey
½ teaspoon kosher salt
¼ teaspoon freshly ground black pepper
1 large pink or ruby red grapefruit, peeled and sectioned

1. Pierce 10 holes on one side of the bottom of a 13 x 9–inch disposable aluminum foil pan. Coat pan with cooking spray. Arrange wood chips over holes inside pan. Spread barley onto opposite side of pan. Place hole side of pan over stovetop burner. Turn burner on high. When wood chips start to smoke, carefully cover pan with foil. Reduce heat to low; smoke 3 minutes. Remove pan from heat; carefully uncover. Rinse and drain barley under cold water; drain well.

2. Trim beets, reserving greens. Remove tough stems from beet greens; tear greens to equal 3 cups, and set aside. Wrap beets together in a large piece of microwave-safe parchment paper. Microwave at HIGH 8 to 9 minutes or until tender; unwrap and cool slightly. Remove skins from beets; cut each beet into 8 wedges. Place beet wedges in a small bowl.

3. Combine oil, vinegar, honey, salt, and pepper in a large bowl, stirring with a whisk. Drizzle 1½ teaspoons vinaigrette over beet wedges; toss to coat. Add barley and beet greens to bowl with remaining vinaigrette; toss gently to coat. Arrange barley mixture in a serving bowl; top with beets and grapefruit.

SERVES 4 *(serving size: about 1 cup)*
CALORIES 201; **FAT** 9.2g (sat 1.3g, mono 6.4g, poly 1.1g); **PROTEIN** 4g; **CARB** 28g; **FIBER** 6g; **SUGARS** 13g (est. added sugars 3g); **CHOL** 0mg; **IRON** 2mg; **SODIUM** 355mg; **CALC** 59mg

MEDITERRANEAN BARLEY WITH CHICKPEAS AND ARUGULA

Are you a weekend warrior type of cook? I try to be—cooking up a big pot of whole grains and using it throughout the week in different incarnations. This main-dish salad offers an easy and delicious use for cooked barley, but you can also use wheat berries, Kamut, spelt, or rye berries.

HANDS-ON TIME: 18 MINUTES TOTAL TIME: 18 MINUTES

3   cups cooked hulled barley
1   cup packed arugula
1   cup finely chopped red
    bell pepper
3   tablespoons finely chopped
    sun-dried tomatoes, packed
    without oil
1   (15½-ounce) can unsalted
    chickpeas, rinsed and drained
2   tablespoons fresh lemon juice
2   tablespoons extra-virgin olive oil
1   teaspoon salt
½   teaspoon crushed red pepper
2   tablespoons chopped pistachios

1. Combine barley, arugula, bell pepper, tomatoes, and chickpeas in a large bowl.

2. Combine lemon juice, oil, salt, and crushed red pepper, stirring with a whisk. Drizzle over barley mixture, and toss. Sprinkle with pistachios.

SERVES 4 *(serving size: 1¼ cups barley mixture and 1½ teaspoons pistachios)*
CALORIES 360; **FAT** 10.1g (sat 1.4g, mono 6.1g, poly 2g); **PROTEIN** 10g; **CARB** 60g; **FIBER** 12g; **SUGARS** 4g (est. added sugars 0g); **CHOL** 0mg; **IRON** 3mg; **SODIUM** 682mg; **CALC** 55mg

MINT AND PISTACHIO TABBOULEH

Based on the classic bulgur and herb salad, this version of tabbouleh incorporates kale and cucumber for more veggie goodness. Serve with chicken, lamb, or beef kebabs or alongside pita sandwiches.

HANDS-ON TIME: 20 MINUTES TOTAL TIME: 20 MINUTES

1 cup cooked bulgur
1 cup chopped stemmed kale
½ cup chopped cucumber
½ cup halved grape tomatoes
¼ cup chopped red onion
¼ cup chopped fresh mint
¼ cup shelled pistachios
1 tablespoon fresh lemon juice
2 teaspoons olive oil
¼ teaspoon kosher salt
¼ teaspoon freshly ground black pepper
Dash of allspice

1. Combine first 7 ingredients in a large bowl. Combine lemon juice and next 4 ingredients (through allspice) in a bowl, stirring with a whisk. Add lemon juice mixture to kale mixture; toss to coat.

SERVES 6 (*serving size: about ⅔ cup*)
CALORIES 81; **FAT** 4g (sat 0.5g, mono 2.3g, poly 0.9g); **PROTEIN** 3g; **CARB** 10g; **FIBER** 3g; **SUGARS** 1g (est. added sugars 0g); **CHOL** 0mg; **IRON** 1mg; **SODIUM** 88mg; **CALC** 32mg

BULGUR SALAD WITH POMEGRANATE AND ORANGE

This salad is reminiscent of one I enjoyed at a Persian restaurant, and it would be absolutely smashing served alongside roast lamb or grilled lamb chops. It's beautiful, with the jewel-like fruit, and the flavor is tangy, sweet, and irresistible. The success of this salad is dependent on the pomegranate molasses, which you'll find at Middle Eastern markets and some gourmet grocery stores. You can also make your own by simmering and reducing pomegranate juice down to a syrup.

HANDS-ON TIME: 13 MINUTES TOTAL TIME: 55 MINUTES

1½ cups water
1 cup uncooked red bulgur
½ teaspoon kosher salt, divided
3 whole cloves
2 tablespoons extra-virgin olive oil
2 tablespoons pomegranate molasses
1 teaspoon honey
¼ teaspoon freshly ground black pepper
1 cup pomegranate arils
1 cup fresh orange sections (about 2 large navel oranges)
½ cup flat-leaf parsley leaves
⅓ cup torn fresh mint
¼ cup chopped pistachios

1. Place 1½ cups water, bulgur, ¼ teaspoon salt, and cloves in a small saucepan; bring to a boil. Cover, reduce heat to low, and simmer 12 minutes. Remove from heat; let stand 10 minutes. Remove and discard cloves (they should have floated to the top). Drain any excess water, if necessary. Spoon bulgur mixture into a large bowl; cool to room temperature.

2. Combine oil, pomegranate molasses, honey, ¼ teaspoon salt, and pepper in a small bowl, stirring well with a whisk. Drizzle over bulgur mixture; toss gently to coat. Add pomegranate arils, oranges, parsley, and mint; toss gently to combine. Sprinkle with pistachios.

MAKE AHEAD

This salad holds up well for about a day—any longer than that, and the orange sections might release too much liquid. Try stirring in some cooked chicken or crumbled feta or goat cheese for a main-dish take with leftovers.

SERVES 6 *(serving size: about 1 cup bulgur mixture and 2 teaspoons chopped pistachios)*
CALORIES 247; **FAT** 7.6g (sat 1g, mono 4.6g, poly 1.2g); **PROTEIN** 5g; **CARB** 41g; **FIBER** 7g; **SUGARS** 12g (est. added sugars 4g); **CHOL** 0mg; **IRON** 2mg; **SODIUM** 168mg; **CALC** 65mg

FARRO, CHERRY, AND WALNUT SALAD

Farro's al dente bite is perfect for this summer salad that holds up well when made ahead. Add juicy cherries, crunchy celery, and a mustardy dressing for the perfect accompaniment to grilled meat, poultry, or fish. If you don't have farro, you can substitute wheat berries, barley, spelt, millet, or quinoa.

HANDS-ON TIME: 55 MINUTES TOTAL TIME: 55 MINUTES

5   cups water
1½ cups uncooked whole-grain farro
½   teaspoon salt, divided
¾   pound sweet cherries, pitted and halved (about 2 cups)
⅔   cup diced celery
½   cup coarsely chopped walnuts, toasted
¼   cup packed flat-leaf parsley leaves
2   tablespoons fresh lemon juice
1   tablespoon whole-grain Dijon mustard
1   tablespoon honey
¼   teaspoon freshly ground black pepper
3   tablespoons extra-virgin olive oil

1. Bring 5 cups water to a boil in a large saucepan. Add farro and ¼ teaspoon salt to boiling water; cook 40 to 45 minutes or until al dente. Drain; cool at room temperature 15 minutes. Combine farro, cherries, celery, walnuts, and parsley in a large bowl.

2. Combine lemon juice, mustard, honey, pepper, and ¼ teaspoon salt, stirring with a whisk. Gradually add oil, stirring constantly with a whisk. Pour dressing over farro mixture; toss to coat.

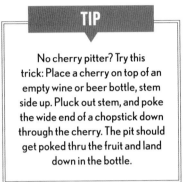

TIP

No cherry pitter? Try this trick: Place a cherry on top of an empty wine or beer bottle, stem side up. Pluck out stem, and poke the wide end of a chopstick down through the cherry. The pit should get poked thru the fruit and land down in the bottle.

SERVES 8 *(serving size: ⅔ cup)*
CALORIES 256; **FAT** 10.6g (sat 1.2g, mono 4.4g, poly 3.9g); **PROTEIN** 7g; **CARB** 37g; **FIBER** 5g; **SUGARS** 7g (est. added sugars 2g); **CHOL** 0mg; **IRON** 2mg; **SODIUM** 201mg; **CALC** 34mg

TUNA, OLIVE, AND WHEAT BERRY SALAD

Be sure to seek out a sustainable type of tuna. A 5-ounce can of Wild Planet's wild albacore tuna in extra-virgin olive oil gives you the correct amount for this salad.

HANDS-ON TIME: 9 MINUTES TOTAL TIME: 9 MINUTES

2   tablespoons chopped
    fresh parsley

2   tablespoons extra-virgin olive oil

2   tablespoons fresh lemon juice

2   teaspoons chopped fresh thyme

½   teaspoon freshly ground
    black pepper

¼   teaspoon kosher salt

2½ cups cooked wheat berries

½   cup thinly vertically sliced
    red onion

10 pitted Castelvetrano
    olives, sliced

4   ounces canned or jarred white
    tuna packed in oil, drained

1. Combine first 6 ingredients in a medium bowl, stirring well with a whisk. Stir in wheat berries and onion; toss to coat. Divide wheat berry mixture among 4 plates. Sprinkle with olives; top with tuna.

SERVES 4 *(serving size: ¾ cup)*
CALORIES 348; **FAT** 12.8g (sat 1.9g, mono 8.2g, poly 2.1g); **PROTEIN** 15g; **CARB** 46g; **FIBER** 8g; **SUGARS** 1g (est. added sugars 0g); **CHOL** 9mg; **IRON** 0mg; **SODIUM** 535mg; **CALC** 10mg

CASHEW, CHICKEN, AND WHEAT BERRY SALAD WITH PEAS

The thigh meat lends an especially moist, rich flavor, but you can use any leftover chicken. If making this salad in winter, when sugar snap peas may taste more starchy than sweet, blanch them in boiling water for 1 minute to brighten the flavor.

HANDS-ON TIME: 14 MINUTES TOTAL TIME: 14 MINUTES

4 teaspoons hoisin sauce
1 tablespoon rice vinegar
1 tablespoon lower-sodium soy sauce
1 tablespoon minced fresh garlic
½ teaspoon freshly ground black pepper
¼ teaspoon kosher salt
2 cups cooked wheat berries
1½ cups chopped cooked chicken thighs
¾ cup sugar snap peas, halved diagonally
½ cup dry-roasted, unsalted cashews
⅓ cup thinly sliced green onions

1. Combine first 6 ingredients in a medium bowl, stirring well with a whisk. Add wheat berries, chicken, and peas; toss well to coat. Stir in cashews and onions.

SERVES 4 *(serving size: 1 cup)*
CALORIES 376; **FAT** 13.3g (sat 3g, mono 6.6g, poly 2.6g); **PROTEIN** 22g; **CARB** 46g; **FIBER** 7g; **SUGARS** 3g (est. added sugars 1g); **CHOL** 71mg; **IRON** 2mg; **SODIUM** 393mg; **CALC** 32mg

WHEAT BERRY SALAD WITH MELON AND FETA

Watermelon-cucumber salads have become a summer classic. This lovely salad starts with that combo and works in tomatoes, wheat berries, and creamy feta cheese for a more substantial take.

HANDS-ON TIME: 22 MINUTES TOTAL TIME: 22 MINUTES

3   tablespoons extra-virgin olive oil
2   tablespoons white wine vinegar
½   teaspoon kosher salt
½   teaspoon freshly ground black pepper
½   teaspoon tomato paste
1½ cups cooked wheat berries
1   cup sliced English cucumber
1   cup chopped watermelon
1   cup yellow grape tomatoes, halved
3   tablespoons chopped fresh mint
2   ounces feta cheese, crumbled (about ½ cup)
2   tablespoons unsalted sunflower seed kernels

1. Combine first 5 ingredients in a large bowl, stirring well with a whisk. Stir in wheat berries; toss to coat. Stir in cucumber, watermelon, tomato, and mint; toss to coat. Sprinkle with cheese and sunflower seeds.

SERVES 4 *(serving size: about 1¼ cups)*
CALORIES 306; **FAT** 16.5g (sat 3.8g, mono 9.2g, poly 2.4g); **PROTEIN** 9g; **CARB** 31g; **FIBER** 5g; **SUGARS** 4g (est. added sugars 0g); **CHOL** 13mg; **IRON** 2mg; **SODIUM** 411mg; **CALC** 103mg

KAMUT SALAD WITH ROASTED CAULIFLOWER AND AVOCADO

The tahini dressing is rich and creamy, pairing well with toasty-roasty cauliflower and chewy Kamut. This salad makes an ideal weekend lunch, and leftovers (minus the avocado) hold up for a day so you can treat yourself to a terrific brown-bag lunch.

HANDS-ON TIME: 20 MINUTES TOTAL TIME: 1 HOUR 30 MINUTES

¾ cup uncooked Kamut berries

4 cups cauliflower florets

2 tablespoons extra-virgin olive oil, divided

Cooking spray

2 tablespoons tahini (roasted sesame seed paste)

2 tablespoons fresh lemon juice

2 tablespoons warm water

¾ teaspoon kosher salt, divided

¼ teaspoon freshly ground black pepper

1 garlic clove, grated

2½ ounces baby arugula

1 ripe peeled avocado, thinly sliced

1. Preheat oven to 475°F.

2. Cook Kamut according to package directions. Drain (if necessary) and rinse with cold water; drain.

3. While Kamut cooks, combine cauliflower and 1 tablespoon oil on a foil-lined jelly-roll pan coated with cooking spray; toss well to coat. Roast at 475°F for 15 minutes or until browned and crisp-tender.

4. Combine 1 tablespoon oil, tahini, lemon juice, 2 tablespoons warm water, ½ teaspoon salt, pepper, and garlic in a large bowl, stirring well with a whisk. Toss cauliflower with 1 tablespoon dressing. Add Kamut and arugula to bowl with remaining dressing; toss gently to coat. Arrange about 1 cup Kamut mixture onto each of 4 plates; divide cauliflower and avocado evenly over servings. Sprinkle avocado evenly with ¼ teaspoon salt.

SERVES 4
CALORIES 338; **FAT** 19.5g (sat 2.7g, mono 11.6g, poly 3.7g); **PROTEIN** 10g; **CARB** 37g; **FIBER** 9g; **SUGARS** 6g (est. added sugars 0g); **CHOL** 0mg; **IRON** 3mg; **SODIUM** 406mg; **CALC** 79mg

CRISPY MILLET SALAD WITH ROASTED RADISHES, ASPARAGUS, AND POACHED EGGS (GF)

Perfect for a light spring meal, this warm salad features two of the season's loveliest vegetables. If you've never tried roasted radishes, you're in for a treat: Roasting makes them sweeter with a juicy texture. Instead of the fried millet, you can use any fried grain you like; I just prefer a small one like millet, quinoa, or bulgur.

HANDS-ON TIME: 8 MINUTES TOTAL TIME: 23 MINUTES

- 1 pound medium-width asparagus spears, trimmed
- 9 Easter egg (multicolored) radishes, trimmed (about 1 bunch)
- 2½ tablespoons extra-virgin olive oil, divided
- ½ teaspoon kosher salt, divided
- 1 tablespoon red wine vinegar
- 2 teaspoons thyme leaves
- 2 teaspoons Dijon mustard
- ¼ teaspoon freshly ground black pepper
- ¾ cup Crunchy Fried Millet (page 32)
- 4 large eggs

1. Preheat oven to 425°F.

2. Place asparagus and radishes on a jelly-roll pan. Drizzle with 1 tablespoon oil; toss gently to coat. Sprinkle with ¼ teaspoon salt. Roast at 425°F for 15 minutes or until crisp-tender and lightly browned, stirring after 8 minutes.

3. Combine 1½ tablespoons oil, ¼ teaspoon salt, vinegar, thyme, mustard, and pepper in a small bowl, stirring well with a whisk. Add 1 tablespoon vinaigrette to Crunchy Fried Millet; toss to coat.

4. Divide radish mixture evenly among 4 plates; drizzle remaining vinaigrette evenly over salads. Spoon about 3 tablespoons Crunchy Fried Millet mixture over each salad.

5. Add water to a large skillet, filling two-thirds full; bring to a boil. Reduce heat; simmer. Break each egg into a custard cup. Gently pour eggs into pan; cook 3 minutes or until desired degree of doneness. Carefully remove eggs from pan using a slotted spoon, placing 1 egg on each salad.

SERVES 4
CALORIES 270; **FAT** 19.2g (sat 3.3g, mono 11.4g, poly 3.8g); **PROTEIN** 11g; **CARB** 15g; **FIBER** 4g; **SUGARS** 3g (est. added sugars 0g); **CHOL** 186mg; **IRON** 4mg; **SODIUM** 378mg; **CALC** 67mg

SHAVED APPLE AND FENNEL SALAD WITH CRUNCHY SPELT

Simply put, apples and fennel are just right together—the flavors are so complementary. I love the way the paper-thin slices intertwine and are punctuated by bright hits of parsley. Canola oil may seem like an odd choice for the dressing, but I wanted to keep the flavors clean and straightforward; you can always use olive oil if you'd like the vinaigrette to assert itself. This is a good potluck or holiday dish; it keeps for an hour or two after everything is tossed together.

HANDS-ON TIME: 20 MINUTES TOTAL TIME: 20 MINUTES

3 tablespoons canola oil
2 tablespoons cider vinegar
1½ teaspoons sugar
1½ teaspoons whole-grain Dijon mustard
⅜ teaspoon kosher salt
¼ teaspoon freshly ground black pepper
1 fennel bulb, halved and cored (about 1¼ cups)
1 small green apple, quartered and cored (about 2 cups)
1 small red apple, quartered and cored (about 2 cups)
1 cup flat-leaf parsley leaves
1 cup Crunchy Fried Spelt (page 32)

1. Combine first 6 ingredients in a large bowl, stirring well with a whisk.

2. Cut fennel and apples into ¹⁄₁₆th-inch slices on a mandoline. Add fennel, apples, parsley, and Crunchy Fried Spelt to vinaigrette; toss well to combine.

SERVES 6 *(serving size: about 1 cup)*
CALORIES 207; **FAT** 11.9g (sat 0.9g, mono 7.1g, poly 3.2g); **PROTEIN** 3g; **CARB** 23g; **FIBER** 5g; **SUGARS** 6g (est. added sugars 1g); **CHOL** 0mg; **IRON** 2mg; **SODIUM** 166mg; **CALC** 43mg

BLACK BEAN–QUINOA SALAD WITH CHIPOTLE STEAK ⒢

The chipotle-rubbed sirloin works beautifully here, but this salad is a wonderful use for any leftover steak.

HANDS-ON TIME: 28 MINUTES TOTAL TIME: 28 MINUTES

- 5 teaspoons olive oil, divided
- ½ teaspoon kosher salt, divided
- ¼ teaspoon chipotle chile powder
- ¼ teaspoon freshly ground black pepper
- 2 (6-ounce) top sirloin steaks
- 2 tablespoons fresh orange juice
- 2 tablespoons red wine vinegar
- 1 tablespoon adobo sauce from canned chipotle chiles in adobo sauce
- ½ teaspoon ground cumin
- ¼ teaspoon honey
- 1½ cups cooked quinoa
- 1½ cups baby spinach leaves
- 1 cup unsalted black beans, rinsed and drained
- ¾ cup chopped red bell pepper
- ¼ cup chopped fresh cilantro
- ¼ cup thinly sliced green onions
- 1 ounce feta cheese, crumbled (about ¼ cup)
- ½ cup ripe peeled avocado, sliced

1. Heat a grill pan over medium-high heat. Combine 1 teaspoon oil, ¼ teaspoon salt, chipotle chile powder, and black pepper; rub evenly over steaks. Add steaks to pan; cook 4 minutes on each side or until desired degree of doneness. Let stand 10 minutes. Cut steaks diagonally across grain into thin slices.

2. Combine 4 teaspoons oil, ¼ teaspoon salt, juice, and next 4 ingredients (through honey) in a large bowl, stirring with a whisk. Stir in quinoa, spinach, beans, bell pepper, cilantro, and green onions; toss to coat. Sprinkle with feta. Place quinoa mixture in each of 4 shallow bowls; top with steak and avocado.

> ## CHANGE IT UP
>
> You can make an equally delicious vegetarian version of this salad by using a 14-ounce package extra-firm, water-packed tofu in place of steak. Cut the tofu into 4 "steaks," coat with the same spice rub, and cook in the grill pan for the same amount of time.

SERVES 4 *(serving size: about 1½ cups)*
CALORIES 340; **FAT** 14.8g (sat 3.5g, mono 7.6g, poly 1.2g); **PROTEIN** 24g; **CARB** 27g; **FIBER** 7g; **SUGARS** 4g (est. added sugars 0g); **CHOL** 51mg; **IRON** 4mg; **SODIUM** 421mg; **CAL** 103mg

KALE-QUINOA CAESAR SALAD WITH ROASTED CHICKEN (GF)

Toasted walnuts replace croutons for a bit of heart-healthy crunch, but the creamy dressing delivers the classic flavor you expect in a Caesar.

HANDS-ON TIME: 23 MINUTES TOTAL TIME: 23 MINUTES

2 tablespoons hot water
2 tablespoons canola mayonnaise
1½ tablespoons olive oil
1 tablespoon fresh lemon juice
½ teaspoon anchovy paste
¼ teaspoon freshly ground black pepper
1 garlic clove, grated
1.5 ounces shaved Parmesan cheese, divided (about 6 tablespoons)
5 cups thinly sliced stemmed Lacinato kale
1½ cups cooked quinoa
1½ cups chopped skinless, boneless rotisserie chicken breast
2 tablespoons chopped toasted walnuts

1. Combine first 7 ingredients in a bowl, stirring well with a whisk. Stir in 3 tablespoons Parmesan cheese. Add kale, quinoa, and chicken; toss to coat. Top with 3 tablespoons Parmesan cheese and walnuts.

SERVES 4 *(serving size: 1 ½ cups)*
CALORIES 344; **FAT** 16.3g (sat 3.3g, mono 6.9g, poly 3.6g); **PROTEIN** 27g; **CARB** 25g; **FIBER** 4g; **SUGARS** 1g (est. added sugars 0g); **CHOL** 61mg; **IRON** 3mg; **SODIUM** 487mg; **CALCIUM** 256mg

CRUNCHY FARRO AND QUINOA SALAD WITH ROASTED TOMATOES

I came up with this salad to serve at a dinner party for a dear friend who was moving away. I was thrilled when guests raved over the alluring combination of crunchy grains, tart vinaigrette, sweet-tangy wilted tomatoes, and robust arugula.

HANDS-ON TIME: 10 MINUTES TOTAL TIME: 20 MINUTES

1 pint grape tomatoes

1 tablespoon extra-virgin olive oil, divided

Cooking spray

1 tablespoon sherry vinegar

1 teaspoon Dijon mustard

1 teaspoon honey

3/8 teaspoon kosher salt

1/4 teaspoon freshly ground black pepper

1 small garlic clove, grated

2/3 cup Crunchy Fried Red Quinoa (page 32)

2/3 cup Crunchy Fried Farro (page 32)

6 cups loosely packed baby arugula

1. Preheat oven to 425°F.

2. Cut tomatoes in half lengthwise; toss with 1 teaspoon oil. Arrange tomatoes, cut sides down, on a foil-lined jelly-roll pan coated with cooking spray. Roast at 425°F for 10 minutes or until tomatoes wilt. Set aside.

3. Combine 2 teaspoons oil, vinegar, and next 5 ingredients (through garlic) in a small bowl, stirring with a whisk.

4. Place Crunchy Fried Red Quinoa and Crunchy Fried Farro in a large bowl. Drizzle with vinaigrette; toss to coat. Add tomatoes and arugula; toss gently to combine.

SERVES 4 *(serving size: 1 cup)*
CALORIES 249; **FAT** 13.8g (sat 1.3g, mono 8.4g, poly 3.4g); **PROTEIN** 5g; **CARB** 26g; **FIBER** 5g; **SUGARS** 5g (est. added sugars 1g); **CHOL** 0mg; **IRON** 2mg; **SODIUM** 223mg; **CALC** 74mg

ROASTED CARROT, CHICKEN, AND GRAPE QUINOA BOWL GF

Caramelized carrots and fresh, juicy grapes impart a welcome sweetness to this main-dish bowl.

HANDS-ON TIME: 20 MINUTES TOTAL TIME: 30 MINUTES

2 cups (¾-inch) diagonally cut carrot

2 teaspoons olive oil

½ teaspoon kosher salt, divided

Cooking spray

5 tablespoons plain 2% reduced-fat Greek yogurt

3 tablespoons fresh lemon juice

2 tablespoons water

1½ tablespoons honey

¾ teaspoon ground cumin

½ teaspoon freshly ground black pepper

1½ cups cooked quinoa

1½ cups shredded skinless, boneless rotisserie chicken breast

1½ cups seedless red grapes, halved

½ cup thinly sliced green onions

½ cup flat-leaf parsley leaves

½ cup toasted sliced almonds

4 cups mixed salad greens

1. Preheat oven to 450°F.

2. Combine carrot, oil, and ¼ teaspoon salt on a jelly-roll pan coated with cooking spray; toss to coat. Roast at 450°F for 15 minutes or until tender.

3. Combine ¼ teaspoon salt, yogurt, and next 5 ingredients (through pepper) in a large bowl, stirring with a whisk. Add carrot, quinoa, and next 5 ingredients (through almonds); toss. Place 1 cup salad greens in each of 4 shallow bowls; top each serving with about 1½ cups quinoa mixture.

SERVES 4
CALORIES 371; **FAT** 12.3g (sat 1.6g, mono 6.2g, poly 2g); **PROTEIN** 25g; **CARB** 44g; **FIBER** 7g; **SUGARS** 21g (est. added sugars 6g); **CHOL** 51mg; **IRON** 3mg; **SODIUM** 502mg; **CALCIUM** 142mg

SORGHUM WITH SUMMER CORN, TOMATOES, AND TARRAGON (GF)

Though sorghum takes a long time to cook, it has become one of my favorite grains; the texture is starchy, like pasta, but heartier in a sense that only a whole grain can embody. The crisp pop of fresh sweet corn makes a lovely pairing.

HANDS-ON TIME: 18 MINUTES   TOTAL TIME: 1 HOUR 30 MINUTES

3   cups unsalted chicken stock (such as Swanson)
1   cup uncooked sorghum
8   teaspoons olive oil
1   tablespoon chopped fresh tarragon
2   tablespoons vinegar
1   teaspoon Dijon mustard
1   teaspoon minced fresh garlic
½   teaspoon kosher salt
¼   teaspoon freshly ground black pepper
2   cups halved cherry tomatoes
1½ cups fresh corn kernels
8   ounces roasted asparagus

1. Combine chicken stock and sorghum in a medium saucepan. Bring to a boil; cover, reduce heat to low, and simmer 1 hour and 10 minutes or until tender. Drain; cool. Combine olive oil and next 6 ingredients (through pepper) in a large bowl, stirring well with a whisk. Add cooked sorghum, tomatoes, corn kernels, and asparagus; toss.

SERVES 6 *(serving size: 1 cup)*
CALORIES 234; **FAT** 8.6g (sat 1.2g, sono 5.4g, poly 1.4g); **PROTEIN** 9g; **CARB** 35g; **FIBER** 4g; **SUGARS** 5g (est. added sugars 0g); **CHOL** 0mg; **IRON** 0mg; **SODIUM** 256mg; **CALCIUM** 0mg

FRESH CORN BLT SALAD (GF)

Simple, crunchy, fresh, and bacony—a pretty offering for any weeknight dinner or a larger gathering (just double the recipe and serve on a bigger platter). Grilled corn takes on some wonderful charred flavor, which complements its natural sweetness.

HANDS-ON TIME: 18 MINUTES TOTAL TIME: 18 MINUTES

3   medium ears shucked corn
Cooking spray
1   tablespoon canola mayonnaise
1   tablespoon canola oil
1   tablespoon cider vinegar
¼   teaspoon kosher salt
¼   teaspoon freshly ground black pepper
3   cups loosely packed baby arugula
1½ cups halved grape tomatoes
3   bacon slices, cooked and crumbled

1. Heat a grill or grill pan over high heat. Coat corn with cooking spray; arrange on grill rack or in pan. Grill corn 8 minutes or until nicely marked, turning frequently. Remove from grill or grill pan; cool slightly. Cut kernels from cobs.

2. Combine mayonnaise and next 4 ingredients (through pepper) in a large bowl, stirring well with a whisk. Place arugula in a medium bowl; drizzle with 1 tablespoon dressing, and toss to coat. Add corn and tomatoes to remaining dressing; toss well to combine. Arrange arugula on a platter or in a large bowl; top with corn mixture. Sprinkle with bacon.

> **MAKE IT FASTER**
>
> Skip the grill, and char ears of corn directly over the flame of three gas burners turned to high. Cook 3 to 5 minutes, turning cobs with tongs until evenly charred.

SERVES 4
CALORIES 155; **FAT** 8.3g (sat 1.4g, mono 4.3g, poly 2g); **PROTEIN** 6g; **CARB** 17g; **FIBER** 3g; **SUGARS** 7g (est. added sugars 0g); **CHOL** 7mg; **IRON** 1mg; **SODIUM** 304mg; **CALC** 36mg

RYE BERRY—SHRIMP SALAD WITH DILL—CRÈME FRAÎCHE DRESSING

Lick-the-bowl good. That's how I describe this easy herb dressing. The salad holds up nicely, so you can take it to work for lunch and make all your colleagues jealous; just let it come to room temp before enjoying it. Rinsing the onion takes away some of its bite, making it more mellow.

HANDS-ON TIME: 15 MINUTES TOTAL TIME: 15 MINUTES

1 pound large shrimp, peeled and deveined

⅓ cup crème fraîche

¼ cup chopped fresh dill

¼ cup nonfat buttermilk

1 tablespoon fresh lemon juice

¾ teaspoon kosher salt

½ teaspoon freshly ground black pepper

1 garlic clove, grated

2 cups cooked rye berries (about ⅔ cup uncooked)

⅓ cup slivered red onion, rinsed in cold water and drained

1 cup shaved baby cucumber

1. Bring a large pot of water to a boil. Add shrimp; reduce heat, and simmer 2 minutes or until shrimp are done. Drain and rinse with cold water; drain.

2. Combine crème fraîche and next 6 ingredients (through garlic) in a large bowl, stirring with a whisk. Add rye berries, onion, and shrimp; toss well to combine. Add cucumber; toss gently to combine.

SERVES 4 *(serving size: about 1⅓ cups)*
CALORIES 378; **FAT** 9.5g (sat 4.6g, mono 1.9g, poly 1.0g); **PROTEIN** 26g; **CARB** 46g; **FIBER** 0g; **SUGARS** 1g (est. added sugars 0g); **CHOL** 162mg; **IRON** 3mg; **SODIUM** 557mg; **CALC** 117mg

BRUSSELS SPROUTS SALAD WITH PICKLED RYE BERRIES

I've become enamored with pickled "hard-shell" grains—rye berries, wheat berries, whole spelt, and Kamut. There's something amazing about how these little nuggets change when soaked in something sour; their texture requires chewing, but the tangy notes make them more dynamic and the chew that much more enjoyable. Here, they go into a gorgeous salad of raw Brussels sprouts leaves and sweet-tangy dried cranberries.

HANDS-ON TIME: 17 MINUTES TOTAL TIME: 17 MINUTES

1 pound Brussels sprouts

1½ tablespoons toasted walnut oil

1 teaspoon cider vinegar

⅜ teaspoon kosher salt

¼ teaspoon freshly ground black pepper

¼ cup slivered red onion, rinsed in cold water and drained

1 cup Pickled Rye Berries (page 35)

¼ cup dried cranberries

3 tablespoons chopped walnuts, toasted

1. Trim bottoms off sprouts; pull off bigger leaves to yield 4 cups leaves. Reserve sprout "hearts" for another use.

2. Combine oil, vinegar, salt, and pepper in a large bowl. Add leaves and onion; toss gently to coat. Arrange leaves and onion on a platter; sprinkle with Pickled Rye Berries, cranberries, and walnuts.

MAKE IT FASTER

While pulling Brussels sprouts leaves might be time-consuming, it's well worth it for the beautiful effect. If you just can't bear to do it, you can use shredded sprouts; you can even find preshredded sprouts in many supermarkets.

SERVES 4 *(serving size: about 1 cup)*
CALORIES 251; **FAT** 9.6g (sat 0.9g, mono 1.7g, poly 6g); **PROTEIN** 8g; **CARB** 36g; **FIBER** 3g; **SUGARS** 9g (est. added sugars 4g); **CHOL** 0mg; **IRON** 2mg; **SODIUM** 319mg; **CALC** 47mg

SOUPS AND STEWS

Friends of mine host an annual soup party, a friendly competition with ballots and prizes for the best soup makers. It's one of the social highlights of the year, and no wonder: Soups and stews speak of communal eating; of casual entertaining; and, above all, of soul-warming, satisfying comfort.

CREAMY TOMATO-BASIL SOUP (GF)

This is the soup you'll want to dunk your grilled cheese into. It has that classic tomato soup taste but comes with a healthier profile—40% less sodium than the canned soup we all grew up with, even with the Parmesan cheese topping!

HANDS-ON TIME: 20 MINUTES TOTAL TIME: 30 MINUTES

2 tablespoons extra-virgin olive oil

1½ cups chopped yellow onion

4 garlic cloves, minced

1 (28-ounce) can unsalted petite diced tomatoes, undrained

2 cups Brown Rice Cream (page 36)

¾ cup coarsely chopped fresh basil (about 1 [1-ounce] package)

⅝ teaspoon kosher salt

½ teaspoon freshly ground black pepper

2 ounces Parmigiano-Reggiano cheese, grated (about ½ cup packed)

1. Heat a Dutch oven over medium-low heat. Add oil; swirl to coat. Add onion and garlic; cook 10 minutes or until tender, stirring occasionally. Add tomatoes; increase heat to medium-high, and bring to a simmer.

2. Place tomato mixture, Brown Rice Cream, and basil in a blender. Remove center piece of blender lid (to allow steam to escape); secure lid on blender. Place a clean towel over opening in blender (to avoid splatters). Blend until smooth (about 3 minutes); pour pureed soup into pan. Heat on medium-low heat until thoroughly heated (about 3 minutes); stir in salt and pepper. Ladle soup into 8 bowls. Sprinkle with cheese.

SERVES 8 *(serving size: about ¾ cup soup and about 1 tablespoon cheese)*
CALORIES 120; **FAT** 5.8g (sat 1.9g, mono 3.1g, poly 0.4g); **PROTEIN** 5g; **CARB** 12g; **FIBER** 2g; **SUGARS** 5g (est. added sugars 0g); **CHOL** 6mg; **IRON** 1mg; **SODIUM** 287mg; **CALC** 140mg

CREAMY BROCCOLI-CHEESE SOUP (GF)

This soup comes out extra chunky, as you only puree about a third of the broccoli mixture in step 3. For a thinner, smoother consistency, just add more soup to the blender.

HANDS-ON TIME: 45 MINUTES TOTAL TIME: 45 MINUTES

- 4 cups unsalted chicken stock (such as Swanson), divided
- ½ cup uncooked instant brown rice
- 1 cup 1% low-fat milk
- 2 teaspoons extra-virgin olive oil
- 1 cup chopped onion
- 3 garlic cloves, minced
- 1¼ pounds broccoli florets, coarsely chopped
- ¾ teaspoon kosher salt
- ½ teaspoon freshly ground black pepper
- 5 ounces extra-sharp cheddar cheese, shredded and divided (about 1¼ cups)

1. Combine 2 cups stock and rice in a small saucepan over medium-high heat; bring to a boil. Cover, reduce heat, and simmer 25 minutes. Remove from heat; let stand 5 minutes. Place rice mixture and milk in a blender. Remove center piece of blender lid (to allow steam to escape); secure blender lid on blender. Place a clean towel over opening in blender lid (to avoid splatters). Blend until smooth.

2. Heat a large saucepan over medium heat. Add oil to pan; swirl to coat. Add onion; sauté 4 minutes, stirring occasionally. Add garlic; cook 30 seconds. Add broccoli and salt; cook 5 minutes, stirring frequently. Add 2 cups stock; bring to a boil. Reduce heat, and simmer 5 minutes or just until broccoli is tender. Add rice mixture; simmer 2 minutes, stirring occasionally.

3. Place 2 cups soup in blender; process until smooth. Return pureed soup to pan. Add pepper and 4 ounces cheese; stir until cheese melts. Ladle soup into each of 6 bowls. Sprinkle with cheese.

SERVES 6 *(serving size: about 1 cup)*
CALORIES 210; **FAT** 10.3g (sat 5.5g, mono 3.5g, poly 0.6g); **PROTEIN** 14g; **CARB** 17g; **FIBER** 4g; **SUGARS** 3g (est. added sugars 0g); **CHOL** 27mg; **IRON** 1mg; **SODIUM** 520mg; **CALC** 290mg

FIERY THAI EGGPLANT SOUP (GF)

The flavor base for this soup is a simplified nam prik, *a Thai chile-based paste. To go old-school, make the paste with a mortar and pestle instead of using the mini food processor. The broiler method is a great way to cook a whole eggplant when it's going to be pureed; it softens wonderfully and picks up slightly charred flavor notes. I encourage you to go with 2 chiles for the biggest flavor hit, but feel free to use less if the heat is too intense.*

HANDS-ON TIME: 43 MINUTES TOTAL TIME: 1 HOUR 13 MINUTES

2 (1-pound) whole eggplants
½ cup chopped shallots (about 2 ounces)
1 tablespoon chopped peeled fresh ginger
2 teaspoons fish sauce
4 garlic cloves
1 or 2 Thai bird chiles, stemmed and coarsely chopped
1 tablespoon canola oil
3 tablespoons unsalted tomato paste
3 cups water
½ cup uncooked quinoa, rinsed and drained
1 cup light coconut milk
¼ cup water
1 tablespoon fresh lime juice
¾ teaspoon kosher salt
½ cup Crunchy Fried Quinoa (page 32)
   Cilantro leaves
   Lime wedges

1. Preheat broiler.

2. Place eggplants on a foil-lined baking sheet; pierce each a few times with tip of a knife. Broil eggplants 20 minutes or until skin is charred and flesh is very soft when tested with a knife, turning occasionally to cook evenly. Cool slightly. Remove and discard skin; set pulp aside.

3. Place shallots and next 4 ingredients (through chiles) in a mini food processor; process until minced and almost paste-like, scraping sides as needed.

4. Heat a Dutch oven over medium-high heat. Add oil to pan; swirl to coat. Add shallot mixture; cook 2 minutes, stirring constantly. Add tomato paste; cook 1 minute, stirring constantly.

Add 3 cups water and uncooked quinoa; bring to a boil over medium-high heat. Cover, reduce heat, and simmer 25 minutes or until quinoa is very tender. Pour mixture into a blender; add eggplant pulp, coconut milk, and ¼ cup water. Remove center piece of blender lid (to allow steam to escape); secure lid on blender. Place a clean towel over opening in blender (to avoid splatters). Blend until smooth (about 2 minutes). Return mixture to pan; stir in lime juice and salt. Heat over medium-low heat 3 minutes or until thoroughly heated.

5. Ladle soup into each of 8 bowls. Top each serving with Crunchy Fried Quinoa. Sprinkle with cilantro leaves; serve with lime wedges.

SERVES 8 *(serving size: about ¾ cup soup and 1 tablespoon Crunchy Fried Quinoa)*
CALORIES 136; **FAT** 5.2g (sat 1.3g, mono 2.2g, poly 1.4g); **PROTEIN** 4g; **CARB** 21g; **FIBER** 6g; **SUGARS** 5g (est. added sugars 0g); **CHOL** 0mg;
IRON 1mg; **SODIUM** 312mg; **CALC** 27mg

ROASTED CAULIFLOWER SOUP WITH CRUNCHY FARRO AND SAGE OIL

Sublimely silky with a flavor that's mildly sweet, nutty, and tinged with a subtle cruciferous twang, this is a hearty main-dish soup. The crunchy topping, flecked with bacon, offers wonderful texture. For the best flavor, roast the cauliflower until it's well browned—those toasty bits are delicious.

HANDS-ON TIME: 16 MINUTES TOTAL TIME: 1 HOUR 11 MINUTES

8 cups cauliflower florets
(1 large head)

4½ tablespoons olive oil, divided

Cooking spray

1 cup chopped yellow onion

3 garlic cloves, minced

2¾ cups unsalted chicken stock
(such as Swanson)

¾ teaspoon kosher salt

⅛ teaspoon ground white pepper

1⅓ cups Millet Cream (page 36)

1½ teaspoons minced fresh sage

6 tablespoons Crunchy Fried
Farro (page 32)

2 bacon slices, cooked
and crumbled

1. Preheat oven to 450°F.

2. Combine cauliflower and 1½ tablespoons oil on a jelly-roll pan coated with cooking spray; toss well to coat. Roast at 450°F for 35 minutes or until tender and browned, stirring every 10 minutes.

3. Heat a Dutch oven over medium-low heat. Add 1½ tablespoons oil; swirl to coat. Add onion and garlic; cook 10 minutes or until very tender, stirring occasionally. Add stock, salt, pepper, and cauliflower; bring to a boil. Cover, reduce heat, and simmer 10 minutes. Place stock mixture and Millet Cream in a blender. Remove center piece of blender lid (to allow steam to escape); secure lid on blender. Place a clean towel over opening in blender (to avoid splatters). Blend until smooth (about 3 minutes). Return mixture to pan; heat on medium heat until thoroughly heated.

4. Combine 1½ tablespoons oil and sage in a small microwave-safe bowl; microwave at HIGH 45 seconds. Combine Crunchy Fried Farro and bacon in a small bowl. Ladle soup into 4 bowls. Top each serving with sage oil and farro mixture.

SERVES 4 *(serving size: about 1½ cups soup, about 1 teaspoon sage oil, and 1½ tablespoons farro mixture)*
CALORIES 363; **FAT** 21.2g (sat 3.5g, mono 13.6g, poly 2.8g); **PROTEIN** 13g; **CARB** 33g; **FIBER** 7g; **SUGARS** 7g (est. added sugars 0g); **CHOL** 7mg; **IRON** 2mg; **SODIUM** 623mg; **CALC** 117mg

BUTTERNUT-LEEK BISQUE WITH SPICED POPPED SORGHUM (GF)

What a great mix of complementary textures: the silky, creamy soup and the fluffy, crunchy topping. The popped sorghum (think of it as baby popcorn) provides a hit of warm spices that play well to the sweetness of butternut squash. Leeks "melt" to buttery softness when cooked slowly over moderate heat and add subtle allium notes.

HANDS-ON TIME: 18 MINUTES TOTAL TIME: 1 HOUR 30 MINUTES

1 (2½-pound) butternut squash
Cooking spray
1½ tablespoons butter
3 cups chopped leeks
¾ teaspoon kosher salt, divided
3 cups water
¾ teaspoon ground cumin, divided
1⅓ cups Millet Cream (page 36)
½ cup Popped Sorghum (page 31)
¼ teaspoon ground cinnamon
⅛ teaspoon kosher salt

1. Preheat oven to 425°F.

2. Cut squash in half lengthwise; discard seeds and membranes. Place squash halves, cut sides down, on a foil-lined jelly-roll pan coated with cooking spray. Roast at 425°F for 50 minutes or until very tender. Cool slightly.

3. Heat a large saucepan over medium-low heat. Add butter; swirl until butter melts. Add leeks and ½ teaspoon salt; cover. Cook 15 minutes or until very tender, stirring frequently. Remove and discard skin from squash. Add ¼ teaspoon salt, squash pulp, 3 cups water, and ½ teaspoon cumin to pan; bring to a simmer. Place squash mixture and Millet Cream in a blender. Remove center piece of blender lid (to allow steam to escape); secure lid on blender. Place a clean towel over opening in blender (to avoid splatters). Blend until smooth (about 2 minutes). Return mixture to pan; heat over medium heat until thoroughly heated.

4. Combine ¼ teaspoon cumin, Popped Sorghum, cinnamon, and ⅛ teaspoon salt; toss to coat. Ladle bisque into 8 bowls. Top each serving with sorghum mixture.

SERVES 8 (serving size: about 1 cup bisque and about 1 tablespoon sorghum mixture)
CALORIES 155; **FAT** 4.3g (sat 1.8g, mono 1.5g, poly 0.7g); **PROTEIN** 4g; **CARB** 28g; **FIBER** 4g; **SUGARS** 5g (est. added sugars 0g); **CHOL** 7mg; **IRON** 2mg; **SODIUM** 248mg; **CALC** 99mg

SPICY FREEKEH MULLIGATAWNY

Mulligatawny *means "pepper water" and is an Indian curry soup that usually includes diced chicken, cream or coconut milk, and rice or lentils. I kept the first two elements and replaced the starch with smoky freekeh. For chile-heads, go with 1½ to 2 serrano peppers; for sensitive palates, stick with 1.*

HANDS-ON TIME: 29 MINUTES TOTAL TIME: 59 MINUTES

2 tablespoons canola oil, divided

1 pound skinless, boneless chicken breast, cut into small pieces

2 cups chopped onion

1 tablespoon minced peeled fresh ginger

5 garlic cloves, minced

1 to 2 serrano peppers, minced (leave seeds in)

1 tablespoon Madras curry powder

3 cups unsalted chicken stock (such as Swanson)

¾ cup uncooked cracked freekeh

1 teaspoon kosher salt

1 (14.5-ounce) can unsalted petite diced tomatoes

1 large Granny Smith apple, peeled and diced (about 1½ cups)

1 cup half-and-half

6 tablespoons coarsely chopped dry-roasted unsalted cashews

Cilantro sprigs (optional)

1. Heat a Dutch oven over medium-high heat. Add 1 tablespoon oil to pan; swirl to coat. Add chicken; cook 5 minutes or until done and lightly browned. Remove chicken from pan.

2. Reduce heat to medium. Add 1 tablespoon oil to pan; swirl to coat. Add onion, ginger, garlic, and serrano; cook 6 minutes, stirring frequently. Stir in curry powder; cook 30 seconds, stirring constantly. Add stock, scraping pan to loosen browned bits. Stir in freekeh, salt, and tomatoes; bring to a boil. Cover, reduce heat, and simmer 15 minutes. Stir in apple; cook 15 minutes or until freekeh is tender. Add chicken and half-and-half; cook 3 minutes or until thoroughly heated. Ladle soup into 6 bowls. Top each serving with cashews. Garnish with cilantro, if desired.

SERVES 6 *(serving size: about 1½ cups mulligatawny and 1 tablespoon cashews)*
CALORIES 369; **FAT** 16g (sat 4.5g, mono 7.5g, poly 2.6g); **PROTEIN** 26g; **CARB** 33g; **FIBER** 5g; **SUGARS** 9g (est. added sugars 0g); **CHOL** 63mg; **IRON** 4mg; **SODIUM** 502mg; **CALC** 104mg

CHICKEN, WILD RICE, AND CORN CHOWDER

Chowder is downright addictive, and for good reason. Thick, creamy, and milk rich, it's the perfect antidote to a cold winter night. This one plays up wild rice's slightly crunchy resistance with crunchy-sweet corn. If you have cooked wild rice on hand (or have some stashed in your freezer), this hearty soup comes together in less than 30 minutes.

HANDS-ON TIME: 44 MINUTES TOTAL TIME: 1 HOUR 34 MINUTES

3 cups water

⅔ cup uncooked wild rice, rinsed and drained

4 applewood-smoked bacon slices, chopped

1½ cups chopped onion

1 cup chopped celery

1 tablespoon chopped fresh thyme

2 bay leaves

1 pound skinless, boneless chicken breast, cut into ½-inch pieces

2¼ ounces all-purpose flour (about ½ cup)

2 cups unsalted chicken stock (such as Swanson)

4 cups 2% reduced-fat milk

1 teaspoon kosher salt

¾ teaspoon freshly ground black pepper

1½ cups frozen corn kernels, thawed

1. Place 3 cups water and wild rice in a medium saucepan; bring to a boil. Cover, reduce heat, and simmer 45 minutes or until done. Drain rice, if necessary.

2. Heat a Dutch oven over medium heat. Add bacon; cook 7 minutes or until crisp, stirring occasionally. Remove bacon from pan with a slotted spoon, reserving 1½ tablespoons drippings (discard remaining drippings). Add onion, celery, thyme, and bay leaves to drippings in pan; cook 8 minutes or until tender, stirring occasionally. Add chicken; cook 3 minutes, stirring occasionally.

3. Weigh or lightly spoon flour into a dry measuring cup; level with a knife. Combine flour and stock, stirring with a whisk until smooth. Add flour mixture, milk, salt, and pepper to pan. Bring to a simmer; stir in rice and corn. Cook 10 minutes, stirring occasionally. Discard bay leaves. Ladle chowder into 8 bowls. Sprinkle with bacon.

SERVES 8 *(serving size: about 1 ½ cups chowder and 2 teaspoons crumbled bacon)*
CALORIES 288; **FAT** 8.4g (sat 3.4g, mono 3g, poly 1g); **PROTEIN** 23g; **CARB** 31g; **FIBER** 2g; **SUGARS** 8g (est. added sugars 0g); **CHOL** 53mg;
IRON 1mg; **SODIUM** 505mg; **CALC** 173mg

CHICKEN AND SAUSAGE GUMBO

I call for all-purpose flour in the roux because whole-grain flours may burn in the pan and become too bitter. But in place of the usual white rice, this deeply spiced stew goes over convenient precooked brown rice.

HANDS-ON TIME: 30 MINUTES TOTAL TIME: 30 MINUTES

6 ounces andouille sausage, finely chopped

2 tablespoons butter

2 tablespoons canola oil

1.5 ounces all-purpose flour (about ⅓ cup)

8 ounces skinless, boneless chicken thighs, cut into bite-sized pieces

1 cup chopped onion

¾ cup chopped green bell pepper (about 1 medium)

½ cup thinly sliced celery

1 tablespoon salt-free Cajun/Creole seasoning

½ teaspoon salt

5 garlic cloves, minced

3 cups unsalted chicken stock (such as Swanson)

1 (14.5-ounce) can unsalted whole tomatoes, drained and crushed

1 cup frozen cut okra

3 cups bagged precooked brown rice

1. Heat a Dutch oven over medium-high heat. Add sausage to pan; sauté 5 minutes, turning to brown on all sides. Remove sausage from pan using a slotted spoon, and drain on paper towels.

2. Melt butter in drippings in pan. Add oil to pan; swirl. Weigh or lightly spoon flour into a dry measuring cup; level with a knife. Stir flour into butter mixture; cook 3 minutes or until flour mixture starts to brown, stirring constantly with a whisk.

3. Add chicken to pan; sauté 4 minutes, stirring frequently. Add onion and next 5 ingredients (through garlic) to pan; sauté 6 minutes or until vegetables are tender, stirring occasionally. Add stock and tomatoes to pan; bring to a boil. Return sausage to pan; stir in okra. Reduce heat, and simmer 6 minutes, stirring occasionally. Divide rice among 6 bowls. Ladle gumbo over rice.

SERVES 6 *(serving size: ½ cup rice and 1 cup gumbo)*
CALORIES 367; **FAT** 16.1g (sat 5.6g, mono 7.3g, poly 2.7g); **PROTEIN** 19g; **CARB** 37g; **FIBER** 4g; **SUGARS** 4g (est. added sugars 0g); **CHOL** 57mg; **IRON** 3mg; **SODIUM** 559mg; **CALCIUM** 70mg

CURRIED CHICKPEA STEW WITH BROWN RICE PILAF GF

This curry hails from the Indian region of Punjab. The cardamom pods puff up to almost twice their size and float to the top, so they're easy to find and discard before serving. Each serving packs plenty of fiber thanks to the brown rice, chickpeas, and vegetables.

HANDS-ON TIME: 20 MINUTES TOTAL TIME: 60 MINUTES

Pilaf:
- 1 tablespoon canola oil
- 1 cup finely chopped onion
- 1 cup uncooked brown rice
- ½ teaspoon ground turmeric
- 3 cardamom pods, crushed
- 1 (3-inch) cinnamon stick
- 1 garlic clove, minced
- 1⅔ cups water
- 1 bay leaf

Stew:
- 1 tablespoon canola oil
- 2 cups chopped onion
- 1 tablespoon grated peeled fresh ginger
- 1 teaspoon ground cumin
- 1 teaspoon ground coriander
- ¾ teaspoon ground turmeric
- ¼ teaspoon ground red pepper
- 4 garlic cloves, minced
- 3 cardamom pods, crushed
- 1 (3-inch) cinnamon stick
- 2½ cups water
- 1 cup diced carrot
- ¼ teaspoon kosher salt
- 1 (15-ounce) can chickpeas (garbanzo beans), rinsed and drained
- 1 (14.5-ounce) can fire-roasted crushed tomatoes, undrained (such as Muir Glen)
- ½ cup plain fat-free yogurt
- ¼ cup chopped fresh cilantro

1. To prepare pilaf, heat a large nonstick skillet over medium heat. Add 1 tablespoon oil; swirl to coat. Add 1 cup onion; cook 6 minutes or until golden, stirring frequently. Add rice and next 4 ingredients (through garlic); cook 1 minute, stirring constantly. Add 1⅔ cups water and bay leaf; bring to a boil. Cover, reduce heat, and simmer 45 minutes. Let stand 5 minutes. Discard cardamom, cinnamon, and bay leaf. Keep warm.

2. To prepare stew, heat a large Dutch oven over medium-high heat. Add 1 tablespoon oil, and swirl to coat. Add 2 cups onion; sauté 6 minutes or until golden. Add ginger and next 7 ingredients (through cinnamon stick); cook 1 minute, stirring constantly. Add 2½ cups water, carrot, ¼ teaspoon salt, chickpeas, and tomatoes; bring to a boil. Cover, reduce heat, and simmer 20 minutes or until carrots are tender and sauce is slightly thick. Discard cardamom and cinnamon stick.

3. Place 1 cup rice mixture in each of 4 bowls; spoon 1¼ cups chickpea mixture over rice. Top each serving with 2 tablespoons yogurt and 1 tablespoon cilantro.

SERVES 4
CALORIES 431; **FAT** 9.6g (sat 1g, mono 5.1g, poly 2.9g); **PROTEIN** 12g; **CARB** 78g; **FIBER** 10g; **SUGARS** 13g (est. added sugars 0g); **CHOL** 1mg; **IRON** 3mg; **SODIUM** 626mg; **CALC** 121mg

BROWN RICE CONGEE

For me, congee—a soupy rice porridge with variations all over Asia—is one of the top three most comforting foods ever, up there with chicken and dumplings and meat loaf (which I have recipes for in this book). I'd always had it made with white rice, but it's also delicious with brown rice; just be sure to use short-grain brown rice. It will seem like you're using a ridiculously large amount of liquid, but trust me, be patient, and go with it. The soup is creamy, rich, savory, and about the best thing to eat when you're chilled or a little under the weather. Leftovers topped with a poached egg for breakfast? Be still my heart!

HANDS-ON TIME: 1 HOUR 58 MINUTES TOTAL TIME: 3 HOURS 13 MINUTES

1 tablespoon canola oil

¾ cup chopped green onion bottoms (white and light green parts)

1 tablespoon minced peeled fresh ginger

4 cups unsalted chicken stock (such as Swanson)

4 cups water

1 cup uncooked short-grain brown rice

2 pounds bone-in chicken thighs, skinned

1 teaspoon kosher salt

1 tablespoon lower-sodium soy sauce

1 tablespoon dark sesame oil

1 tablespoon Sriracha (hot chile sauce, such as Huy Fong)

½ cup chopped green onion tops (dark green parts)

1. Heat a Dutch oven over medium-high heat. Add canola oil; swirl to coat. Add green onion bottoms and ginger; sauté 2 minutes. Add stock and next 3 ingredients (through chicken); bring to a boil. Cover, reduce heat, and simmer 1 hour.

2. Remove chicken from pan; cool slightly. Remove meat from bones; discard bones. Shred meat; cover and set aside in refrigerator.

3. Continue simmering rice mixture, uncovered, an additional 1 hour 45 minutes, stirring occasionally, or until rice is broken down and mixture is very creamy. Stir in salt.

4. Spoon about 1 cup rice mixture into each of 6 bowls. Drizzle ½ teaspoon soy sauce, ½ teaspoon sesame oil, and ½ teaspoon Sriracha over each serving. Divide chicken evenly among servings; sprinkle evenly with green onion tops.

SERVES 6
CALORIES 298; **FAT** 9g (sat 1.4g, mono 3.7g, poly 2.4g); **PROTEIN** 24g; **CARB** 29g; **FIBER** 2g; **SUGARS** 1g (est. added sugars 0g); **CHOL** 86mg; **IRON** 2mg; **SODIUM** 635mg; **CALC** 52mg

CHICKEN, KALE, AND QUINOA SOUP (GF)

This tasty soup was inspired by taking four of the top recipe search categories from the Cooking Light *website—chicken, kale, quinoa, and soups—and combining them into a dish that is sure to become a new favorite. Rinse the quinoa to ensure that any bitter coating is removed.*

HANDS-ON TIME: 59 MINUTES TOTAL TIME: 59 MINUTES

4 center-cut bacon slices

1½ cups chopped onion

¾ cup chopped carrot

1 teaspoon kosher salt, divided

6 garlic cloves, minced

Cooking spray

1 pound skinless, boneless chicken thighs, cut into ¾-inch pieces

½ teaspoon freshly ground black pepper, divided

6 cups unsalted chicken stock (such as Swanson)

2 bay leaves

⅔ cup uncooked quinoa

6 cups chopped kale

2 teaspoons thyme leaves

1. Cook bacon in a Dutch oven over medium heat until crisp. Remove bacon from pan, reserving drippings. Crumble bacon; set aside.

2. Increase heat to medium-high. Add onion, carrot, and ¼ teaspoon salt to drippings in pan; sauté 5 minutes, stirring occasionally. Add garlic; sauté 2 minutes. Remove mixture from pan.

3. Coat pan with cooking spray. Add chicken to pan; sprinkle with ¼ teaspoon salt and ¼ teaspoon pepper. Sauté 6 minutes or until chicken is browned and done. Stir in onion mixture, chicken stock, bay leaves, ½ teaspoon salt, and ¼ teaspoon pepper; bring to a boil.

4. Place quinoa in a fine sieve; place sieve in a large bowl. Cover quinoa with water. Using your hands, rub grains together for 30 seconds; rinse and drain. Repeat procedure twice. Drain well. Add quinoa to pan; cover and simmer 15 minutes. Add kale and thyme to pan; simmer, uncovered, 5 minutes or until kale is tender. Discard bay leaves. Ladle soup into 6 bowls. Sprinkle with bacon.

SERVES 6 *(serving size: about 1²/₃ cups soup and about 1 teaspoon bacon)*
CALORIES 262; **FAT** 6.2g (sat 1.7g, mono 1.4g, poly 1.6g); **PROTEIN** 27g; **CARB** 26g; **FIBER** 4g; **SUGARS** 3g (est. added sugars 0g); **CHOL** 77mg; **IRON** 3mg; **SODIUM** 650mg; **CALC** 147mg

TURKEY MEATBALL SOUP WITH GREENS ⓖⓕ

The tenderness of lacinato kale is a nice way to round out this soup, but you can easily substitute other varieties.

HANDS-ON TIME: 40 MINUTES TOTAL TIME: 60 MINUTES

- 1 pound ground turkey breast
- ½ cup cooked quinoa
- 2 ounces Parmigiano-Reggiano cheese, grated and divided (about ½ cup)
- 2 tablespoons chopped fresh flat-leaf parsley
- 2 tablespoons chopped fresh basil
- ¾ teaspoon kosher salt, divided
- ½ teaspoon freshly ground black pepper, divided
- 6 garlic cloves, minced and divided
- 1 large egg, lightly beaten
- 4 teaspoons extra-virgin olive oil, divided
- ½ cup chopped shallots
- ½ cup chopped celery
- 8 cups trimmed chopped lacinato kale (about 1 pound)
- ¼ teaspoon crushed red pepper
- 5 cups unsalted chicken stock (such as Swanson)
- Lemon wedges (optional)

1. Combine turkey, quinoa, ¼ cup cheese, parsley, basil, ¼ teaspoon salt, ¼ teaspoon black pepper, 2 garlic cloves, and egg in a large bowl; mix gently just until combined. Working with damp hands, shape turkey mixture into 24 meatballs (about 2 tablespoons each).

2. Heat a large Dutch oven over medium-high heat. Add 1 teaspoon oil to pan; swirl to coat. Add 12 meatballs; cook 8 minutes, turning to brown on all sides. Remove from pan. Repeat procedure with 1 teaspoon oil and 12 meatballs.

3. Add 2 teaspoons oil to pan; swirl to coat. Add shallots and celery to pan; sauté 5 minutes. Add 4 garlic cloves; sauté 1 minute. Add kale, ½ teaspoon salt, ¼ teaspoon black pepper, and red pepper; cook 2 minutes, stirring occasionally. Add stock; bring to a boil. Return meatballs to pan. Reduce heat; simmer 10 minutes or until kale is tender and meatballs are done.

4. Ladle soup into 6 bowls. Sprinkle remaining cheese over each serving. Serve with lemon wedges, if desired.

SERVES 6 *(serving size: 1¹/₃ cups soup and 2 teaspoons cheese)*
CALORIES 264; **FAT** 8.5g (sat 2.7g, mono 3.3g, poly 0.9g); **PROTEIN** 31g; **CARB** 18g; **FIBER** 3g; **SUGARS** 2g (est. added sugars 0g); **CHOL** 70mg; **IRON** 3mg; **SODIUM** 608mg; **CALC** 271mg

CLASSIC BEEF AND BARLEY STEW

A hearty combination of tender stew meat and well-cooked barley, this recipe is old-school comfort defined. The grains get so soft that my kids think they are pasta.

HANDS-ON TIME: 12 MINUTES TOTAL TIME: 2 HOURS 38 MINUTES

- 2 tablespoons canola oil, divided
- 2 pounds beef stew meat
- 1½ cups chopped onion
- 1 cup chopped celery
- 6 garlic cloves, minced
- 3 tablespoons unsalted tomato paste
- 1 cup water
- 4 cups unsalted beef stock (such as Swanson)
- ⅔ cup uncooked hulled barley
- 5 thyme sprigs
- 2 bay leaves
- 2 cups sliced carrot
- 1 teaspoon kosher salt
- ½ teaspoon freshly ground black pepper

1. Heat a Dutch oven over medium-high heat. Add 1 tablespoon oil; swirl to coat. Add half of beef; cook 10 minutes, turning to brown well on all sides. Remove beef from pan. Repeat procedure with remaining beef; remove from pan.

2. Add 1 tablespoon oil to pan; swirl to coat. Add onion, celery, and garlic; sauté 5 minutes. Add tomato paste; cook 1 minute, stirring constantly. Add 1 cup water, scraping pan to loosen browned bits. Stir in beef, stock, barley, thyme, and bay leaves. Bring mixture to a boil; cover, reduce heat, and simmer 1 hour. Add carrot; simmer 45 minutes to 1 hour or until beef is tender. Discard thyme and bay leaves; stir in salt and pepper.

MAKE AHEAD

To freeze, cool the soup to room temperature, and pour into a heavy-duty zip-top plastic bag. To thaw, microwave at LOW for 4 minutes or until pliable. Pour soup into a saucepan, and heat over medium heat 20 minutes or until bubbly and thoroughly heated.

SERVES 8 *(serving size: about 1 cup)*
CALORIES 276; **FAT** 9.1g (sat 2.5g, mono 4.9g, poly 1.6g); **PROTEIN** 29g; **CARB** 21g; **FIBER** 5g; **SUGARS** 4g (est. added sugars 0g); **CHOL** 73mg; **IRON** 3mg; **SODIUM** 439mg; **CALC** 49mg

FRENCH ONION SOUP WITH BARLEY

This Cooking Light *favorite adds whole-grain barley to update the classic soup. Pearl barley may be quick cooking, but it's not whole grain; choose whole-grain barley, sometimes labeled 'hulled barley.' You may be able to find it in the bulk foods section of your grocery store.*

HANDS-ON TIME: 18 MINUTES TOTAL TIME: 1 HOUR 25 MINUTES

6 cups water
1 cup uncooked hulled barley
2 tablespoons canola oil
1½ pounds yellow onions, peeled and vertically sliced
1 pound sweet onions, peeled and vertically sliced
¾ teaspoon kosher salt, divided
6 garlic cloves, thinly sliced
¼ cup dry sherry
6 cups unsalted beef stock (such as Swanson)
½ teaspoon freshly ground black pepper
3 thyme sprigs
1 bay leaf
1½ tablespoons thyme leaves
3 ounces French bread baguette, cut into 18 thin slices
3 ounces cave-aged Gruyère cheese, shredded (about ¾ cup)
2 ounces part-skim mozzarella cheese, shredded (about ½ cup)

1. Bring 6 cups water and barley to a boil in a large saucepan; cover, reduce heat, and simmer 1 hour or until done. Drain.

2. While barley cooks, heat a Dutch oven over medium-high heat. Add oil to pan; swirl to coat. Add onions; cook 5 minutes, stirring frequently. Add ¼ teaspoon salt and garlic; reduce heat to medium-low, and cook 45 minutes or until onions are caramelized and very tender, stirring occasionally.

3. Increase heat to medium-high. Add sherry; cook 2 minutes or until liquid almost evaporates. Stir in stock, pepper, thyme sprigs, and bay leaf; bring to a boil. Reduce heat, and simmer 30 minutes. Discard thyme sprigs and bay leaf. Stir in barley, thyme leaves, and ½ teaspoon salt.

4. Preheat broiler.

5. Arrange bread in a single layer on a baking sheet; broil 30 seconds on each side or until toasted. Ladle 1⅓ cups soup into each of 6 ovenproof bowls. Arrange 3 toast pieces in each bowl; divide cheeses over toasts. Place bowls on baking sheet. Broil 2 minutes or until cheese melts and begins to brown.

MAKE IT FASTER

You can cut about 30 minutes from this soup with two simple changes: First, use whole-grain farro in place of barley. Second, speed up the caramelized onion process by stirring ¼ teaspoon baking soda into the onion mixture after the initial 5 minutes.

SERVES 6
CALORIES 380; **FAT** 11.7g (sat 4.2g, monot 4.9g, poly 2g); **PROTEIN** 16g; **CARB** 51g; **FIBER** 9g; **SUGARS** 8g (est. added sugars 0g); **CHOL** 22mg; **IRON** 2mg; **SODIUM** 590mg; **CALC** 279mg

RYE BERRY, CABBAGE, AND CARAWAY SOUP WITH SAUSAGE

I adore cabbage, with its silky cooked texture and satisfying sweetness. The rye berries here, which I toast first for more depth, offer a wonderfully chewy foil to the cabbage. With rye, my thoughts turned to rye bread and its characteristic caraway twang. All come together in a slightly sweet, slightly sour warming bowl of rustic comfort.

HANDS-ON TIME: 10 MINUTES   TOTAL TIME: 2 HOURS

¾   cup uncooked rye berries

1½   tablespoons canola oil

1½   cups chopped onion

1   tablespoon chopped fresh thyme

1½   teaspoons caraway seeds

4   garlic cloves, minced

3   tablespoons unsalted tomato paste

6   cups unsalted beef stock (such as Swanson)

1   cup water

1   cup thinly sliced carrot

1   tablespoon sugar

1   teaspoon freshly ground black pepper

⅝   teaspoon kosher salt

2   (14.5-ounce) cans unsalted diced tomatoes, undrained

2   bay leaves

1½   pounds cabbage, thinly sliced and cut into 2-inch-long pieces

12   ounces andouille sausage, thinly sliced

1½   tablespoons red wine vinegar

¼   cup chopped fresh dill

1. Heat a large Dutch oven over medium heat. Add rye berries; cook 6 to 8 minutes or until browned and fragrant, stirring frequently. Add water to 2 inches above rye berries; bring to a boil. Reduce heat, and simmer 35 to 45 minutes or until chewy-tender. Drain.

2. Heat pan over medium-low heat. Add oil to pan; swirl to coat. Add onion, thyme, caraway, and garlic; cook 10 minutes, stirring occasionally. Add tomato paste; cook 2 minutes, stirring constantly. Stir in stock and next 8 ingredients (through cabbage); bring to a boil. Stir in rye berries; cover, reduce heat, and simmer 45 minutes or until cabbage is tender. Add sausage and vinegar; cook 10 minutes or until thoroughly heated. Ladle soup into each of 8 bowls. Sprinkle with dill.

MAKE AHEAD

This is one of those soups that tastes better when made the day before. The cabbage will be slightly softer after reheating the soup, and the rye berries (unlike pasta or some other grains) won't soak up all the liquid.

SERVES 8 *(serving size: 2 cups soup and 1½ teaspoons dill)*
CALORIES 337; **FAT** 11.2g (sat 3.4g, mono 5.3g, poly 2.3g); **PROTEIN** 16g; **CARB** 43g; **FIBER** 4g; **SUGARS** 10g (est. added sugars 2g); **CHOL** 30mg; **IRON** 4mg; **SODIUM** 644mg; **CALC** 88mg

LAMB, TOASTED RYE BERRY, AND APRICOT TAGINE

Tagines *(fragrant Moroccan stews)* are often served over couscous, but here rye berries cook in the stew and soak up all the rich, meaty goodness. If you can't find lamb shoulder, you can also use an equal amount of trimmed boneless leg of lamb; it cooks in the same amount of time.

HANDS-ON TIME: 38 MINUTES TOTAL TIME: 2 HOURS 23 MINUTES

¾ cup uncooked rye berries

Cooking spray

1½ pounds cubed trimmed lamb shoulder

1½ teaspoons canola oil

2½ cups chopped onion

10 garlic cloves, minced

1½ teaspoons ground cumin

1 teaspoon ground cinnamon

½ teaspoon ground red pepper

3 tablespoons unsalted tomato paste

4 cups unsalted beef stock (such as Swanson)

1 cup quartered dried apricots (about 6 ounces)

1 tablespoon honey

1½ teaspoons kosher salt

¼ cup cilantro leaves

1. Heat a Dutch oven over medium heat. Add rye berries; cook 6 minutes or until browned and fragrant, stirring occasionally. Remove from pan.

2. Increase heat to medium-high. Coat pan with cooking spray. Add half of lamb; cook 5 minutes, turning to brown on all sides. Remove lamb from pan; repeat procedure with cooking spray and remaining lamb. Remove lamb from pan.

3. Reduce heat to medium. Add oil to pan; swirl to coat. Add onion and garlic; cook 5 minutes, stirring frequently. Add cumin, cinnamon, and pepper; cook 30 seconds, stirring constantly. Add tomato paste; cook 1 minute, stirring constantly. Add stock, scraping pan to loosen browned bits. Stir in lamb, rye berries, apricots, honey, and salt; bring to a boil. Cover, reduce heat to medium-low, and simmer 1 hour 45 minutes or until lamb is tender and rye berries are chewy-tender. Ladle stew into each of 8 bowls. Sprinkle with cilantro.

CHANGE IT UP

If you're not a fan of lamb, switch to inexpensive beef stew meat or skinless, boneless chicken thighs. The stew meat will need to cook the same amount of time as the lamb, but the chicken only needs to go about 30 minutes.

SERVES 8 *(serving size: about 1 cup stew and 1½ teaspoons cilantro)*
CALORIES 426; **FAT** 18g (sat 7g, mono 7.3g, poly 1.9g); **PROTEIN** 22g; **CARB** 44g; **FIBER** 3g; **SUGARS** 14g (est. added sugars 2g); **CHOL** 60mg; **IRON** 4mg; **SODIUM** 496mg; **CALC** 64mg

AFRICAN SWEET POTATO, TEFF, AND GREENS STEW (GF)

Tiny teff grains swell and thicken this delicious vegetarian stew. It gets its flavor from Berbere seasoning, a spicy Ethiopian flavoring that typically includes ground chiles, ginger, fenugreek, cardamom, turmeric, and more. Look at the label closely; if the kind you buy includes salt, you'll need to decrease the amount of salt added at the end.

HANDS-ON TIME: 50 MINUTES TOTAL TIME: 50 MINUTES

2 tablespoons canola oil

2 cups chopped onion

4 garlic cloves, minced

1 tablespoon Berbere spice blend

4 cups unsalted vegetable stock (such as Kitchen Basics)

1 cup water

1 cup uncooked teff

1¼ pounds sweet potatoes, peeled and cubed

1 (14.5-ounce) can unsalted diced tomatoes, undrained

8 cups thinly sliced trimmed collard greens

¼ cup creamy peanut butter

1½ teaspoons kosher salt

Lemon wedges

1. Heat a large Dutch oven over medium heat. Add oil to pan; swirl to coat. Add onion and garlic; cook 6 minutes, stirring frequently. Add Berbere spice blend; cook 30 seconds, stirring constantly. Add stock, 1 cup water, teff, sweet potatoes, and tomatoes; bring to a boil. Cover, reduce heat, and simmer 20 minutes, stirring occasionally.

2. Add greens; cover and simmer 10 minutes or until greens wilt and sweet potatoes are tender. Add peanut butter and salt, stirring well. Ladle stew into bowls. Serve with lemon wedges.

SERVES 10 *(serving size: about 1 cup)*
CALORIES 281; **FAT** 8.4g (sat 1.3g, mono 4.3g, poly 2.5g); **PROTEIN** 9g; **CARB** 45g; **FIBER** 7g; **SUGARS** 8g (est. added sugars 1g); **CHOL** 0mg; **IRON** 3mg; **SODIUM** 574mg; **CALC** 143mg

WHITE BEAN AND HOMINY CHILI

Vegetarian chipotle sausage packs quite a punch, adding savory depth to the entire pot. Use any leftover chili to make nachos, or ladle onto baked potatoes.

HANDS-ON TIME: 20 MINUTES TOTAL TIME: 40 MINUTES

2 (15-ounce) cans unsalted cannellini beans or other white beans, rinsed, drained, and divided

1 tablespoon olive oil

1 (4-ounce) meatless Mexican chipotle sausage (such as Field Roast), finely chopped

1½ cups chopped white onion

3 garlic cloves, minced

2 poblano chiles, seeded and chopped

2 teaspoons chili powder

1 teaspoon ground cumin

1½ cups water

2 tablespoons chopped fresh oregano

2 teaspoons hot pepper sauce (such as Tabasco)

½ teaspoon salt

1 (15.5-ounce) can white hominy, rinsed and drained

2 tablespoons thinly sliced green onions

2 tablespoons chopped fresh cilantro

8 lime wedges

1. Mash ⅔ cup beans with a fork.

2. Heat a large Dutch oven over medium heat. Add oil to pan; swirl to coat. Add sausage, and sauté 4 minutes. Add onion, garlic, and poblanos; sauté 6 minutes. Add chili powder and cumin; cook 30 seconds, stirring constantly. Add mashed beans, whole beans, 1½ cups water, and next 4 ingredients (through hominy). Bring to a boil. Cover, reduce heat, and simmer 20 minutes or until slightly thick. Stir in green onions and cilantro. Ladle chili into each of 4 bowls. Serve with lime wedges.

SERVES 4 *(serving size: 1½ cups chili and 2 lime wedges)*
CALORIES 261; **FAT** 6.1g (sat 0.6g, mono 3g, poly 1.6g); **PROTEIN** 14g; **CARB** 41g; **FIBER** 10g; **SUGARS** 6g (est. added sugars 0g); **CHOL** 0mg; **IRON** 3mg; **SODIUM** 596mg; **CALC** 89mg

FARRO MINESTRONE WITH BRUSSELS SPROUTS, BUTTERNUT SQUASH, AND CHESTNUTS

In place of the usual pasta or rice, farro goes into this minestrone that's packed with winter vegetables.

HANDS-ON TIME: 40 MINUTES TOTAL TIME: 1 HOUR 25 MINUTES

1 cup uncooked whole-grain farro
1 tablespoon extra-virgin olive oil
1 cup coarsely chopped onion
½ cup finely chopped carrot (about 1 small)
⅓ cup finely chopped celery
3 ounces pancetta, chopped
2 garlic cloves, minced
5 cups fat-free, lower-sodium chicken broth (such as Swanson)
⅓ cup dry white wine
1½ cups bottled chestnuts, halved
1 cup diced peeled butternut squash
1 cup quartered Brussels sprouts (about 5 ounces)
¼ teaspoon freshly ground black pepper
1 cup grape tomatoes, halved
1 ounce shaved pecorino Romano cheese (about ¼ cup)

1. Place farro in a large saucepan. Cover with water to 2 inches above farro; bring to a boil. Reduce heat, and simmer 40 to 45 minutes or until tender. Drain; set aside.

2. Heat a Dutch oven over medium-high heat. Add oil to pan; swirl to coat. Add onion, carrot, celery, pancetta, and garlic; sauté 8 minutes or until mixture is very fragrant and beginning to brown. Stir in broth and wine, scraping pan to loosen browned bits. Add chestnuts, squash, Brussels sprouts, and pepper; bring to a boil. Reduce heat, and simmer, uncovered, 10 minutes. Stir in farro and tomatoes; cover and cook 10 minutes. Ladle soup into each of 6 bowls. Sprinkle with cheese.

CHANGE IT UP

If you'd like to make a meatless version, omit the pancetta, switch to vegetable stock, and stir in a tablespoon of white miso to add back some umami depth. If you don't have miso, simmer the soup with a piece of pecorino Romano rind.

SERVES 6 *(serving size: about 1 cup soup and about 2 teaspoons cheese)*
CALORIES 333; **FAT** 10.1g (sat 3.4g, mono 2.5g, poly 0.7g); **PROTEIN** 12g; **CARB** 53g; **FIBER** 5g; **SUGARS** 9g (est. added sugars 0g); **CHOL** 15mg; **IRON** 3mg; **SODIUM** 638mg; **CALC** 125mg

CHICKEN AND WHOLE-GRAIN DUMPLINGS

Thanks to delicate whole-wheat pastry flour, these dumplings simmer to puffy, light perfection. This is the type of recipe that epitomizes the point I've tried to make in this book: You can rethink classic recipes using healthier whole grains, without compromising flavor or texture.

HANDS-ON TIME: 27 MINUTES TOTAL TIME: 1 HOUR 5 MINUTES

Cooking spray
1 pound skinless, boneless chicken thighs, cut into bite-sized pieces
1 tablespoon canola oil
1 cup chopped onion
1 cup cubed peeled turnip
¾ cup thinly sliced celery
¾ cup chopped carrot
1 tablespoon chopped fresh thyme
4 cups unsalted chicken stock (such as Swanson)
1 bay leaf
1 teaspoon kosher salt, divided
½ teaspoon freshly ground black pepper
1½ tablespoons whole-wheat pastry flour
3 tablespoons water
4 ounces whole-wheat pastry flour (about 1 cup)
1 teaspoon baking powder
2 tablespoons chilled butter, cut into small pieces
¼ cup chopped fresh flat-leaf parsley
½ cup nonfat buttermilk

1. Heat a Dutch oven over medium-high heat. Coat pan with cooking spray. Add chicken to pan; cook 6 minutes, turning to brown on all sides. Remove chicken from pan.

2. Add oil to pan; swirl to coat. Add onion, turnip, celery, and carrot; sauté 5 minutes. Add thyme; sauté 1 minute. Add stock, bay leaf, ⅝ teaspoon salt, and pepper; bring to a boil. Cover, reduce heat, and simmer 20 minutes or until vegetables are tender. Place 1½ tablespoons flour in a small bowl; gradually add 3 tablespoons water, stirring with a whisk until smooth. Stir water mixture into stew; cook 1 minute or until slightly thick. Stir in chicken.

3. Weigh or lightly spoon 4 ounces flour into a dry measuring cup; level with a knife. Combine 4 ounces flour, baking powder, and ⅜ teaspoon salt in a medium bowl. Cut in butter with a pastry blender or 2 knives until mixture resembles coarse meal. Stir in parsley. Add buttermilk, stirring just until moist. Spoon dough by rounded tablespoonfuls into stew to form 18 dumplings; cover and simmer 10 minutes or until dumplings are done. Discard bay leaf. Ladle stew into each of 6 bowls. Top each serving with dumplings.

SERVES 6 *(serving size: about 1 cup stew and 3 dumplings)*
CALORIES 276; **FAT** 9.8g (sat 3.4g, mono 3.6g, poly 1.5g); **PROTEIN** 22g; **CARB** 25g; **FIBER** 5g; **SUGARS** 3g (est. added sugars 0g); **CHOL** 82mg; **IRON** 2mg; **SODIUM** 632mg; **CALC** 130mg

MISO SOBA BOWL WITH SOFT-BOILED EGG

Miso is one of our flavor-bomb secret weapons at Cooking Light, *instantly providing rich umami depth. So, too, do dried shiitake mushrooms, which infuse the broth with earthy, savory flavor. It's easy to overcook soba, so watch it closely, and be sure to rinse it with cold water as soon as it's done to stop the cooking process. The steaming method for the eggs cooks them perfectly and makes the shells easy to remove.*

HANDS-ON TIME: 35 MINUTES TOTAL TIME: 1 HOUR 30 MINUTES

3 cups water

1 ounce dried shiitake mushrooms

1 tablespoon dark sesame oil

½ cup sliced green onion bottoms (white and light green parts)

6 (¼-inch) slices peeled fresh ginger

5 garlic cloves, minced

4 cups unsalted vegetable stock (such as Kitchen Basics)

3 tablespoons yellow or white miso

1 tablespoon lower-sodium soy sauce

6 large eggs in shells, refrigerator-cold

9 ounces uncooked soba (buckwheat noodles)

1 tablespoon rice vinegar

1 (14-ounce) package water-packed extra-firm tofu, drained and cubed

3 baby bok choy, halved vertically (about 1 pound)

½ cup sliced green onion tops (dark green parts)

1. Bring 3 cups water to a boil in a small saucepan. Add mushrooms; cover, remove from heat, and let stand 20 minutes or until mushrooms are tender. Remove mushrooms from pan with a slotted spoon, reserving liquid. Thinly slice mushrooms.

2. Heat a Dutch oven over medium heat. Add oil to Dutch oven; swirl to coat. Add green onion bottoms, ginger, and garlic; cook 3 minutes, stirring frequently. Add mushrooms, mushroom soaking liquid, stock, miso, and soy sauce; bring to a boil. Reduce heat, and simmer 15 minutes.

3. While stock mixture simmers, bring 1 inch of water to a boil in a large saucepan. Place eggs in a vegetable steamer basket; lower basket into pan. Cover and cook 6 minutes 45 seconds; plunge eggs into ice water. Let stand 3 minutes. Drain and peel.

4. Cook soba in boiling water 2 minutes or until al dente; drain and rinse with cold water. Drain.

5. Stir vinegar and tofu into stock mixture. Arrange bok choy on top; cover and simmer 5 minutes. Place about ¾ cup soba and 1 bok choy half in each of 6 bowls; ladle about 1¼ cups simmering stock mixture over noodles. Sprinkle each serving with 1½ tablespoons green onion tops. Cut each egg in half; nestle 2 egg halves into each bowl.

SERVES 6 *(serving size: 1 bowl)*
CALORIES 371; **FAT** 11.5g (sat 2.4g, mono 4.2g, poly 4.5g); **PROTEIN** 22g; **CARB** 48g; **FIBER** 7g; **SUGARS** 5g (est. added sugars 0g); **CHOL** 186mg; **IRON** 4mg; **SODIUM** 653mg; **CALC** 186mg

MAINS

I believe in moving meat from the theoretical center of the plate to the outskirts. The way I usually cook at home is more about combined dishes—whole grains tossed with a little meat (or none) and lots of vegetables. That's not to say that you can't have your comfort-food favorites, like meat loaf or chicken casserole; they're represented here, too, with a healthier spin.

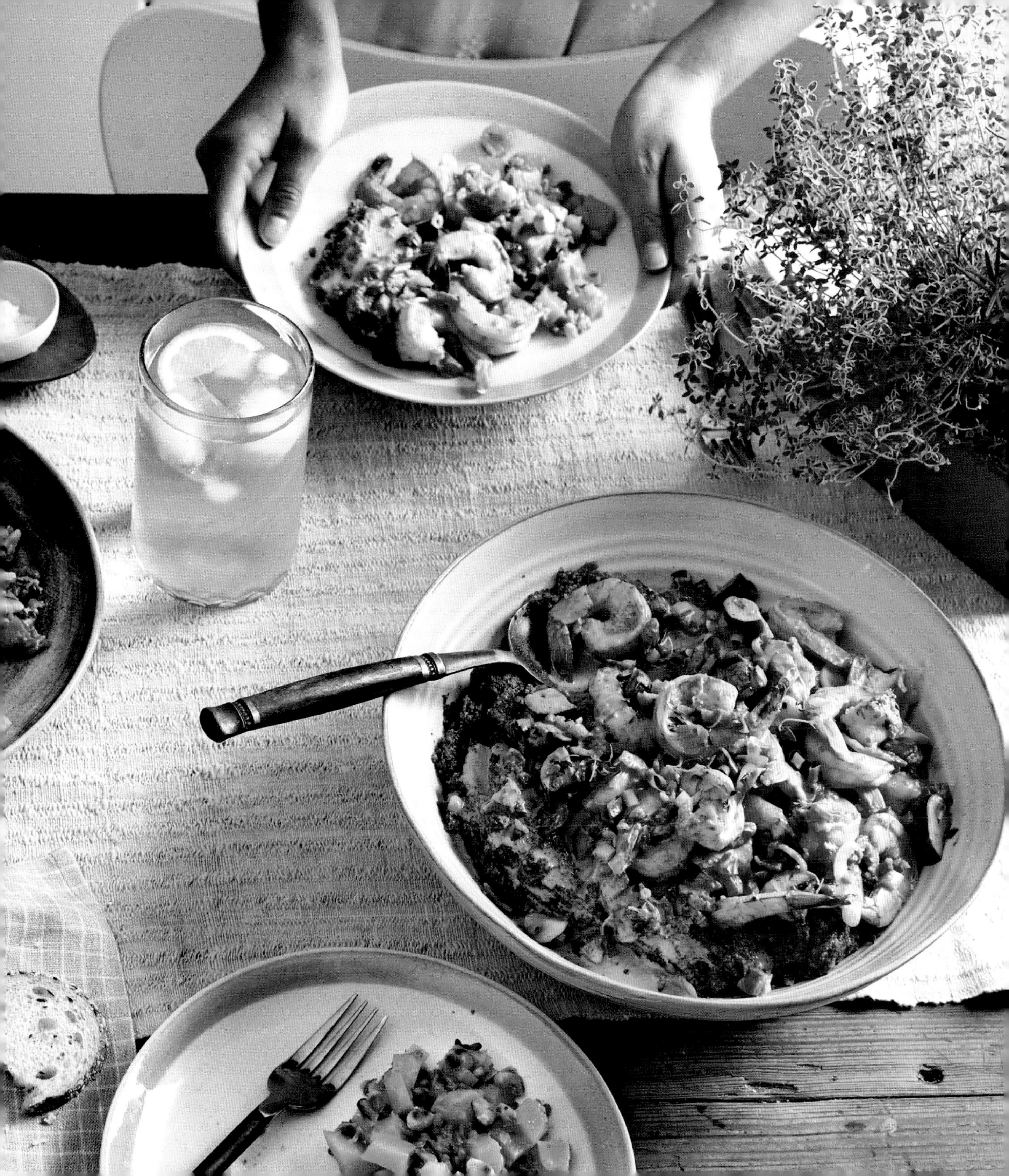

WHEAT BERRY, PORCINI, AND ROOT VEGETABLE POTPIES

Admittedly, there are a few steps to this recipe, but the results are worth it: a rich vegetarian dinner of chewy grains, sweet root vegetables, and deeply savory porcini gravy all under a flaky whole-wheat crust. To get 2 cups cooked wheat berries or spelt, start with ⅔ cup uncooked.

HANDS-ON TIME: 37 MINUTES TOTAL TIME: 2 HOURS 17 MINUTES

Crust:

- 6 ounces whole-wheat pastry flour (scant 1½ cups)
- ½ teaspoon kosher salt
- ¼ cup extra-virgin olive oil
- ¼ cup 2% reduced-fat milk

Filling:

- 3 cups (½-inch) cubed peeled celery root
- 1½ cups (¼-inch) sliced carrot
- 1¼ cups (¼-inch) sliced parsnips (cut any large rounds into half-moons)
- Cooking spray
- 1 tablespoon extra-virgin olive oil
- 1 ounce dried porcini mushrooms
- 3 cups boiling water
- 1 tablespoon butter
- ⅔ cup finely chopped shallots
- 1 tablespoon chopped fresh thyme
- 4 garlic cloves, minced
- ¼ cup Madeira wine
- ⅔ cup 2% reduced-fat milk
- 1.33 ounces whole-wheat pastry flour (about ⅓ cup)
- 1 teaspoon kosher salt
- 1 teaspoon freshly ground black pepper
- 2 cups cooked wheat berries or spelt berries

1. Preheat oven to 425°F.

2. To prepare crust, weigh or lightly spoon 6 ounces pastry flour into dry measuring cups; level with a knife. Combine flour and ½ teaspoon salt in a medium bowl. Combine ¼ cup oil and ¼ cup milk; add to flour mixture. Stir mixture until dough forms. Wrap dough in plastic wrap; chill 30 minutes.

3. Meanwhile, to prepare filling, combine celery root, carrot, and parsnips on a foil-lined jelly-roll pan coated with cooking spray. Drizzle with 1 tablespoon oil; toss to coat. Cover pan with foil. Bake at 425°F for 15 minutes; uncover and bake an additional 30 minutes or until vegetables are tender and lightly browned. Remove from oven (do not turn oven off).

4. Place porcini in a medium bowl; cover with 3 cups boiling water. Cover and let stand 15 minutes or until mushrooms are tender; strain through a sieve over a 2-cup glass measuring cup, reserving liquid. Chop mushrooms.

5. Heat a large nonstick skillet over medium-high heat. Add butter; swirl until butter melts. Add shallots, thyme, and garlic; sauté 3 minutes. Add wine; cook 1 minute or until liquid mostly evaporates. Slowly pour in porcini soaking liquid, leaving grit behind in bottom of measuring cup; bring to a boil. Combine ⅔ cup milk and 1.33 ounces flour, stirring with a whisk. Add milk mixture to pan, stirring constantly; cook 2 minutes or until mixture thickens. Stir in 1 teapoon salt, pepper, wheat berries or spelt, mushrooms, and vegetables; remove from heat.

6. Remove dough from refrigerator; cut into 6 equal pieces. Roll each dough piece into a ball. Roll each dough ball between sheets of plastic wrap into a 5-inch circle. Divide filling evenly among 6 (10-ounce) ramekins; top each with 1 dough circle. Tuck edges of dough under, or loosely pleat around edge. Cut slits in dough to vent. Place ramekins on a foil-lined jelly-roll pan. Bake at 425°F for 25 minutes or until crust is browned and filling is bubbly.

SERVES 6 *(serving size: 1 potpie)*
CALORIES 458; **FAT** 15.6g (sat 3.5g, mono 9.2g, poly 1.7g); **PROTEIN** 12g; **CARB** 68g; **FIBER** 12g; **SUGARS** 8g (est. added sugars 0g); **CHOL** 8mg; **IRON** 4mg; **SODIUM** 623mg; **CALC** 136mg

White Pizza with Asparagus

Pepperonata Pizza, page 180

PIZZAS FOUR WAYS

As far as I'm concerned, pizza night should be a weekly thing. I'm talking homemade here—pies you put your personal stamp on by having fun with the toppings. While it's easy to go overboard when cheese, sauce, and meat hit flatbread, these thin-crust pies are perfectly balanced and perfectly portioned. Just remember: The pizza is your entrée; fill half your plate with a salad to round out the meal.

WHITE PIZZA WITH ASPARAGUS

Long, slender pieces of asparagus look beautiful on this pizza, but you can use 2-inch diagonally-cut pieces if you want to simplify prep.

HANDS-ON TIME: 10 MINUTES TOTAL TIME: 26 MINUTES

¾ cup part-skim ricotta cheese

1.5 ounces Parmigiano-Reggiano cheese, grated (about ⅓ cup)

2 tablespoons 2% reduced-fat milk

1 large garlic clove, grated

1 tablespoon extra-virgin olive oil, divided

8 ounces trimmed asparagus spears, halved lengthwise

1 portion White Wheat Pizza Dough (page 37)

2 ounces very thinly sliced prosciutto, torn into pieces

1. Place a pizza stone or heavy baking sheet in oven. Preheat oven to 500°F (leave stone in oven as it heats).

2. Combine first 4 ingredients in a bowl, stirring well to combine.

3. Heat a large skillet over medium-high heat. Add 1½ teaspoons oil to pan; swirl to coat. Add asparagus; sauté 3 minutes or just until asparagus starts to soften.

4. Roll White Wheat Pizza Dough into a 13-inch circle on a piece of parchment paper. Spread ricotta mixture evenly over dough, leaving a ½-inch border. Top evenly with asparagus. Brush 1½ teaspoons oil on edge of dough. Transfer pizza (still on parchment) onto hot pizza stone. Bake at 500°F for 13 minutes or until crust is browned. Remove from oven; top evenly with prosciutto. Cut into 8 wedges.

SERVES 4 *(serving size: 2 wedges)*
CALORIES 360; **FAT** 14.7g (sat 5.4g, mono 6.9g, poly 1g); **PROTEIN** 21g; **CARB** 34g; **FIBER** 6g; **SUGARS** 2g (est. added sugars 1g); **CHOL** 31mg; **IRON** 4mg; **SODIUM** 668mg; **CALC** 310mg

PEPPERONATA PIZZA

This colorful vegetarian pizza boasts a sweet-salty flavor profile, with oil-simmered bell peppers and meaty olives. Though I call for different colored bell peppers and tomatoes, you can go for a dramatic monochrome of all yellow, orange, or red instead.

HANDS-ON TIME: 8 MINUTES TOTAL TIME: 41 MINUTES

2½ tablespoons extra-virgin olive oil, divided

⅔ cup vertically sliced shallots

4 garlic cloves, thinly sliced

1 red bell pepper, cut into strips

1 yellow bell pepper, cut into strips

1 tablespoon chopped fresh oregano

1 tablespoon balsamic vinegar

¼ teaspoon kosher salt

1 portion White Wheat Pizza Dough (page 37)

2 ounces pitted Castelvetrano olives, halved

3 ounces fresh mozzarella cheese, thinly sliced

1 cup halved yellow cherry tomatoes

Oregano leaves (optional)

1. Place a pizza stone or heavy baking sheet in oven. Preheat oven to 500°F (leave stone in oven as it heats).

2. Heat a large skillet over medium heat. Add 2 tablespoons oil to pan; swirl to coat. Add shallots, garlic, and bell peppers; reduce heat to medium-low, and cook 20 minutes or until very tender, stirring occasionally. Remove from heat; stir in chopped oregano, vinegar, and salt.

3. Roll White Wheat Pizza Dough into a 13-inch circle on a piece of parchment paper. Top evenly with bell pepper mixture, leaving a ½-inch border. Top evenly with olives, cheese, and tomatoes. Brush 1½ teaspoons oil on edge of dough. Transfer pizza (still on parchment) onto hot pizza stone. Bake at 500°F for 13 minutes or until crust is browned and cheese melts. Sprinkle with oregano leaves, if desired. Cut into 8 wedges.

SERVES 4 (serving size: 2 wedges)
CALORIES 401; **FAT** 19.5g (sat 4.8g, mono 10.9g, poly 1.6g); **PROTEIN** 13g; **CARB** 41g; **FIBER** 8g; **SUGARS** 8g (est. added sugars 1g); **CHOL** 17mg; **IRON** 3mg; **SODIUM** 648mg; **CALC** 63mg

SUPER-GREEN PIZZA

In the Pittman house, where broccoli appears at least three nights each week, this pie is a big hit. It's powerfully good, with the kale pesto base and broccoli floret topping. It feels mighty virtuous, too—so much so that I just had to add some bacon. (It's still delicious without it if you want to keep it meatless.)

HANDS-ON TIME: 16 MINUTES TOTAL TIME: 29 MINUTES

3 ounces chopped curly kale
¼ cup water, divided
3 cups small broccoli florets
1 ounce Parmigiano-Reggiano cheese, grated (about ¼ cup)
3 tablespoons pine nuts, toasted
1 large garlic clove
2 tablespoons extra-virgin olive oil
1 portion White Wheat Pizza Dough (page 37)
2 ounces shredded part-skim mozzarella cheese (about ½ cup)
¼ teaspoon kosher salt
2 bacon slices, cooked and crumbled

1. Place a pizza stone or heavy baking sheet in oven. Preheat oven to 500°F (leave stone in oven as it heats).

2. Place kale in a large microwave-safe bowl; drizzle with 2 tablespoons water. Cover with plastic wrap; pierce once with a knife to vent. Microwave at HIGH 3 minutes; drain and place in a mini food processor. Place broccoli in bowl; drizzle with 2 tablespoons water. Cover with plastic wrap; pierce once with a knife to vent. Microwave at HIGH 3 minutes; drain and rinse with cold water. Drain.

3. Add Parmigiano-Reggiano, pine nuts, and garlic to kale in processor; pulse until finely chopped. With processor on, slowly drizzle oil through food chute until mixture is paste-like.

4. Roll White Wheat Pizza Dough into a 13-inch circle on a piece of parchment paper. Spread kale mixture over dough, leaving a ½-inch border. Sprinkle with mozzarella, and top with broccoli. Sprinkle evenly with salt. Transfer pizza (still on parchment) onto hot pizza stone. Bake at 500°F for 13 minutes or until crust is browned and cheese melts. Sprinkle with bacon. Cut pizza into 8 wedges.

SERVES 4 *(serving size: 2 wedges)*
CALORIES 404; **FAT** 21g (sat 4.9g, mono 10g, poly 3.6g); **PROTEIN** 18g; **CARB** 35g; **FIBER** 7g; **SUGARS** 1g (est. added sugars 1g); **CHOL** 17mg; **IRON** 4mg; **SODIUM** 664mg; **CALC** 277mg

SAUSAGE, ONION, AND JALAPEÑO PIZZA

Nothing too fancy here, just classic pizzeria-style deliciousness. I like shredding the mozzarella from a block, as I find it to be creamier—but you can use preshredded to save time.

HANDS-ON TIME: 5 MINUTES TOTAL TIME: 23 MINUTES

- 4 ounces sweet (pork) Italian sausage, casings removed
- 1 tablespoon olive oil
- 1 garlic clove, grated
- 1 portion White Wheat Pizza Dough (page 37)
- ½ cup lower-sodium marinara sauce (such as Dell'Amore)
- 4 ounces part-skim mozzarella cheese, shredded (about 1 cup)
- ½ cup thinly vertically sliced red onion
- 1 red jalapeño pepper, thinly sliced

Small basil leaves (optional)

1. Place a pizza stone or heavy baking sheet in oven. Preheat oven to 500°F (leave stone in oven as it heats).

2. Heat a medium nonstick skillet over medium-high heat. Add sausage to pan; cook 5 minutes or until browned, stirring to crumble.

3. Combine oil and garlic in a small microwave-safe bowl; microwave at HIGH 30 seconds.

4. Roll White Wheat Pizza Dough into a 13-inch circle on a piece of parchment paper. Spread marinara over dough, leaving a ½-inch border; top evenly with cheese, sausage, onion, and jalapeño. Brush oil mixture on edge of dough. Transfer pizza (still on parchment) onto hot pizza stone. Bake at 500°F for 13 minutes or until crust and cheese are browned. Sprinkle with basil, if desired. Cut into 8 wedges.

SERVES 4 *(serving size: 2 wedges)*
CALORIES 369; **FAT** 15.8g (sat 4.8g, mono 6.8g, poly 0.9g); **PROTEIN** 20g; **CARB** 34g; **FIBER** 6g; **SUGARS** 3g (est. added sugars 1g); **CHOL** 24mg; **IRON** 3mg; **SODIUM** 632mg; **CALC** 257mg

CLASSIC LASAGNA WITH MEAT SAUCE

Whole-grain pasta can sometimes be a hard sell with the family—but not when it's tucked inside saucy, cheesy layers. Extra-lean ground beef (which can cook up dry) works well here because it's combined with marinara to keep it moist.

HANDS-ON TIME: 16 MINUTES TOTAL TIME: 1 HOUR 6 MINUTES

1½   cups fat-free ricotta cheese

6   ounces part-skim mozzarella cheese, shredded (about 1½ cups)

¼   cup flat-leaf parsley leaves, divided

1½   tablespoons unsalted butter, melted

1   tablespoon finely chopped fresh oregano

5   garlic cloves, minced and divided

1   large egg, lightly beaten

12   ounces extra-lean ground beef (93% lean)

½   teaspoon freshly ground black pepper

¼   teaspoon crushed red pepper

1   (25-ounce) jar lower-sodium marinara sauce (such as Dell'Amore)

Cooking spray

6   whole-grain lasagna noodles, cooked

1   ounce Parmigiano-Reggiano cheese, grated (about ¼ cup)

1. Preheat oven to 375°F.

2. Combine ricotta, 2 ounces (about ½ cup) mozzarella, 2 tablespoons parsley, butter, oregano, 1 garlic clove, and egg; set aside.

3. Place beef in a large nonstick skillet over medium-high heat; sprinkle with peppers and 4 garlic cloves. Cook 9 minutes or until beef is browned, stirring to crumble; drain. Return beef mixture to pan; stir in marinara sauce, and remove from heat.

4. Spread ½ cup meat sauce in bottom of a broiler-safe 11 x 7–inch glass or ceramic baking dish coated with cooking spray. Cut bottom third off each noodle to form 6 long and 6 short noodles; cut short noodles in half to form 12 pieces. Arrange 2 long noodles along outside edges of dish; arrange 4 short noodle pieces along center of dish. Top noodles with 1 cup meat sauce. Top with 2 long noodles and 4 short noodle pieces, all of ricotta mixture, and 1 cup meat sauce. Arrange 2 long noodles and 4 short noodle pieces on top. Spread remaining meat sauce over top of noodles. Sprinkle evenly with 4 ounces (1 cup) mozzarella cheese and Parmigiano-Reggiano cheese. Cover with foil coated with cooking spray. Bake at 375°F for 30 minutes. Uncover and bake an additional 10 minutes or until bubbly.

5. Preheat broiler. (Keep lasagna in oven.)

6. Broil lasagna 1 to 2 minutes or until cheese is golden brown and sauce is bubbly. Remove from oven; let stand 10 minutes. Sprinkle with 2 tablespoons parsley; cut into 6 pieces.

SERVES 6 *(serving size: 1 piece)*
CALORIES 415; **FAT** 16.3g (sat 6.5g, mono 3.7g, poly 0.7g); **PROTEIN** 32g; **CARB** 34g; **FIBER** 6g; **SUGARS** 9g (est. added sugars 2g); **CHOL** 100mg; **IRON** 3mg; **SODIUM** 602mg; **CALC** 414mg

WHOLE-WHEAT SPAGHETTI WITH KALE, POACHED EGGS, AND TOASTED BREADCRUMBS

Born of the cucina povera (literally translated "poor kitchen") tradition, this dish transforms humble ingredients into something rather elegant. Lacinato kale, sometimes labeled cavalo nero, Tuscan, or black kale, has dark leaves that are richly flavored. If you can't find lacinato kale, you can use regular curly kale. Or try Swiss chard instead, and cut the cooking time for the greens in half.

HANDS-ON TIME: 55 MINUTES TOTAL TIME: 55 MINUTES

1 (2-ounce) piece whole-wheat baguette, cubed

2 tablespoons extra-virgin olive oil, divided

3 cups sliced onion (about 1 medium)

14 cups stemmed, coarsely chopped lacinato kale (about 18 ounces)

½ cup water

¼ teaspoon crushed red pepper

4 garlic cloves, chopped

2¼ teaspoons kosher salt, divided

4 large eggs

8 ounces whole-wheat spaghetti

2 ounces pecorino Romano cheese, divided

½ teaspoon coarsely ground black pepper

1. Preheat oven to 400°F.

2. Place bread in a food processor; pulse until 1 cup fine breadcrumbs form. Combine breadcrumbs and 2 teaspoons oil on a baking sheet. Bake at 400°F for 8 minutes or until toasted, stirring occasionally.

3. Heat a large nonstick skillet over medium-high heat. Add 1 teaspoon oil; swirl to coat. Add onion; sauté 8 minutes or until golden, stirring frequently. Gradually add kale, stirring to wilt after each addition. Stir in ½ cup water, red pepper, and garlic. Reduce heat to medium; cook, uncovered, 12 minutes or until kale is tender, stirring occasionally. Stir in ¼ teaspoon salt. Keep warm.

4. Bring a large pot of water and 2 teaspoons salt to a simmer. Working with 1 egg at a time, crack each egg into a small bowl or ramekin. Gently slide eggs into water; cook 3 minutes or until whites are just set. Carefully remove eggs from water with a slotted spoon; set aside. Remove any remaining egg solids from water with a slotted spoon, and discard.

[CONTINUED]

5. Bring water to a boil. Add pasta; cook 10 minutes or until al dente. Drain and place in a large bowl. Grate 1 ounce cheese. Add cheese, 1 tablespoon oil, and black pepper to pasta; toss to coat. Place about ¾ cup kale in bottom of each of 4 shallow bowls. Top each serving with about 1 cup pasta mixture, 1 egg, and ¼ cup breadcrumbs. Shave 1 ounce cheese evenly over servings.

SERVES 4
CALORIES 519; **FAT** 16.4g (sat 4g, mono 7.8g, poly 2.5g); **PROTEIN** 26; **CARB** 76g; **FIBER** 13g; **SUGARS** 5g (est. added sugars 0g); **CHOL** 216mg; **IRON** 7mg; **SODIUM** 569mg; **CALC** 438mg

"FARROTTO" WITH BUTTERNUT, GRUYÈRE, AND HAZELNUTS

Cubes of butternut squash hold their shape and bite, and stand out wonderfully against the farro background. Grated Gruyère cheese and chopped hazelnuts add the perfect touch of fat and salt at the end of this vegetarian main dish.

HANDS-ON TIME: 50 MINUTES TOTAL TIME: 1 HOUR 20 MINUTES

1 tablespoon olive oil

1½ cups thinly sliced leek (about 1 large)

1 cup uncooked whole-grain farro

1 garlic clove, minced

½ cup white wine

4 cups water, divided

4 cups (½-inch) cubed peeled butternut squash

1 tablespoon chopped fresh sage

¾ teaspoon kosher salt

½ teaspoon freshly ground black pepper

2 ounces Gruyère cheese, grated (about ½ cup packed)

½ cup chopped hazelnuts, toasted

1. Heat a Dutch oven over medium-high heat. Add oil to pan; swirl to coat. Add leek; sauté 5 minutes or until tender, stirring frequently. Add farro and garlic; cook 1 minute, stirring constantly. Stir in wine; cook 1 minute or until wine evaporates. Add 1 cup water; cook 8 minutes or until liquid is nearly absorbed, stirring frequently. Add 2 cups water, 1 cup at a time, stirring until each portion is absorbed before adding the next (about 40 minutes total). Stir in 1 cup water, squash, sage, salt, and pepper. Cover, reduce heat, and simmer 30 minutes or until squash is just tender, stirring occasionally. Stir in cheese; sprinkle with nuts. Serve immediately.

SERVES 4 *(serving size: about 1⅓ cups)*
CALORIES 449; **FAT** 17.7g (sat 3.7g, mono 10.4g, poly 1.8g); **PROTEIN** 15g; **CARB** 58g; **FIBER** 10g; **SUGARS** 5g (est. added sugars 0g); **CHOL** 15mg; **IRON** 4mg; **SODIUM** 417mg; **CALC** 261mg

FREEKEH-TURKEY SLOPPY JOES

Here's a great way to incorporate more whole grains into your family's diet while inconspicuously reducing your meat consumption. Hearty freekeh replaces much of the ground meat in a typical sloppy Joe mix, and its texture is completely satisfying.

HANDS-ON TIME: 13 MINUTES TOTAL TIME: 54 MINUTES

½ cup uncooked cracked freekeh
2 tablespoons canola oil
¾ cup finely chopped onion
5 garlic cloves, minced
8 ounces ground turkey
1 tablespoon chili powder
1 tablespoon brown sugar
⅛ teaspoon ground red pepper
2 cups canned crushed tomatoes
¾ teaspoon kosher salt
6 Bibb lettuce leaves (optional)
6 (1½-ounce) whole-wheat hamburger buns, toasted
6 (⅛-inch-thick) slices red onion

1. Cook freekeh according to package directions.

2. Heat a large skillet over medium-high heat. Add oil to pan; swirl to coat. Add onion and garlic; sauté 5 minutes. Add turkey to pan; sprinkle with chili powder, sugar, and pepper. Cook 6 minutes or until turkey is done, stirring to crumble. Add cooked freekeh and tomatoes; reduce heat to medium, and cook 10 minutes or until mixture thickens. Stir in salt. Remove from heat; let stand 5 minutes.

3. Place 1 lettuce leaf on bottom half of each bun, if desired. Spoon about ⅔ cup freekeh mixture over lettuce. Top each sandwich with 1 onion slice and top half of bun.

CHANGE IT UP

For taco night, try this variation: Remove the sugar and add a teaspoon of ground cumin; stuff the filling into warm corn tortillas with the usual taco toppers.

SERVES 6 *(serving size: 1 sandwich)*
CALORIES 309; **FAT** 10.2g (sat 1.5g, mono 4.7g, poly 3.3g); **PROTEIN** 15g; **CARB** 44g; **FIBER** 7g; **SUGARS** 11g (est. added sugars 2g); **CHOL** 26mg; **IRON** 4mg; **SODIUM** 589mg; **CALC** 105mg

MEXICAN STUFFED POBLANOS

This vegetarian dish is so hearty it will satisfy any avid meat-eater. Poblano chiles are stuffed with beans and veggies and smothered with cheese for an indulgent dish you will adore.

HANDS-ON TIME: 45 MINUTES TOTAL TIME: 1 HOUR 5 MINUTES

4 poblano chiles

½ cup organic vegetable broth (such as Swanson)

½ cup uncooked bulgur

1 tablespoon olive oil

1 cup chopped onion

3 garlic cloves, minced

2 teaspoons ground cumin

1 (15-ounce) can unsalted pinto beans, drained

1 (4-ounce) can chopped green chiles, undrained

Cooking spray

3 ounces shredded Monterey Jack cheese (about ¾ cup)

2 cups chopped seeded tomato (about 2)

½ cup finely chopped red onion

¼ cup chopped fresh cilantro

2 tablespoons fresh lime juice

¼ teaspoon kosher salt

⅛ teaspoon ground red pepper

1 jalapeño pepper, seeded and finely chopped

1. Preheat broiler.

2. Place poblanos on a foil-lined baking sheet. Broil 5 minutes on each side or until blackened and charred. Wrap poblanos in foil; fold to close tightly. Let stand 15 minutes; peel. Cut a slit lengthwise in each poblano; discard seeds, keeping chiles intact. Set aside.

3. Reduce oven temperature to 400°F.

4. Bring vegetable broth to a boil in a medium saucepan; gradually stir in bulgur. Remove from heat; cover and let stand 30 minutes.

5. Heat a large nonstick skillet over medium-high heat. Add oil to pan; swirl to coat. Add onion and garlic to pan; sauté 5 minutes or until onion is lightly browned. Add cumin, beans, and green chiles. Bring to a boil, reduce heat, and simmer 10 minutes or until thick, stirring occasionally. Remove from heat; let stand 10 minutes. Stir in cooked bulgur.

6. Divide bean mixture evenly among poblanos. Press poblanos gently to close. Place poblanos, seam-side up, on a foil-lined baking sheet coated with cooking spray. Top each poblano with 3 tablespoons cheese. Bake poblanos at 400°F for 15 minutes or until lightly browned.

7. Combine tomato and next 6 ingredients (through jalapeño) in a medium bowl. Serve with poblanos.

SERVES 4 *(serving size: 1 poblano and ⅓ cup salsa)*
CALORIES 307; **FAT** 10.7g (sat 4.6g, mono 4.4g, poly 0.8g); **PROTEIN** 14g; **CARB** 42g; **FIBER** 11g; **SUGARS** 8g (est. added sugars 0g); **CHOL** 19mg; **IRON** 3mg; **SODIUM** 442mg; **CALC** 256mg

QUINOA-STUFFED HEIRLOOM TOMATOES WITH ROMESCO (GF)

Old-fashioned stuffed tomatoes get a 21st-century update with a dilly quinoa-chickpea filling and smoky romesco accompaniment.

HANDS-ON TIME: 60 MINUTES TOTAL TIME: 1 HOUR 30 MINUTES

Romesco Sauce:

- 1 cup bottled roasted red bell peppers, rinsed and drained (about 5 ounces)
- ¼ cup unsalted dry-roasted almonds
- 2 tablespoons water
- 1 tablespoon olive oil
- 1½ teaspoons red wine vinegar
- 1 teaspoon minced fresh garlic
- ⅛ teaspoon kosher salt
- ⅛ teaspoon ground red pepper
- ⅛ teaspoon freshly ground black pepper

Filling:

- 1 tablespoon olive oil
- ¼ cup thinly sliced onion
- 1 teaspoon minced fresh garlic
- 1 teaspoon minced peeled fresh ginger
- ¾ cup uncooked quinoa, rinsed and drained
- 1¾ cups organic vegetable broth (such as Swanson)
- ⅜ teaspoon kosher salt
- ¼ teaspoon freshly ground black pepper
- 3 tablespoons chopped fresh Italian parsley
- 2 tablespoons chopped fresh dill
- 1 (15-ounce) can unsalted chickpeas (garbanzo beans), drained and coarsely chopped
- 8 medium heirloom tomatoes

1. To prepare romesco sauce, place first 9 ingredients in a blender or food processor; process until smooth.

2. To prepare filling, heat a medium saucepan over medium-high heat. Add 1 tablespoon oil to pan; swirl to coat. Add onion; sauté 4 minutes or until onion begins to brown. Add 1 teaspoon garlic and ginger; sauté 30 seconds, stirring constantly. Stir in quinoa; cook 1 minute, stirring constantly. Add broth, ⅜ teaspoon salt, and ¼ teaspoon black pepper; bring to a boil. Cover and simmer 20 minutes or until quinoa is tender and liquid is absorbed.

3. Combine quinoa mixture, parsley, dill, and chickpeas in a bowl. Cut tops off tomatoes; set aside. Carefully scoop out tomato pulp, leaving shells intact; discard pulp. Divide quinoa mixture evenly among tomato shells; replace tomato tops. Spoon romesco sauce around stuffed tomatoes.

> **MAKE AHEAD**
>
> The quick-and-easy pepper sauce can be made ahead and refrigerated in an airtight container for up to 4 days.

SERVES 4 *(serving size: 2 stuffed tomatoes and about ¼ cup sauce)*
CALORIES 387; **FAT** 15.4g (sat 1.7g, mono 8.7g, poly 3.8g); **PROTEIN** 14g; **CARB** 52g; **FIBER** 11g; **SUGARS** 10g (est. added sugars 0g); **CHOL** 0mg; **IRON** 3mg; **SODIUM** 614mg; **CALC** 102mg

CHICKEN AND VEGETABLE BIRYANI GF

Biryani *is an Indian rice casserole, often baked and typically made with white basmati rice. Here, I keep it all stovetop and use brown basmati. The yogurt and butter stirred in at the end add richness and a hint of tanginess.*

HANDS-ON TIME: 25 MINUTES TOTAL TIME: 1 HOUR 15 MINUTES

Cooking spray

- 1 pound skinless, boneless chicken thighs, cut into ¾-inch pieces
- 1 teaspoon kosher salt, divided
- 1½ tablespoons canola oil
- 1½ cups chopped onion
- 1 tablespoon minced peeled fresh ginger
- 5 garlic cloves, minced
- 1 teaspoon ground cumin
- 1 teaspoon ground coriander
- ½ teaspoon ground turmeric
- ¼ teaspoon ground red pepper
- ⅛ teaspoon ground cardamom
- 1 cup uncooked brown basmati rice
- 1½ cups water
- 2 cups chopped cauliflower florets
- ⅔ cup frozen green peas, thawed
- ½ cup plain 2% reduced-fat Greek yogurt
- 1 tablespoon butter

1. Heat a large sauté pan or skillet over medium-high heat. Coat pan with cooking spray. Add chicken to pan; sprinkle with ¼ teaspoon salt. Cook chicken 8 minutes, turning to brown on all sides. Remove from pan.

2. Add oil to pan; swirl to coat. Add onion, ginger, and garlic; sauté 5 minutes, stirring occasionally. Add cumin, coriander, turmeric, pepper, and cardamom; cook 1 minute, stirring constantly. Add rice; cook 30 seconds, stirring constantly. Add 1½ cups water, scraping pan to loosen browned bits; bring to a boil. Cover, reduce heat, and simmer 30 minutes or until rice is almost tender. Add additional 2 tablespoons water, if needed. Stir in chicken, cauliflower, and ¾ teaspoon salt; cover and cook 10 minutes. Stir in peas, yogurt, and butter; cover and cook 10 minutes or until rice is tender.

SERVES 4 (serving size: about 1½ cups)
CALORIES 432; **FAT** 15.4g (sat 3.9g, mono 5.7g, poly 2.7g); **PROTEIN** 31g; **CARB** 46g; **FIBER** 6g; **SUGARS** 7g (est. added sugars 0g); **CHOL** 117mg; **IRON** 3mg; **SODIUM** 660mg; **CALC** 74mg

TARRAGON CHICKEN SALAD WITH PICKLED GRAINS

Any pickle would offer tangy little flavor bursts to chicken salad, but pickled grains one-up ordinary pickles by providing a unique chew and slightly nutty flavor. I like this best with pickled rye berries, but you can also use wheat berries, spelt, or Kamut.

HANDS-ON TIME: 10 MINUTES TOTAL TIME: 35 MINUTES

2 bay leaves

1½ pounds skinless, boneless chicken breast

⅓ cup 2% reduced-fat Greek yogurt

¼ cup canola mayonnaise

2 tablespoons chopped fresh flat-leaf parsley

1 tablespoon finely chopped fresh tarragon

½ teaspoon freshly ground black pepper

⅜ teaspoon kosher salt

¾ cup Pickled "Hard-Shell" Grains (page 35)

¼ cup slivered red onion

8 Bibb lettuce leaves

1. Fill a large skillet about two-thirds full with water; add bay leaves, and bring to a boil. Add chicken to pan; reduce heat and simmer, partially covered, 14 minutes or until chicken is done, turning after 7 minutes. Remove chicken from pan; discard liquid and bay leaves. Cool chicken slightly; shred with 2 forks.

2. Combine yogurt and next 5 ingredients (through salt) in a large bowl, stirring with a whisk. Add Pickled "Hard-Shell" Grains and onion; toss to coat. Add chicken; toss well to combine. Serve over lettuce leaves.

SERVES 4 *(serving size: 2 lettuce leaves and about 1 cup salad)*
CALORIES 332; **FAT** 9.1g (sat 1.2g, mono 3.6g, poly 2.1g); **PROTEIN** 42g; **CARB** 18g; **FIBER** 0g; **SUGARS** 3g (est. added sugars 2g); **CHOL** 110mg; **IRON** 2mg; **SODIUM** 555mg; **CALC** 45mg

BROCCOLI-QUINOA CASSEROLE WITH CHICKEN AND CHEDDAR

In my updated spin on chicken-rice casserole, whole-grain quinoa stands in for the typical white rice. It's a modern interpretation that still has loads of old-school comfort-food appeal.

HANDS-ON TIME: 20 MINUTES TOTAL TIME: 55 MINUTES

1½ tablespoons canola oil, divided

1 cup uncooked quinoa, rinsed and drained

1¼ cups water

1 (12-ounce) package microwave-in-bag fresh broccoli florets

Cooking spray

12 ounces skinless, boneless chicken breast, cut into bite-sized pieces

½ teaspoon kosher salt, divided

½ teaspoon freshly ground black pepper, divided

1½ cups chopped onion

6 garlic cloves, minced

½ cup 1% low-fat milk

2½ tablespoons all-purpose flour

1½ cups unsalted chicken stock (such as Swanson)

2 ounces Parmesan cheese, grated (about ½ cup)

½ cup canola mayonnaise

4 ounces sharp cheddar cheese, shredded (about 1 cup)

1. Heat a medium saucepan over medium-high heat. Add 1½ teaspoons oil; swirl to coat. Add quinoa; cook 2 minutes or until toasted, stirring frequently. Add 1¼ cups water; bring to a boil. Cover, reduce heat, and simmer 15 minutes or until quinoa is tender. Remove from heat; let stand 5 minutes. Fluff with a fork.

2. Preheat oven to 400°F.

3. Cook broccoli in microwave according to package directions, reducing cook time to 2½ minutes.

4. Heat a Dutch oven over medium-high heat. Coat pan with cooking spray. Add chicken to pan; sprinkle with ⅛ teaspoon salt and ⅛ teaspoon pepper. Cook 5 minutes or until browned, turning occasionally; remove from pan.

5. Add 1 tablespoon oil to pan; swirl to coat. Add onion and garlic; sauté 5 minutes. Combine milk and flour, stirring with a whisk. Add milk mixture, stock, ⅜ teaspoon salt, and ⅜ teaspoon pepper to pan. Bring to a boil, stirring frequently; cook 2 minutes or until thick. Remove from heat; cool slightly. Add Parmesan, stirring until cheese melts. Stir in quinoa, broccoli, chicken, and mayonnaise. Spoon mixture into a 2-quart glass or ceramic baking dish coated with cooking spray. Sprinkle with cheddar. Bake at 400°F for 15 minutes or until casserole is bubbly and cheese melts.

SERVES 6 *(serving size: 1⅓ cups)*
CALORIES 449; **FAT** 21.3g (sat 6.7g, mono 9g, poly 4.5g); **PROTEIN** 34g; **CARB** 29g; **FIBER** 4g; **SUGARS** 4g (est. added sugars 0g); **CHOL** 75mg; **IRON** 3mg; **SODIUM** 668mg; **CALC** 333mg

CHEESY VEGETABLE MOUSSAKA

Broiling the eggplant coaxes out a deeper, more complex flavor. I like to keep the antioxidant-packed skin on, but feel free to peel the eggplant before broiling. You can garnish the dish with extra basil leaves.

HANDS-ON TIME: 40 MINUTES TOTAL TIME: 1 HOUR 30 MINUTES

- 2 tablespoons olive oil, divided
- 2 cups finely chopped onion
- 6 garlic cloves, chopped
- 1 cup water
- ½ cup uncooked quinoa, rinsed and drained
- 2 tablespoons unsalted tomato paste
- ⅜ teaspoon kosher salt
- ¼ teaspoon freshly ground black pepper
- 1 (28-ounce) can unsalted diced tomatoes, undrained
- 2 tablespoons chopped fresh basil
- 2 large eggplants, cut into (½-inch-thick) slices (about 2½ pounds)
- Cooking spray
- 3 (8-ounce) packages presliced mushrooms
- ½ cup dry white wine
- 2 tablespoons lower-sodium soy sauce
- 2 tablespoons chopped fresh dill
- 1½ cups plain fat-free Greek yogurt
- 2.5 ounces feta cheese, crumbled (about ⅔ cup)
- 2 large eggs
- 1 large egg white
- 1 ounce vegetarian Parmesan cheese, grated (about ¼ cup)

1. Heat a medium saucepan over medium-high heat. Add 1 tablespoon oil to pan; swirl to coat. Add onion; cook 6 minutes or until onion is tender. Add garlic; cook 1 minute. Add 1 cup water, quinoa, tomato paste, salt, pepper, and tomatoes. Bring to a boil; reduce heat, and simmer 20 minutes. Remove from heat; stir in basil.

2. Preheat broiler.

3. Place half of eggplant slices on a foil-lined baking sheet coated with cooking spray; lightly coat both sides of eggplant slices with cooking spray. Broil 5 inches from heat 5 minutes on each side or until browned. Repeat procedure with remaining eggplant. Set eggplant aside.

4. Reduce oven temperature to 350°F.

5. Heat a large skillet over medium-high heat. Add 1 tablespoon oil to pan; swirl to coat. Add mushrooms; cook 8 minutes. Add wine and soy sauce; simmer 4 minutes. Remove from heat; stir in dill.

6. Combine yogurt, feta cheese, eggs, and egg white in a bowl, stirring well with a whisk until smooth.

7. Spread half of tomato sauce in bottom of a 13 x 9-inch glass or ceramic baking dish coated with cooking spray. Arrange half of eggplant slices over sauce. Spread mushroom mixture over eggplant; sprinkle with Parmesan cheese. Spoon remaining tomato sauce over cheese; top with remaining eggplant slices. Spoon yogurt mixture evenly over eggplant. Bake at 350°F for 45 minutes or until topping is lightly browned.

SERVES 6 *(serving size: ⅙ of moussaka)*
CALORIES 335; **FAT** 11.9g (sat 4g, mono 5.1g, poly 1.8g); **PROTEIN** 21g; **CARB** 38g; **FIBER** 10g; **SUGARS** 16g (est. added sugars 1g); **CHOL** 77mg; **IRON** 4mg; **SODIUM** 586mg; **CALC** 247mg

ZUCCHINI, WALNUT, AND FETA CAKES WITH CUCUMBER-YOGURT SAUCE (GF)

Uncooked quinoa instead of flour binds these tasty cakes. It's protein rich, adding an extra 3 grams per serving. Simply pulse in a mini food processor until finely ground.

HANDS-ON TIME: 25 MINUTES TOTAL TIME: 25 MINUTES

½   cup uncooked quinoa, rinsed and drained

¼   cup chopped walnuts

4½ cups grated zucchini (about 2 medium)

½   teaspoon kosher salt, divided

3   ounces feta cheese, crumbled (about ⅔ cup)

¼   cup thinly sliced green onions

3   tablespoons chopped fresh dill

¾   teaspoon freshly ground black pepper, divided

2   large eggs, lightly beaten

2   tablespoons olive oil, divided

1   (6-ounce) container plain fat-free Greek yogurt

1   cucumber, halved lengthwise, seeded, and thinly sliced (about 1½ cups)

1   garlic clove, minced

4   cups mixed salad greens (about 2 ounces)

1. Place quinoa in a mini food processor; process 1 minute or until finely ground. Add chopped walnuts to processor; process until smooth.

2. Place zucchini in a colander, and sprinkle with ¼ teaspoon salt. Toss well. Let stand 10 minutes, tossing occasionally. Press zucchini between paper towels until barely moist.

3. Combine zucchini, cheese, green onions, dill, ½ teaspoon pepper, ¼ teaspoon salt, and eggs in a large bowl; stir to combine. Sprinkle quinoa mixture over zucchini mixture; stir well to combine.

4. Heat a large nonstick skillet over medium heat. Add 1 tablespoon oil to pan; swirl to coat. Add 4 (⅓-cup) zucchini batter mounds to pan; flatten into 3-inch cakes. Cook 4 minutes on each side or until browned. Remove from pan; keep warm. Repeat procedure with 1 tablespoon oil and remaining batter to yield 8 cakes total.

5. Combine ¼ teaspoon pepper, yogurt, cucumber, and garlic in a small bowl. Divide greens evenly among 4 plates. Top each serving with cakes and cucumber mixture. Serve immediately.

SERVES 4 (serving size: 1 cup greens, 2 cakes, and about ¼ cup sauce)
CALORIES 336; **FAT** 19.2g (sat 4.7g, mono 6.9g, poly 5.5g); **PROTEIN** 18g; **CARB** 27g; **FIBER** 5g; **SUGARS** 7g (est. added sugars 0g); **CHOL** 101mg; **IRON** 3mg; **SODIUM** 589mg; **CALC** 175mg

PORK WITH FIGS AND FARRO

Stuffing a butterflied pork tenderloin is easier than you may think, and it makes for an impressive celebration- or holiday-worthy centerpiece.

HANDS-ON TIME: 35 MINUTES TOTAL TIME: 1 HOUR 15 MINUTES

2 cups water
⅔ cup uncooked whole-grain farro
1 (3-inch) cinnamon stick
1½ tablespoons olive oil, divided
¾ cup minced onion
1 garlic clove, minced
½ cup chopped dried figs
¼ cup chopped fresh flat-leaf parsley
1¼ teaspoons kosher salt, divided
¾ teaspoon freshly ground black pepper, divided
1 teaspoon sherry vinegar
⅛ teaspoon ground allspice
⅛ teaspoon ground cloves
1 large egg, lightly beaten
2 (1-pound) pork tenderloins, trimmed

1. Combine first 3 ingredients in a saucepan; bring to a boil. Cover and simmer 40 to 45 minutes or until al dente. Drain; discard cinnamon stick.

2. Heat a medium skillet over medium heat. Add 1½ teaspoons oil to pan; swirl to coat. Add onion; sauté 6 minutes or until tender. Add garlic; sauté 1 minute, stirring constantly.

3. Combine farro, onion mixture, figs, parsley, ½ teaspoon salt, ¼ teaspoon pepper, and next 4 ingredients (through egg) in a medium bowl.

4. Preheat oven to 425°F.

5. Slice pork lengthwise, cutting to, but not through, other side. Open halves. Place pork between sheets of plastic wrap; pound to ¼-inch thickness. Top pork with farro mixture, leaving a ½-inch border. Roll, starting with long side; secure pork with wooden picks.

6. Sprinkle pork evenly with ¾ teaspoon salt and ½ teaspoon pepper. Heat a large ovenproof skillet over medium-high heat. Add 1 tablespoon olive oil to pan; swirl to coat. Add pork; cook 6 minutes, browning all sides. Place pan in oven; bake pork at 425°F for 15 minutes or until a thermometer registers 145°F. Remove pork from pan; let stand 5 minutes. Slice.

MAKE AHEAD

Assemble the pork (through step 5) up to a day ahead, wrapping the rolled pork in plastic wrap and refrigerating until shortly before cooking. Let the pork stand at room temperature 15 minutes, discard the plastic wrap, and proceed with step 6.

SERVES 8 *(serving size: 4 ounces)*
CALORIES 202; **FAT** 5.8g (sat 1.3g, mono 3g, poly 0.8g); **PROTEIN** 26g; **CARB** 12g; **FIBER** 2g; **SUGARS** 5g (est. added sugars 0g); **CHOL** 96mg; **IRON** 3mg; **SODIUM** 371mg; **CALC** 31mg

CHEESY BUCKWHEAT WITH KALE AND MUSHROOMS (GF)

With its strong, almost hoppy flavor, buckwheat overpowers delicate ingredients. Here, it's matched nicely by robust kale and garlicky sautéed mushrooms. Coating the groats with egg is a trick that allows them to remain separate and fluffy (as in a traditional pilaf); otherwise, the cooked buckwheat would be a bit sticky.

HANDS-ON TIME: 33 MINUTES TOTAL TIME: 33 MINUTES

1 cup uncooked buckwheat groats

1 large egg, lightly beaten

1½ cups water

½ teaspoon kosher salt

2 ounces shredded Gruyère cheese (about ½ cup)

2 tablespoons grated fresh Parmesan cheese

1 tablespoon canola oil

8 ounces presliced mushrooms

½ cup diced onion

1 tablespoon sliced garlic

6 cups chopped kale

¼ teaspoon freshly ground black pepper

¼ cup toasted walnuts

2 center-cut bacon slices, cooked and crumbled

1. Combine buckwheat and egg in a bowl; toss. Heat a saucepan over medium heat. Add buckwheat mixture to pan; cook 3 minutes or until grains are dry and separated, stirring frequently. Stir in 1½ cups water and salt; bring to a boil. Cover, reduce heat, and simmer 15 minutes or until water is absorbed. Remove from heat; stir in Gruyère cheese and Parmesan cheese.

2. Heat a large nonstick skillet over medium heat. Add oil to pan; swirl to coat. Add mushrooms, onion, and garlic; cook 7 minutes. Add kale and pepper to pan; cook 2 minutes. Add kale mixture to buckwheat mixture. Sprinkle with walnuts and bacon.

SERVES 6 *(serving size: ¾ cup)*
CALORIES 268; **FAT** 11.6g (sat 3.4g, mono 3.5g, poly 3.1g); **PROTEIN** 13g; **CARB** 32g; **FIBER** 4g; **SUGARS** 2g (est. added sugars 0g); **CHOL** 45mg; **IRON** 2mg; **SODIUM** 309mg; **CALC** 227mg

BIBIMBOP

My Korean mom taught me that there are infinite versions of bibimbop, *a dish we explained to others as "a bunch of stuff on rice." Koreans take great care in arranging ingredients over the rice, varying colors and textures, with an egg in the center of it all.*

HANDS-ON TIME: 50 MINUTES TOTAL TIME: 66 MINUTES

8   ounces extra-firm tofu, drained
⅓   cup water
¼   cup apple cider vinegar
2   teaspoons sugar, divided
2   teaspoons minced fresh garlic, divided
1   teaspoon minced peeled fresh ginger, divided
¼   teaspoon crushed red pepper
1   cup julienne-cut carrot
2   tablespoons lower-sodium soy sauce
3   tablespoons plus 2 teaspoons dark sesame oil, divided
3   cups hot cooked short-grain brown rice
1   cup fresh bean sprouts
1   (5-ounce) package sliced shiitake mushroom caps
1   (9-ounce) package fresh baby spinach
1   teaspoon unsalted butter
4   large eggs
4   teaspoons gochujang (Korean chili paste, such as Annie Chun's)
¼   teaspoon kosher salt

1. Cut tofu into ¾-inch-thick slices. Place tofu in a single layer on several layers of paper towels; cover with additional paper towels. Let stand 30 minutes, pressing down occasionally.

2. Meanwhile, combine ⅓ cup water, vinegar, 1 teaspoon sugar, ½ teaspoon garlic, ½ teaspoon ginger, and crushed red pepper in a small saucepan. Bring to a boil. Add carrot, and remove from heat; let stand 30 minutes. Drain.

3. Remove tofu from paper towels; cut into ¾-inch cubes. Place tofu in a medium bowl. Combine 1 teaspoon sugar, ½ teaspoon garlic, ½ teaspoon ginger, soy sauce, and 1 tablespoon oil, stirring with a whisk. Add 1 tablespoon soy sauce mixture to tofu; toss gently. Let stand 15 minutes.

4. Heat a 10-inch cast-iron skillet over high heat 4 minutes. Add 1 tablespoon sesame oil; swirl to coat. Add rice to pan in a single layer; cook 1 minute (do not stir). Remove from heat; let stand 20 minutes.

5. Heat a large nonstick skillet over medium-high heat. Add 1 teaspoon oil; swirl to coat. Add 1½ teaspoons soy sauce mixture and bean sprouts to pan; sauté 1 minute. Remove sprouts from pan; keep warm. Add 1 teaspoon oil to pan; swirl to coat. Add mushrooms to pan; sauté 2 minutes. Stir in 1½ teaspoons soy sauce mixture; sauté 1 minute. Remove mushrooms from pan; keep warm. Add 2 teaspoons oil to pan; swirl to coat. Add tofu to pan; sauté 7 minutes or until golden brown. Remove tofu from pan; keep warm. Add 1 teaspoon oil to pan; swirl to coat. Add 1 teaspoon garlic and 1 tablespoon soy sauce mixture; sauté 30 seconds. Add spinach to pan; sauté 1 minute or until spinach wilts. Remove spinach from pan; keep warm. Reduce heat to medium. Melt butter in pan. Crack eggs into pan; cook 4 minutes or until whites are set. Remove from heat.

6. Place ¾ cup rice in each of 4 shallow bowls. Top each serving evenly with carrots, sprouts, mushrooms, tofu, and spinach. Top each serving with 1 egg and 1 teaspoon chili paste. Sprinkle evenly with salt.

SERVES 4 *(serving size: 1 bowl)*
CALORIES 508; **FAT** 24.5g (sat 4.8g, mono 10.3g, poly 7.8g); **PROTEIN** 21g; **CARB** 59g; **FIBER** 8g; **SUGARS** 6g (est. added sugars 2g); **CHOL** 189mg; **IRON** 5mg; **SODIUM** 710mg; **CALC** 204mg

SOBA NOODLES WITH SPICY CUMIN LAMB

This aromatic, fiery main course may be just the thing to spice up a ho-hum weeknight. Soba, made from buckwheat, is one of the quickest-cooking whole-grain noodles you can find and milder in flavor than most whole-wheat pastas.

HANDS-ON TIME: 20 MINUTES TOTAL TIME: 20 MINUTES

7	ounces uncooked soba noodles
½	cup fat-free, lower-sodium chicken broth (such as Swanson)
2	tablespoons rice vinegar
4½	teaspoons hoisin sauce
1	teaspoon minced fresh garlic
¼	teaspoon five-spice powder
8	ounces ground lamb
1	tablespoon dark sesame oil
1	teaspoon cumin seeds
⅜	teaspoon crushed red pepper
1½	cups broccoli florets
1	cup snow peas, trimmed
½	cup thinly sliced red bell pepper
9	baby carrots, halved lengthwise

1. Cook noodles according to package directions. Drain and rinse; drain well.

2. Combine chicken broth and next 4 ingredients (through five-spice powder) in a small bowl, stirring with a whisk.

3. Heat a large wok or skillet over medium-high heat. Add lamb; cook 2½ minutes or until browned, stirring to crumble. Remove lamb from pan with a slotted spoon; set aside.

4. Return pan to medium-high heat. Add oil to drippings in pan; swirl to coat. Add cumin and red pepper; cook 30 seconds or until seeds begin to pop, stirring frequently. Add broccoli, peas, bell pepper, and carrots to pan; cook 5 minutes, stirring frequently. Add lamb and broth mixture; cook 1½ minutes or until liquid is slightly reduced. Serve over noodles.

SERVES 4 *(serving size: 1 cup noodles and 1 cup lamb mixture)*
CALORIES 409; **FAT** 16.5g (sat 5.4g, mono 6.4g, poly 2.5g); **PROTEIN** 23g; **CARB** 45g; **FIBER** 2g; **SUGARS** 5g (est. added sugars 2g); **CHOL** 55mg; **IRON** 4mg; **SODIUM** 621mg; **CALC** 65mg

THAI BUCKWHEAT LARB (GF)

This dish is not for the faint of heart: It's a flavor explosion—nothing subtle about it, with its chile fire and garlicky punch. It tastes surprisingly authentic, too, thanks to full-flavored buckwheat, which takes the place of much of the usual ground meat. Three chiles are definitely my style, but that makes for a rather incendiary dish; go for two or, sigh, even one if you just can't take the heat. Larb is often served as a salad over a bed of cabbage, but I choose to go cabbage-cup style here. If the ribs of the cabbage leaves are particularly thick, shave them off with a paring knife to make the leaves more pliable.

HANDS-ON TIME: 12 MINUTES   TOTAL TIME: 33 MINUTES

1 cup water
⅔ cup uncooked buckwheat groats
6 ounces ground pork
1 tablespoon sugar
2 tablespoons fresh lime juice
2 tablespoons fish sauce*
4 garlic cloves, grated
2 or 3 Thai bird chiles, thinly sliced
½ cup thinly vertically sliced red onion
⅓ cup torn basil leaves
⅓ cup torn mint leaves
¼ cup cilantro leaves
8 Savoy cabbage leaves

1. Bring 1 cup water to a boil in a small saucepan. Add buckwheat; cover, reduce heat, and simmer 10 minutes. Remove from heat; let stand, covered, 5 minutes. Drain any excess liquid.

2. Heat a large nonstick skillet over medium-high heat. Add pork to pan; cook 5 minutes or until browned, stirring to crumble. Stir in buckwheat.

3. Combine sugar and next 4 ingredients (through chiles), stirring until sugar dissolves. Add sugar mixture to pan; cook 1 minute, stirring constantly. Remove pan from heat; cool slightly. Stir in onion, basil, mint, and cilantro. Serve with cabbage leaves.

Note: Not all fish sauces are gluten-free. Make sure to check the label.

SERVES 4 *(serving size: about 1 cup larb and 2 cabbage leaves)*
CALORIES 258; **FAT** 9.9g (sat 3.4g, mono 4g, poly 0.9g); **PROTEIN** 13g; **CARB** 31g; **FIBER** 4g; **SUGARS** 7g (est. added sugars 3g); **CHOL** 31mg; **IRON** 2mg; **SODIUM** 608mg; **CALC** 39mg

MIDDLE EASTERN MEAT LOAF WITH POMEGRANATE GLAZE

This unique meat loaf lies somewhere between kibbeh *(ground meat mixed with bulgur) and* kofta *(ground meat mixed with lots of herbs and spices that's shaped into oval patties on skewers and grilled)—an exotic take on an old standby. Pomegranate molasses makes the ideal glaze, lending a tartness that cuts the richness of the meat.*

HANDS-ON TIME: 30 MINUTES TOTAL TIME: 1 HOUR 10 MINUTES

1 cup water
½ cup uncooked bulgur
1 small onion (about 4 ounces)
1 cup chopped fresh flat-leaf parsley
½ cup whole-wheat panko (Japanese breadcrumbs; such as Kikkoman)
½ cup chopped fresh cilantro
1 teaspoon kosher salt
1 teaspoon ground coriander
¾ teaspoon ground cumin
⅜ teaspoon ground cinnamon
¼ teaspoon ground allspice
¼ teaspoon ground red pepper
1 large egg, lightly beaten
1 pound ground sirloin (90% lean)
Cooking spray
1½ tablespoons pomegranate molasses
1½ teaspoons honey

1. Bring 1 cup water to a boil in a small saucepan. Add bulgur; cover, reduce heat, and simmer 12 minutes. Remove from heat; let stand, covered, 5 minutes. Spoon bulgur into a large bowl; cool slightly.

2. Preheat oven to 350°F.

3. Shred onion using large holes of a grater onto several layers of paper towels. Add onion, parsley, and next 9 ingredients (through egg) to bulgur; stir well. Add beef; mix well to incorporate. Spoon mixture into a 9 x 5–inch loaf pan coated with cooking spray. Bake at 350°F for 30 minutes or until a thermometer inserted in middle registers 160°F. Remove from oven; let stand 5 minutes. Combine pomegranate molasses and honey; brush over loaf. Cut into 8 slices.

MAKE IT FASTER

You can cut the cook time by half (or more) by spooning the meat mixture into muffin tins and baking individual meat muffins.

SERVES 4 *(serving size: 2 slices)*
CALORIES 381; **FAT** 13.3g (sat 5.1g, mono 5.5g, poly 0.8g); **PROTEIN** 29g; **CARB** 36g; **FIBER** 5g; **SUGARS** 8g (est. added sugars 6g); **CHOL** 120mg; **IRON** 6mg; **SODIUM** 598mg; **CALC** 83mg

SMOKED EINKORN TACOS

Vegetarian tacos have never tasted so meaty! Einkorn berries take on luscious smoky flavor (thanks to the stovetop smoking method) that's enhanced by the tangy kick of salsa verde.

HANDS-ON TIME: 35 MINUTES TOTAL TIME: 35 MINUTES

Cooking spray

⅓ cup cherry or apple wood chips

1¾ cups cooked einkorn berries (about ⅔ cup uncooked)

2 tablespoons olive oil

1 cup fresh corn kernels

5 garlic cloves, minced

1 teaspoon ground cumin

¼ teaspoon salt

1 (7-ounce) can salsa verde (such as Herdez)

12 (6-inch) corn tortillas

⅓ cup crema Mexicana

¾ cup chopped tomato

3 ounces queso fresco, crumbled (about ¾ cup)

⅓ cup cilantro leaves

1 ripe avocado, peeled and diced

1. Pierce 10 holes on one side of the bottom of a 13 x 9–inch disposable aluminum foil pan. Coat pan with cooking spray. Arrange wood chips over holes inside pan. Spread einkorn onto opposite side of pan. Place hole side of pan over stovetop burner. Turn burner on high. When wood chips start to smoke, carefully cover pan with foil. Reduce heat to low; cook 3 minutes. Remove pan from heat; carefully uncover. Remove einkorn from pan; set aside.

2. Heat a large skillet over medium-high heat. Add oil; swirl to coat. Add corn and garlic; sauté 2 minutes. Add cumin; cook 30 seconds, stirring almost constantly. Add smoked einkorn, salt, and salsa verde; cook on medium heat 5 minutes or until most of liquid evaporates.

3. Heat each tortilla directly over burner or in a dry skillet for 15 seconds on each side or until lightly charred. Spoon about 3 tablespoons einkorn mixture onto center of each tortilla; top each with about 1½ teaspoons crema, 1 tablespoon tomato, and 1 tablespoon cheese. Divide cilantro and avocado evenly over tacos.

SERVES 6 *(serving size: 2 tacos)*
CALORIES 367; **FAT** 18.6g (sat 5.4g, mono 7.6g, poly 2g); **PROTEIN** 10g; **CARB** 44g; **FIBER** 8g; **SUGARS** 4g (est. added sugars 0g); **CHOL** 10mg; **IRON** 1mg; **SODIUM** 571mg; **CALC** 124mg

AMARANTH FALAFEL FRITTERS

Tiny amaranth grains lend themselves to this falafel riff; they cook up thick and viscous, so the fritters stay creamy and moist inside while browning nicely on the outside. Toasting the amaranth flour alleviates it from its hyper-grassy flavor and enhances overall savoriness. The sauce is thick—similar in texture to hummus—but if it's too thick for your taste, stir in a little water to thin it out.

HANDS-ON TIME: 36 MINUTES TOTAL TIME: 61 MINUTES

Fritters:

1¾ cups water

⅔ cup uncooked amaranth

1 ounce amaranth flour (about ¼ cup)

⅔ cup chopped onion

½ cup coarsely chopped fresh flat-leaf parsley

½ cup coarsely chopped fresh cilantro

3 garlic cloves, chopped

⅔ cup whole-wheat panko (Japanese breadcrumbs; such as Kikkoman)

1½ teaspoons ground cumin

1½ teaspoons ground coriander

1 teaspoon kosher salt

⅛ teaspoon ground red pepper

1 large egg, lightly beaten

2 tablespoons canola oil, divided

Sauce:

¼ cup plain 2% reduced-fat Greek yogurt

1 tablespoon tahini

1½ teaspoons fresh lemon juice

⅛ teaspoon kosher salt

1 garlic clove, grated

Remaining ingredient:

2 cups sliced English cucumber

1. To prepare fritters, bring 1¾ cups water to a boil. Add amaranth; cover, reduce heat, and simmer 20 minutes, stirring occasionally. Remove from heat; let stand, covered, 5 minutes. Carefully pour off any standing water from top of amaranth. Cool amaranth slightly.

2. Weigh or lightly spoon flour into a dry measuring cup; level with a knife. Heat a small skillet over medium heat. Add flour to pan; cook 5 minutes or until browned and toasty-fragrant (no longer grassy-fragrant), stirring frequently. Pour into a small bowl; cool slightly.

3. Place onion, parsley, cilantro, and garlic in a food processor; pulse until minced. Add amaranth, amaranth flour, panko, and next 5 ingredients (through egg); pulse until well combined.

4. Heat a large nonstick skillet over medium-high heat. Add 1 tablespoon oil; swirl to coat. Add amaranth mixture in 2½ tablespoon mounds to form 16 fritters; cook 3 minutes on each side or until browned. Remove from pan. Repeat procedure with 1 tablespoon oil and remaining amaranth mixture.

5. To prepare sauce, combine yogurt and next 4 ingredients (through grated garlic). Serve sauce and cucumber with fritters.

SERVES 4 *(serving size: 4 fritters, about 1 tablespoon sauce, and ½ cup cucumber)*
CALORIES 336; **FAT** 14g (sat 2g, mono 6.2g, poly 4g); **PROTEIN** 12g; **CARB** 43g; **FIBER** 6g; **SUGARS** 4g (est. added sugars 0g); **CHOL** 47mg;
IRON 5mg; **SODIUM** 590mg; **CALC** 122mg

CRISPY HERBED SALMON

Breaded fish is a surefire family hit, and this version is arguably the crispiest you'll ever try. If you have a batch of Crunchy Fried Bulgur, Quinoa, or Millet in your freezer (as I encourage on page 32), this entrée comes together in less than 25 minutes.

HANDS-ON TIME: 10 MINUTES TOTAL TIME: 22 MINUTES

¾ cup Crunchy Fried Bulgur (page 32)

2 tablespoons chopped fresh flat-leaf parsley

2 tablespoons chopped fresh chives

3 tablespoons canola mayonnaise

1 teaspoon Dijon mustard

4 (6-ounce) salmon fillets

Cooking spray

⅜ teaspoon kosher salt

¼ teaspoon freshly ground black pepper

1. Preheat oven to 425°F.

2. Combine first 3 ingredients in a small bowl, tossing well.

3. Combine mayonnaise and mustard in a small bowl, stirring well. Arrange fish on a baking sheet coated with cooking spray. Sprinkle fish evenly with salt and pepper; spread mayonnaise mixture evenly over fish. Carefully pat Crunchy Fried Bulgur mixture evenly over fish. Bake at 425°F for 10 to 12 minutes or until desired degree of doneness.

SERVES 4 *(serving size: 1 fillet)*
CALORIES 366; **FAT** 18.1g (sat 1.8g, mono 7.1g, poly 5g); **PROTEIN** 38g; **CARB** 10g; **FIBER** 1g; **SUGARS** 1g (est. added sugars 0g); **CHOL** 89mg; **IRON** 2mg; **SODIUM** 421mg; **CALC** 30mg

QUICK FRIED BROWN RICE WITH SHRIMP AND SNAP PEAS

Stir up your weeknight meal routine by serving up this easy 20-minute dish. Thanks to unseasoned, precooked brown rice—a great option when time is short—the dish comes together lickety-split.

HANDS-ON TIME: 20 MINUTES TOTAL TIME: 20 MINUTES

1½ (8.8-ounce) pouches precooked brown rice (such as Uncle Ben's)
2 tablespoons lower-sodium soy sauce
1 tablespoon sambal oelek (ground fresh chile paste)
1 tablespoon honey
2 tablespoons peanut oil, divided
10 ounces medium shrimp, peeled and deveined
3 large eggs, lightly beaten
1½ cups sugar snap peas, diagonally sliced
⅓ cup unsalted, dry-roasted peanuts
⅛ teaspoon salt
3 garlic cloves, crushed

1. Heat rice according to package directions.

2. Combine soy sauce, sambal oelek, and honey in a large bowl. Combine 1 teaspoon peanut oil and shrimp in a medium bowl; toss to coat. Heat a wok or large skillet over high heat. Add shrimp to pan, and stir-fry 2 minutes. Add shrimp to soy sauce mixture; toss to coat shrimp. Add 1 teaspoon peanut oil to pan; swirl to coat. Add eggs to pan; cook 45 seconds or until set. Remove eggs from pan; cut into bite-sized pieces.

3. Add 1 tablespoon oil to pan; swirl to coat. Add rice; stir-fry 4 minutes. Add rice to shrimp mixture. Add 1 teaspoon oil to pan; swirl to coat. Add sugar snap peas, peanuts, salt, and garlic to pan; stir-fry 2 minutes or until peanuts begin to brown. Add shrimp mixture and egg to pan, and cook 2 minutes or until thoroughly heated.

SERVES 4 *(serving size: 1½ cups)*
CALORIES 418; **FAT** 19.8g (sat 3.6g, mono 8.5g, poly 5.9g); **PROTEIN** 22g; **CARB** 39g; **FIBER** 3g; **SUGARS** 6g (est. added sugars 4g); **CHOL** 229mg; **IRON** 2mg; **SODIUM** 587mg; **CALC** 82mg

CAJUN-SPICED SHRIMP ON CREAMY CHEDDAR TEFF (GF)

Like shrimp and grits? Then this dish is right up your alley, with creamy teff standing in for the grits. Teff's nutty, earthy flavor calls for more robust flavors in the shrimp mixture, hence the smoky bacon, woodsy bay leaf, and cayenne kick.

HANDS-ON TIME: 25 MINUTES TOTAL TIME: 1 HOUR 11 MINUTES

2 cups 1% low-fat milk

1¾ cups unsalted chicken stock (such as Swanson), divided

1 cup uncooked teff

2 ounces reduced-fat shredded sharp white cheddar cheese (about ½ cup)

¾ teaspoon kosher salt, divided

3 applewood-smoked bacon slices, cut crosswise into thin strips

1½ pounds peeled and deveined large shrimp

8 ounces cremini mushrooms, quartered

⅔ cup sliced green onion bottoms (white part)

4 garlic cloves, thinly sliced

½ teaspoon freshly ground black pepper

⅜ teaspoon ground red pepper

1 (14.5-ounce) can unsalted petite diced tomatoes, undrained

1 bay leaf

⅓ cup heavy whipping cream

2 teaspoons thyme leaves

6 tablespoons sliced green onion tops (green part)

1. Bring milk and 1½ cups stock to a boil in a medium saucepan. Stir in teff; reduce heat and simmer 25 to 30 minutes or until liquid is absorbed and mixture is thick, stirring occasionally. Stir in cheese and ½ teaspoon salt. (If teff stiffens, whisk in a little warm water to loosen.)

2. While teff cooks, cook bacon in a large skillet over medium heat until crisp (about 5 minutes). Remove bacon with a slotted spoon; drain on paper towels. Pour bacon drippings into a small bowl.

3. Increase heat to medium-high. Add shrimp to pan; sauté 4 minutes or until done. Remove shrimp from pan. Add 1 tablespoon bacon drippings to pan; discard remaining drippings. Add mushrooms to pan; sauté 5 minutes or until browned, stirring occasionally. Add onion bottoms and garlic; sauté 2 minutes, stirring frequently. Stir in ¼ cup stock, peppers, tomatoes, bay leaf, and ¼ teaspoon salt; reduce heat to medium-low, and cook 4 to 5 minutes or until slightly thickened. Stir in cream and thyme. Return shrimp to pan; cook 1 minute or until thoroughly heated. Discard bay leaf. Serve shrimp mixture over teff; sprinkle with bacon and green onion tops.

SERVES 6 (serving size: about ½ cup teff, ⅔ cup shrimp mixture, 2 teaspoons bacon, and 1 tablespoon green onion tops)
CALORIES 400; **FAT** 14.1g (sat 6.9g, mono 2.9g, poly 1g); **PROTEIN** 30g; **CARB** 37g; **FIBER** 5g; **SUGARS** 8g (est. added sugars 0g); **CHOL** 179mg; **IRON** 3mg; **SODIUM** 703mg; **CALC** 352mg

STEEL-CUT OATS JAMBALAYA (GF)

The Creole classic gets a fun makeover with toothsome steel-cut oats in place of rice. But I wouldn't dare change the heart of the recipe—the trinity of onion, bell pepper, and celery. Be sure to use quick-cooking steel-cut oats for the best results.

HANDS-ON TIME: 51 MINUTES TOTAL TIME: 51 MINUTES

Cooking spray

1 pound skinless, boneless chicken thighs, cut into ½-inch pieces

1¼ teaspoons kosher salt, divided

8 ounces andouille sausage, thinly sliced

2 tablespoons canola oil

2 cups chopped white onion

1 cup diced celery

1 cup finely chopped green bell pepper

1 cup finely chopped red bell pepper

8 garlic cloves, minced

2 teaspoons paprika

1 teaspoon freshly ground black pepper

¾ teaspoon dried oregano

½ teaspoon ground red pepper

2 bay leaves

1 cup uncooked quick-cooking steel-cut oats

2½ cups unsalted chicken stock (such as Swanson)

1 (14.5-ounce) can unsalted diced tomatoes, undrained

12 ounces peeled and deveined medium shrimp

½ cup sliced green onions

1. Heat a Dutch oven over medium-high heat. Coat pan with cooking spray. Add chicken to pan, and sprinkle with ¼ teaspoon salt; cook 4 minutes, turning to brown on all sides. Add sausage; sauté 2 minutes. Remove mixture from pan.

2. Add oil to pan; swirl to coat. Add white onion, celery, bell peppers, and garlic; sauté 8 minutes or until tender, scraping pan occasionally to loosen browned bits. Stir in 1 teaspoon salt, paprika, and next 4 ingredients (through bay leaves); sauté 1 minute. Add oats; cook 1 minute, stirring constantly. Add stock and tomatoes; bring to a boil. Reduce heat, and simmer, uncovered, 4 minutes. Return chicken mixture to pan; add shrimp, and cook 5 minutes or until shrimp and oats are done and mixture thickens. Sprinkle with green onions.

SERVES 8 *(serving size: 1⅛ cups jambalaya and 1 tablespoon green onions)*
CALORIES 296; **FAT** 9.8g (sat 2g, mono 3.1g, poly 1.7g); **PROTEIN** 27g; **CARB** 25g; **FIBER** 5g; **SUGARS** 5g (est. added sugars 0g); **CHOL** 138mg; **IRON** 3mg; **SODIUM** 628mg; **CALC** 115mg

SIDES

Side dishes are familiar territory for whole grains, which lend themselves naturally to pilafs and the like. These workhorse dishes pair well with "salt-and-pepper proteins"—entrées that stay simple so the sides can do the heavy lifting at the table. They also work beautifully for holidays and other special occasions; you'll find something to complement any meal.

FREEKEH WITH CHARD AND ROASTED CARROTS

If you can find rainbow chard, use it here for its glorious array of colors; if not, the beet-red stems of standard ruby chard will be lovely, too. Because this dish combines vegetables and starch, it is all you need to complete the perfect roast chicken dinner.

HANDS-ON TIME: 35 MINUTES TOTAL TIME: 42 MINUTES

  3 medium carrots
 12 ounces rainbow Swiss chard
  2 tablespoons extra-virgin olive oil, divided
  ½ teaspoon kosher salt, divided
  ¾ cup finely chopped onion
  ¾ teaspoon ground cumin
1¾ cups unsalted chicken stock (such as Swanson)
  1 cup uncooked cracked freekeh
  ¼ teaspoon freshly ground black pepper
     Assorted fresh herbs (such as parsley, basil, and oregano; optional)

1. Preheat oven to 425°F.

2. Cut carrots in half lengthwise; cut each half into 1½-inch-long pieces. Cut thicker pieces in half lengthwise. Remove leaves from chard stems; tear leaves, and set aside. Cut stems into 1½-inch-long pieces; set aside. Combine carrots and 1 tablespoon oil on a small jelly-roll pan; toss to coat. Cover pan with foil. Roast at 425°F for 10 minutes. Remove pan from oven (leave oven on). Add chard stems to pan with carrots; sprinkle with ⅛ teaspoon salt, and toss to combine. Roast, uncovered, at 425°F for 12 minutes or until tender.

3. Heat a large sauté pan or skillet over medium-high heat. Add 1 tablespoon oil; swirl to coat. Add onion; sauté 3 minutes. Add cumin; sauté 30 seconds, stirring constantly. Add stock and freekeh; bring to a boil. Cover, reduce heat, and simmer 20 minutes or until liquid is absorbed. Add chard leaves; cover and cook 5 minutes or until chard wilts. Stir well to combine. Stir in ⅜ teaspoon salt and pepper. Add carrots and chard stems; toss gently to combine. Top with herbs, if desired.

SERVES 6 *(serving size: about ¾ cup)*
CALORIES 166; **FAT** 5.4g (sat 0.7g, mono 3.7g, poly 0.7g); **PROTEIN** 7g; **CARB** 26g; **FIBER** 5g; **SUGARS** 3g (est. added sugars 0g); **CHOL** 0mg; **IRON** 4mg; **SODIUM** 341mg; **CALC** 65mg

CHEESY SORGHUM AND SHAVED SQUASH PILAF (GF)

Long, slender ribbons of butternut squash make for a beautiful and unusual presentation; just be gentle when stirring so you don't break all those gorgeous pieces. Try to find a squash with a long neck—that straight surface works best for ribboning.

HANDS-ON TIME: 34 MINUTES TOTAL TIME: 34 MINUTES

1 cup water
½ ounce dried porcini mushrooms
12 ounces peeled butternut squash
2 tablespoons olive oil
8 ounces sliced cremini mushrooms
½ cup finely chopped shallots
1 tablespoon thyme leaves
3 garlic cloves, minced
3 cups cooked sorghum (about 1 cup uncooked grains)
1 teaspoon kosher salt
½ teaspoon freshly ground black pepper
3 ounces cave-aged Gruyère cheese, finely shredded (about ¾ cup)
Flat-leaf parsley and oregano leaves (optional)

1. Combine 1 cup water and porcini in a 2-cup glass measuring cup. Microwave at HIGH 3 minutes. Let stand 10 minutes. Remove mushrooms with a slotted spoon, reserving liquid in cup. Finely chop porcini.

2. Cut squash into long, 1½-inch-wide pieces. Shave into ribbons using a mandoline or vegetable peeler to yield about 6 cups.

3. Heat a large (14-inch) skillet over medium-high heat. Add oil to pan; swirl to coat. Add cremini, shallots, thyme, and garlic; sauté 9 minutes. Stir in porcini, sorghum, salt, and pepper. Pour in porcini soaking liquid, stopping before grit at very bottom of measuring cup reaches opening. Arrange squash ribbons on top; cover and cook 4 minutes. Gently stir squash into sorghum mixture; cook 2 minutes or until most of liquid evaporates.

4. Remove from heat. Sprinkle with cheese; gently fold in cheese until it melts. Sprinkle with parsley and oregano, if desired.

CHANGE IT UP

In place of butternut, try carrot, parsnip, or zucchini ribbons. If using zucchini, stir into the mixture and cook for only 2 minutes.

SERVES 8 *(serving size: about ¾ cup)*
CALORIES 197; **FAT** 7.8g (sat 2.6g, mono 3.8g, poly 0.9g); **PROTEIN** 8g; **CARB** 27g; **FIBER** 4g; **SUGARS** 3g (est. added sugars 0g); **CHOL** 12mg; **IRON** 2mg; **SODIUM** 282mg; **CALC** 143mg

GRILLED RADICCHIO AND SORGHUM PILAF ⒼⒻ

The deep maroon hues come from radicchio and dried cranberries, whose bitter and sweet flavors add depth. When toasted, sorghum takes on a rich malty taste; just be prepared that it takes a long simmer to get it tender. Don't be alarmed if, while toasting the grains on the front end, a few pop—just fish them out and continue with the recipe.

HANDS-ON TIME: 15 MINUTES TOTAL TIME: 2 HOURS 4 MINUTES

1 cup uncooked sorghum
1 tablespoon butter
1½ cups chopped onion
3 cups unsalted chicken stock (such as Swanson)
⅔ cup water
⅝ teaspoon kosher salt, divided
¼ teaspoon freshly ground black pepper
½ cup dried sweetened cranberries
1 (12-ounce) head radicchio
1½ tablespoons olive oil
¼ cup chopped walnuts, toasted

1. Heat a large saucepan over medium heat. Add sorghum; cook 4 minutes or until toasted, stirring occasionally. Remove from pan. Add butter to pan; swirl until butter melts. Add onion; cook 5 minutes, stirring occasionally. Add sorghum, stock, ⅔ cup water, ½ teaspoon salt, and pepper; bring to a boil. Cover, reduce heat to medium-low, and simmer 1 hour and 40 minutes or until grains are chewy-tender. (Liquid may not all be absorbed, but reserve this flavorful cooking liquid for another use such as soup broth.) Stir in cranberries; cover and keep warm.

2. Heat a large grill pan over high heat. Cut radicchio into quarters, leaving core intact. Brush all sides of radicchio with oil. Arrange radicchio in grill pan; grill 10 minutes, turning to brown on all sides. Remove from pan; coarsely chop, removing and discarding cores. Add radicchio to sorghum mixture; toss well to combine. Sprinkle with nuts.

SERVES 6 *(serving size: about 1 cup)*
CALORIES 259; **FAT** 9.8g (sat 2.2g, mono 3.7g, poly 3.3g); **PROTEIN** 8g; **CARB** 39g; **FIBER** 4g; **SUGARS** 9g (est. added sugars 3g); **CHOL** 5mg; **IRON** 2mg; **SODIUM** 297mg; **CALC** 45mg

QUINOA WITH BROCCOLI AND BACON (GF)

Dress up a plain quinoa dish with bacon crumbles and sautéed broccoli for a fresh and colorful side.

HANDS-ON TIME: 10 MINUTES TOTAL TIME: 25 MINUTES

¾ cup uncooked quinoa, rinsed and drained

1 cup water

1 teaspoon olive oil

2 cups broccoli florets

2 tablespoons water

2 teaspoons olive oil

⅛ teaspoon salt

2 bacon slices, cooked and crumbled

1. Heat a small saucepan over medium-high heat. Add quinoa; sauté 2 minutes. Add 1 cup water; bring to a boil. Cover, reduce heat, and simmer 13 minutes. Remove from heat; let stand 2 minutes. Heat a medium saucepan over medium-high heat. Add 1 teaspoon olive oil to pan; swirl to coat. Add broccoli florets; sauté 2 minutes. Add 2 tablespoons water; cover and reduce heat. Cook 2 minutes. Combine quinoa, broccoli, 2 teaspoons olive oil, salt, and bacon.

SERVES 4 *(serving size: about 1 cup)*
CALORIES 170; **FAT** 6.4g (sat 1.2g, mono 3g, poly 1.5g); **PROTEIN** 7g; **CARB** 22g; **FIBER** 3g; **SUGARS** 2g (est. added sugars 0g); **CHOL** 4mg; **IRON** 2mg; **SODIUM** 139mg; **CALC** 32mg

BALSAMIC AND GRAPE QUINOA (GF)

The color and texture of red quinoa makes this a little more elegant, but regular quinoa also works well.

HANDS-ON TIME: 17 MINUTES TOTAL TIME: 17 MINUTES

1⅔ cups water
1 cup uncooked red quinoa, rinsed and drained
2 tablespoons chopped fresh flat-leaf parsley
1 tablespoon white balsamic vinegar
2 teaspoons extra-virgin olive oil
¼ teaspoon kosher salt
20 seedless red grapes, halved

1. Bring 1⅔ cups water and quinoa to a boil in a medium saucepan. Reduce heat to low, and simmer 12 minutes or until quinoa is tender; drain. Place quinoa in a bowl. Add parsley, vinegar, oil, salt, and grapes, stirring to combine.

> **MAKE AHEAD**
>
> This dish also tastes great cold, so you can make it up to 2 days in advance and serve it straight from the fridge.

SERVES 4 *(serving size: about ¾ cup)*
CALORIES 201; **FAT** 4.8g (sat 0.3g, mono 2g, poly 0.4g); **PROTEIN** 6g; **CARB** 34g; **FIBER** 2g; **SUGARS** 4g (est. added sugars 0g); **CHOL** 0mg; **IRON** 3mg; **SODIUM** 133mg; **CALC** 26mg

NUTTY ALMOND-SESAME RED QUINOA (GF)

Toasty dark sesame oil amplifies the nuttiness of almonds so that a small handful tastes like much more.

HANDS-ON TIME: 17 MINUTES TOTAL TIME: 17 MINUTES

1⅔ cups water
1 cup red quinoa, rinsed and drained
¼ cup sliced almonds, toasted
2 tablespoons fresh lemon juice
2 teaspoons olive oil
2 teaspoons dark sesame oil
¼ teaspoon kosher salt
3 green onions, thinly sliced

1. Bring 1⅔ cups water and quinoa to a boil in a medium saucepan. Reduce heat to low, and simmer 12 minutes or until quinoa is tender; drain. Stir in almonds, juice, oils, salt, and onions.

SERVES 4 *(serving size: about ½ cup)*
CALORIES 238; **FAT** 10g (sat 0.9g, mono 4.4g, poly 19g); **PROTEIN** 8g; **CARB** 32g; **FIBER** 3g; **SUGARS** 3g (est. added sugars 0g); **CHOL** 0mg; **IRON** 3mg; **SODIUM** 132mg; **CALCIUM** 44mg

WILTED KALE WITH FARRO AND WALNUTS

A hint of maple syrup balances the earthiness of kale and walnuts. If you don't have maple on hand, use an equal amount of brown sugar or honey.

HANDS-ON TIME: 8 MINUTES TOTAL TIME: 50 MINUTES

1	cup uncooked whole-grain farro
4	teaspoons walnut oil, divided
3½	cups lacinato kale, stemmed and chopped
⅓	cup unsalted chicken stock (such as Swanson)
4	teaspoons sherry vinegar
1	teaspoon maple syrup
¼	teaspoon kosher salt
2	tablespoons chopped walnuts, toasted

1. Cook farro according to package directions.

2. Heat a Dutch oven over medium-low heat. Add 2 teaspoons oil and chopped kale; cook 2 minutes. Add chicken stock; cover and cook 4 minutes. Combine vinegar and maple syrup in a large bowl. Add farro, 2 teaspoons oil, and salt. Add kale mixture and walnuts; toss to combine.

SERVES 4 *(serving size: ¾ cup)*
CALORIES 251; **FAT** 6.1g (sat 0.5g, mono 0.9g, poly 3.4g); **PROTEIN** 10g; **CARB** 43g; **FIBER** 6g; **SUGARS** 1g (est. added sugars 1g); **CHOL** 0mg; **IRON** 3mg; **SODIUM** 156mg; **CALC** 106mg

BROWN RICE PILAF WITH PECANS (GF)

For me, this dish goes on heavy rotation come fall, when I'll serve it with roasted pork tenderloin or seared pork chops. I love that when I don't have much time to spend on dinner, I can gussy up precooked rice with a few aromatic ingredients.

HANDS-ON TIME: 20 MINUTES TOTAL TIME: 20 MINUTES

1 (8.8-ounce) package precooked whole-grain brown rice blend (such as Uncle Ben's)

2 teaspoons olive oil

2 cups sliced shiitake mushroom caps

1 thinly sliced leek (white and light green parts only)

¼ cup water

3 tablespoons chopped toasted pecans

¼ teaspoon salt

¼ teaspoon freshly ground black pepper

1. Heat rice according to package directions. Heat a large skillet over medium heat. Add oil to pan; swirl to coat. Add mushroom caps and leek; sauté 4 minutes or until tender, stirring occasionally. Add ¼ cup water, scraping pan to loosen browned bits. Stir in rice, pecans, salt, and black pepper.

SERVES 4 *(serving size: ½ cup)*
CALORIES 162; **FAT** 7.5g (sat 0.7g, mono 3.7g, poly 1.4g); **PROTEIN** 4g; **CARB** 22g; **FIBER** 3g; **SUGARS** 2g (est. added sugars 0g); **CHOL** 0g; **IRON** 1mg; **SODIUM** 160mg; **CALC** 18mg

DIRTY BROWN RICE (GF)

This Creole dish gets its name from the "dirtying" effect of cooking rice (typically white, but here updated to quick-cooking brown rice) with bits of chicken liver and/or ground meat. It's a deeply savory, delicious side that goes well with barbecue shrimp, roast chicken, or pork chops. Don't fret too much about the chicken livers: They do a similar thing that, for example, anchovies do—They add umami richness but don't contribute a pronounced "livery" taste. Try using leftovers as an omelet stuffing—delicious with a little pepper-Jack cheese.

HANDS-ON TIME: 28 MINUTES TOTAL TIME: 28 MINUTES

2 (3½-ounce) bags boil-in-bag brown rice (such as Uncle Ben's)
6 ounces cleaned chicken livers
1½ tablespoons butter
½ cup finely chopped onion
½ cup finely chopped green bell pepper
½ cup finely chopped celery
1 tablespoon chopped fresh thyme
4 garlic cloves, minced
1 teaspoon smoked paprika
¼ teaspoon ground red pepper
½ cup unsalted chicken stock (such as Swanson)
½ teaspoon kosher salt
⅓ cup thinly sliced green onions

1. Cook rice according to package directions; drain.

2. While rice cooks, place chicken livers in a mini food processor; pulse until ground. Set aside.

3. Heat a large skillet over medium heat. Add butter; swirl until butter melts. Add onion, bell pepper, and celery; cook 5 minutes, stirring occasionally. Add thyme and garlic; cook 3 minutes, stirring occasionally.

Push vegetable mixture to outside rim of pan. Add chicken livers to open center part of pan; cook 1 minute without stirring. Cook 3 minutes or until browned, stirring occasionally. Stir into vegetable mixture. Add paprika and pepper; cook 1 minute, stirring constantly. Add rice, stock, and salt; cook 2 minutes or until liquid is absorbed. Remove from heat; stir in green onions.

SERVES 6 *(serving size: about ¾ cup)*
CALORIES 195; **FAT** 5.4g (sat 2.3g, mono 1.1g, poly 0.5g); **PROTEIN** 9g; **CARB** 29g; **FIBER** 2g; **SUGARS** 1g (est. added sugars 0g); **CHOL** 105mg; **IRON** 3mg; **SODIUM** 227mg; **CALC** 23mg

WILD RICE WITH SQUASH (GF)

The butternut squash adds just the right amount of sweetness to this simple wild rice dish. Combined with woodsy rosemary, it's fragrant and full of autumnal flair.

HANDS-ON TIME: 12 MINUTES TOTAL TIME: 60 MINUTES

5 cups water

⅔ cup uncooked wild rice

1½ tablespoons olive oil

1½ cups (½-inch) cubed peeled butternut squash

1 shallot, chopped

1 teaspoon chopped fresh rosemary

⅛ teaspoon salt

⅛ teaspoon freshly ground black pepper

¼ teaspoon salt

1. Place 5 cups water and rice in a saucepan; bring to a boil. Cover, reduce heat, and simmer 30 minutes. Turn off heat; let stand, covered, 25 minutes. Drain.

2. Heat a large skillet over medium heat. Add olive oil to pan; swirl to coat. Add squash, shallot, rosemary, and ⅛ teaspoon salt; cook 10 minutes. Add rice, pepper, and ¼ teaspoon salt, stirring to combine.

SERVES 4 *(serving size: about 1 cup)*
CALORIES 169; **FAT** 5.4g (sat 0.8g, mono 3.7g, poly 0.7g); **PROTEIN** 5g; **CARB** 27g; **FIBER** 3g; **SUGARS** 2g (est. added sugars 0g); **CHOL** 0mg; **IRON** 1mg; **SODIUM** 185mg; **CALC** 34mg

GRILLED ZUCCHINI—BULGUR PILAF

This super-easy dish makes good use of summer's bumper zucchini crop.

HANDS-ON TIME: 20 MINUTES TOTAL TIME: 20 MINUTES

1 tablespoon olive oil
¾ cup chopped onion
⅓ cup chopped celery
2 cups water
1 cup uncooked bulgur
Cooking spray
1 medium zucchini
¼ cup chopped fresh
　flat-leaf parsley
½ teaspoon salt
¼ teaspoon black pepper
6 lemon wedges

1. Heat a medium saucepan over medium-high heat. Add oil to pan; swirl to coat. Add onion and celery; sauté 3 minutes. Add 2 cups water and bulgur; bring to a boil. Cover, reduce heat, and simmer 11 minutes or until liquid is absorbed.

2. Heat a grill pan over medium-high heat; coat with cooking spray. Quarter zucchini lengthwise. Add zucchini to grill pan, and grill 5 minutes; dice. Combine bulgur, zucchini, parsley, salt, and pepper. Serve with lemon wedges.

SERVES 6 *(serving size: ⅔ cup and 1 lemon wedge)*
CALORIES 116; **FAT** 2.8g (sat 0.4g, mono 1.7g, poly 0.4g); **PROTEIN** 4g; **CARB** 21g; **FIBER** 5g; **SUGARS** 2g (est. added sugars 0g); **CHOL** 0mg;
IRON 1mg; **SODIUM** 210mg; **CALC** 26mg

CREAMY GORGONZOLA TEFF WITH HERB-ROASTED TOMATOES GF

If you like polenta or grits, give teff a try. It cooks up thick and has a deep, toasty flavor.

HANDS-ON TIME: 15 MINUTES TOTAL TIME: 30 MINUTES

1½ cups unsalted chicken stock
　(such as Swanson)
1½ cups 2% reduced-fat milk
1 cup uncooked teff
½ teaspoon kosher salt
2 ounces crumbled Gorgonzola
　cheese (about ½ cup)
¼ cup fat-free sour cream
¼ teaspoon black pepper
¼ cup oven-roasted cherry
　tomatoes
Thyme leaves

1. Combine chicken stock and milk in a medium saucepan; bring to a boil. Stir in teff and salt. Cover and simmer 20 minutes or until liquid is absorbed, stirring occasionally. Remove pan from heat; stir in crumbled Gorgonzola, sour cream, and pepper. Place teff mixture on 6 plates. Top each with tomatoes; sprinkle with fresh thyme.

SERVES 6 *(serving size: about ½ cup teff and about ¼ cup tomato mixture)*
CALORIES 219; **FAT** 7g (sat 3.1g, mono 2g, poly 0.4g); **PROTEIN** 10g; **CARB** 30g; **FIBER** 5g; **SUGARS** 5g (est. added sugars 0g); **CHOL** 14mg;
IRON 2mg; **SODIUM** 375mg; **CALC** 204mg

SMOKED POLENTA WITH SAGE BROWNED BUTTER GF

As a stand-alone side dish, this creamy polenta has a hint of smokiness that makes it truly memorable. It can also serve as an excellent beginning to something more wonderful: I would serve braised short ribs or oxtail ragu over it, and then die of joy.

HANDS-ON TIME: 13 MINUTES TOTAL TIME: 13 MINUTES

⅓ cup apple or cherry wood chips
5 ounces whole-grain cornmeal (about 1 cup)
2 cups water
2 cups 1% low-fat milk
1 teaspoon kosher salt
3 tablespoons butter
16 small sage leaves

1. Pierce 10 holes on one side of the bottom of a 13 x 9–inch heavy-duty disposable aluminum foil pan. Arrange wood chips over holes inside pan. Spread cornmeal onto far opposite side of pan. Place hole side of pan over stovetop burner. Turn burner on high. When wood chips start to smoke, carefully cover pan with foil. Reduce heat to low; cook 2 minutes. Remove pan from heat; uncover pan, reserving foil. Carefully remove wood chips with tongs; place on foil. Wipe any wood fragments out with a damp paper towel. Pour cornmeal into a bowl.

2. Bring 2 cups water, milk, and salt to a boil in a large saucepan. Gradually add cornmeal, stirring constantly with a whisk. Reduce heat, and simmer, uncovered, 5 minutes or until thick, stirring frequently. Cover and keep warm.

3. Place butter and sage in a small skillet over medium heat; cook 3 minutes or until sage crisps and butter turns brown and smells very toasty-fragrant. Spoon polenta into each of 8 bowls; top each serving with sage leaves and butter.

SERVES 8 *(serving size: ½ cup polenta, 2 sage leaves, and about 1¼ teaspoons butter)*
CALORIES 119; **FAT** 5.5g (sat 3.2g, mono 1.4g, poly 0.4g); **PROTEIN** 3g; **CARB** 15g; **FIBER** 1g; **SUGARS** 3g (est. added sugars 0g); **CHOL** 15mg; **IRON** 1mg; **SODIUM** 312mg; **CALC** 82mg

CORN ON THE COB WITH SMOKY RED PEPPER MAYO AND BASIL (GF)

The sauce is basically a creamy romesco—delicious with charred corn.

HANDS-ON TIME: 12 MINUTES TOTAL TIME: 12 MINUTES

4 ears shucked corn

Cooking spray

2 tablespoons chopped bottled
   roasted red bell peppers

1½ tablespoons canola mayonnaise

½ teaspoon minced fresh garlic

½ teaspoon fresh lemon juice

⅛ teaspoon smoked paprika

⅛ teaspoon kosher salt

Dash of ground red pepper

4 teaspoons chopped fresh basil

1. Preheat grill to high heat. Place corn on grill rack coated with cooking spray; grill 8 minutes or until lightly charred, turning occasionally.

2. Place roasted red bell pepper, canola mayonnaise, minced garlic, lemon juice, paprika, salt, and ground red pepper in a mini food processor; process until smooth. Drizzle mixture over corn. Sprinkle with chopped fresh basil.

SERVES 4 *(serving size: 1 corn cob)*
CALORIES 105; **FAT** 2.9g (sat 0.3g, mono 1.3g, poly 1g); **PROTEIN** 3g; **CARB** 19g; **FIBER** 2g; **SUGARS** 6g (est. added sugars 0g); **CHOL** 0mg;
IRON 1mg; **SODIUM** 126mg; **CALC** 4mg

CORN ON THE COB WITH FETA AND MINT BUTTER (GF)

This is a Greek twist on the Mexican street-cart classic elote, *with mint and feta lending bright, tangy notes.*

HANDS-ON TIME: 17 MINUTES TOTAL TIME: 17 MINUTES

4 ears shucked corn

Cooking spray

2 tablespoons crumbled feta

1 tablespoon unsalted
   butter, softened

1 tablespoon minced fresh mint

1½ teaspoons fresh lime juice

1. Preheat grill to high heat. Place corn on grill rack coated with cooking spray; grill 8 minutes or until lightly charred, turning occasionally.

2. Place feta, butter, mint, and lime juice in a small bowl. Mash with a fork to combine. Press mixture onto slightly cooled cobs using hands.

SERVES 4 *(serving size: 1 corn cob)*
CALORIES 128; **FAT** 5.4g (sat 2.9g, mono 1.4g, poly 0.6g); **PROTEIN** 4g; **CARB** 19g; **FIBER** 2g; **SUGARS** 7g (est. added sugars 0g); **CHOL** 12mg;
IRON 1mg; **SODIUM** 68mg; **CALC** 27mg

BUTTERY CREAMED CORN GF ▶

For a chunky texture (as shown), pulse the corn mixture in a food processor. To make this silky-smooth, puree the kernels in a blender until the mixture resembles polenta.

HANDS-ON TIME: 26 MINUTES TOTAL TIME: 26 MINUTES

8 medium ears shucked corn
2 cups 1% low-fat milk, divided
2 tablespoons cornstarch
5/8 teaspoon kosher salt
1/4 teaspoon freshly ground black pepper
2 tablespoons butter

1. Cut kernels from ears of corn to measure 4 cups. Using dull side of a knife blade, scrape milk and remaining pulp from cobs. Place kernels, corn milk and pulp, and 1¾ cups milk in a large saucepan; bring to a simmer over medium heat. Reduce heat to low, and simmer 8 minutes, stirring occasionally.

2. Pour corn mixture into a food processor. Process until smooth (about 2 minutes). Return mixture to pan. Combine ¼ cup milk and cornstarch in a small bowl, stirring with a whisk. Stir cornstarch mixture, salt, and pepper into corn mixture; cook over medium heat 3 minutes or until thick and bubbly. Remove from heat; add butter, stirring until butter melts.

SERVES 6 *(serving size: about ¾ cup)*
CALORIES 162; **FAT** 5.9g (sat 3.3g, mono 1.6g, poly 0.6g); **PROTEIN** 6g; **CARB** 25g; **FIBER** 2g; **SUGARS** 10g (est. added sugars 0g); **CHOL** 14mg; **IRON** 1mg; **SODIUM** 284mg; **CALC** 105mg

GRITS-STYLE BULGUR WITH CORN-BASIL RELISH

Think of this dish as a spin on cheese grits: Cooking bulgur with a little extra water makes it creamy and porridge-like.

HANDS-ON TIME: 20 MINUTES TOTAL TIME: 20 MINUTES

2¼ cups water
1 cup uncooked bulgur
2 ounces shredded extra-sharp cheddar cheese (about ½ cup)
1/4 teaspoon salt
1 cup fresh corn kernels
1/4 cup finely chopped fresh basil
1 tablespoon minced shallots
1 tablespoon white wine vinegar
1/8 teaspoon salt

1. Bring 2¼ cups water and bulgur to a boil in a small saucepan. Cover, reduce heat, and cook 8 minutes. Stir in cheese and ¼ teaspoon salt.

2. Combine corn kernels, basil, shallots, vinegar, and ⅛ teaspoon salt in a small bowl. Top bulgur mixture with corn mixture.

SERVES 4 *(serving size: ⅔ cup bulgur and ¼ cup corn relish)*
CALORIES 209; **FAT** 5.5g (sat 3.2g, mono 0.2g, poly 0.4g); **PROTEIN** 9g; **CARB** 34g; **FIBER** 7g; **SUGARS** 3g (est. added sugars 0g); **CHOL** 13mg; **IRON** 1mg; **SODIUM** 324mg; **CALC** 120mg

CRUNCHY ZUCCHINI CHIPS

My kids fell in love with these tempting chips. Besides the savory seasoning, these zucchini rounds have a secret weapon: amaranth in the breading. It makes them amazingly crunchy without overpowering the vegetable. They make a great accompaniment for burgers, sandwiches, or grilled chicken drumsticks.

HANDS-ON TIME: 15 MINUTES TOTAL TIME: 41 MINUTES

⅓ cup whole-wheat panko (Japanese breadcrumbs; such as Kikkoman)

1 ounce Parmesan cheese, finely grated (about ¼ cup)

3 tablespoons uncooked amaranth

½ teaspoon garlic powder

¼ teaspoon kosher salt

¼ teaspoon freshly ground black pepper

12 ounces zucchini, cut into (¼-inch-thick) slices

1 tablespoon olive oil

Cooking spray

1. Preheat oven to 425°F.

2. Combine first 6 ingredients in a shallow dish. Combine zucchini and oil in a large bowl; toss well to coat. Dredge zucchini in panko mixture, pressing gently to adhere. Place coated slices on an ovenproof wire rack coated with cooking spray; place rack on a baking sheet or jelly-roll pan. Bake at 425°F for 26 minutes or until browned and crisp. Serve immediately.

SERVES 4 *(serving size: 8 to 10 chips)*
CALORIES 132; **FAT** 6.5g (sat 1.9g, mono 3.3g, poly 0.8g); **PROTEIN** 6g; **CARB** 14g; **FIBER** 2g; **SUGARS** 2g (est. added sugars 0g); **CHOL** 5mg; **IRON** 1mg; **SODIUM** 249mg; **CALC** 113mg

GREEN BEAN CASSEROLE WITH CRUNCHY MILLET TOPPING

Here's a modern play on a traditional holiday side dish. I use fresh green beans, tons of cremini mushrooms, and leave out the condensed soup. It's still creamy, and the fried grains work to give the topping a crunch upgrade. It may seem redundant to use onion and shallots, but it's not—they contribute different types of flavor and add nice complexity to the sauce.

HANDS-ON TIME: 45 MINUTES TOTAL TIME: 1 HOUR 15 MINUTES

2 pounds green beans, trimmed

1 tablespoon canola oil

¾ cup chopped onion

½ cup chopped shallots

1 pound sliced cremini mushrooms

2 teaspoons chopped fresh thyme

¼ cup dry sherry

1 tablespoon lower-sodium soy sauce

2 cups 2% reduced-fat milk

1.19 ounces white whole-wheat flour (about ¼ cup)

2 ounces Parmigiano-Reggiano cheese, grated (about ½ cup)

½ teaspoon kosher salt

½ teaspoon freshly ground black pepper

Cooking spray

1 cup Crunchy Fried Millet or Crunchy Fried Quinoa (page 32)

Chopped fresh parsley and thyme leaves (optional)

1. Preheat oven to 350°F.

2. Cook green beans in a large pot of boiling water 5 to 6 minutes or until almost tender. Drain and plunge into ice water; drain and pat dry.

3. Heat a Dutch oven over medium heat. Add oil to pan; swirl to coat. Add onion and shallots; cook 6 minutes, stirring occasionally. Add mushrooms; increase heat to medium-high, and cook 8 minutes or until mushroom liquid evaporates. Stir in thyme. Combine sherry and soy sauce. Add sherry mixture to pan; cook 4 minutes or until liquid evaporates. Combine milk and flour, stirring well with a whisk. Stir milk mixture into pan; cook 2 minutes or until bubbly and thick, stirring constantly. Remove from heat; stir in cheese, salt, and pepper. Add green beans; toss gently to coat.

4. Spoon mixture into a 3-quart glass or ceramic baking dish coated with cooking spray. Sprinkle Crunchy Fried Millet evenly over top. Bake at 350°F for 30 minutes or until filling is bubbly. Garnish with parsley and thyme leaves, if desired.

CHANGE IT UP

The creamy sauce and crunchy topping would be great with other vegetables, too. You can sub in halved Brussels sprouts, or try broccoli florets (reduce cook time for broccoli in step 2 to 2 to 3 minutes).

SERVES 12 *(serving size: about ½ cup)*
CALORIES 148; **FAT** 6.1g (sat 1.6g, mono 2.8g, poly 1.4g); **PROTEIN** 7g; **CARB** 16g; **FIBER** 4g; **SUGARS** 6g (est. added sugars 0g); **CHOL** 6mg; **IRON** 2mg; **SODIUM** 227mg; **CALC** 144mg

SAVORY HARVEST VEGETABLE TART WITH TOASTED QUINOA CRUST (GF)

This tart is a favorite with the entire Cooking Light *team. The brilliant use of whole-grain quinoa for a press-in-the-pan tart shell hits all the right marks. Browning the grains first lends an extra flavor boost. Peppered goat cheese and a colorful crown of caramelized veggies make this dish simply spectacular.*

HANDS-ON TIME: 25 MINUTES TOTAL TIME: 35 MINUTES

1 cup uncooked quinoa, rinsed and drained

½ cup almond meal

1 tablespoon cornstarch

¼ teaspoon kosher salt

2 tablespoons olive oil

1 large egg, beaten

Cooking spray

2 ounces ⅓-less-fat cream cheese, softened (about ¼ cup)

2 ounces goat cheese, softened (about ¼ cup)

2 tablespoons chopped fresh parsley

1 tablespoon finely minced shallots

½ teaspoon coarsely ground black pepper

2 cups chopped leftover roasted vegetables (such as carrots, acorn squash, Brussels sprouts, onions, and parsnips), at room temperature

2 tablespoons torn parsley or thyme leaves

1 tablespoon balsamic glaze

1. Preheat oven to 350°F.

2. Place quinoa on a jelly-roll pan. Bake at 350°F for 10 minutes or until golden brown; cool. Place half of quinoa in a food processor; pulse 30 seconds. Transfer to a large bowl. Add remaining toasted quinoa, almond meal, cornstarch, and salt to bowl; stir to combine. Add oil and egg; stir until mixture is crumbly but holds together when pressed. Press into bottom and up sides of a 4 x 13–inch removable-bottom tart pan coated with cooking spray. Bake at 350°F for 15 minutes or until golden and crisp; cool completely on a wire rack.

3. While crust cools, combine cream cheese, goat cheese, chopped parsley, shallots, and black pepper, stirring until smooth; spread evenly in bottom of crust. Arrange vegetables evenly over cheese mixture; top with parsley leaves. Remove tart from pan; drizzle with balsamic glaze.

SERVES 12 *(serving size: 1 [2-inch] wedge)*
CALORIES 145; **FAT** 8.6g (sat 2.1g, mono 3g, poly 1g); **PROTEIN** 5g; **CARB** 13g; **FIBER** 2g; **SUGARS** 3g (est. added sugars 1g); **CHOL** 21mg; **IRON** 1mg; **SODIUM** 115mg; **CALCIUM** 26mg

BBQ BAKED BARLEY

Chewy-tender barley gets the baked beans treatment, sauced up with molasses-sweetened tomato sauce and flavored with smoky bacon. It's a fantastic update to your backyard barbecues.

HANDS-ON TIME: 30 MINUTES TOTAL TIME: 1 HOUR 15 MINUTES

1   cup uncooked hulled barley
3   hickory-smoked bacon slices, chopped
1   cup finely chopped onion
1   teaspoon ground cumin
½   teaspoon smoked paprika
⅛   teaspoon ground red pepper
¼   cup molasses
1   teaspoon kosher salt
1   (15-ounce) can unsalted tomato sauce
Thyme sprigs (optional)

1. Heat a large heavy saucepan over medium heat. Add barley to pan; cook 10 minutes or until evenly toasty-brown and fragrant, stirring frequently. Add water to cover by 3 inches; bring to a boil. Reduce heat, and simmer 45 minutes or until chewy-tender. Drain, or reserve liquid for Korean Roasted Barley Tea (page 93).

2. Preheat oven to 350°F.

3. Heat a large ovenproof skillet over medium-high heat. Add bacon to pan; cook 6 to 8 minutes or until crisp, stirring occasionally. Remove bacon from pan with a slotted spoon; set aside. Remove all but 1 tablespoon bacon drippings from pan. Add onion to drippings in pan; sauté 4 minutes or until tender. Add cumin, paprika, and pepper; cook 1 minute, stirring constantly. Add molasses, salt, and tomato sauce; bring to a simmer. Remove from heat; stir in barley.

4. Bake at 350°F for 35 to 40 minutes or until bubbly. Sprinkle with bacon. Garnish with thyme, if desired.

SERVES 8 *(serving size: about ½ cup)*
CALORIES 167; **FAT** 3.7g (sat 1.2g, mono 1.4g, poly 0.6g); **PROTEIN** 5g; **CARB** 30g; **FIBER** 5g; **SUGARS** 9g (est. added sugars 6g); **CHOL** 5mg; **IRON** 2mg; **SODIUM** 325mg; **CALC** 42mg

CLASSIC CORN BREAD DRESSING

This is the quintessential Southern Thanksgiving side dish. It's made with crumbled corn bread—no French or sourdough bread to cut it—so the texture is truly unique. This is one of my favorites, probably because it's what I grew up with. Loads of aromatics are crucial; don't be tempted to use less. Garnish with extra herbs to perk up the color.

HANDS-ON TIME: 20 MINUTES TOTAL TIME: 1 HOUR 20 MINUTES

- 3 tablespoons canola oil
- 2 cups chopped white onion
- 1½ cups diced celery
- 2 tablespoons finely chopped fresh thyme
- 2 tablespoons finely chopped fresh sage
- 1 teaspoon freshly ground black pepper
- ½ teaspoon kosher salt
- 1 loaf Whole-Grain Corn Bread (page 254), cooled
- 2½ cups unsalted chicken stock (such as Swanson)
- ¼ cup chopped fresh flat-leaf parsley
- 2 large eggs, lightly beaten
- Cooking spray

1. Preheat oven to 375°F.

2. Heat a large nonstick skillet over medium heat. Add oil to pan; swirl to coat. Add onion and celery; cook 10 minutes or until tender, stirring occasionally. Add thyme, sage, pepper, and salt; cook 1 minute, stirring frequently. Remove from heat; cool slightly.

3. Crumble Whole-Grain Corn Bread into a large bowl. Add onion mixture, stock, parsley, and eggs; stir well to combine. Spoon mixture into a 2-quart shallow glass or ceramic baking dish coated with cooking spray. Bake at 375°F for 50 minutes or until lightly browned (cover with foil if top is getting too brown last 15 minutes of bake time). Let stand 10 minutes before serving.

SERVES 15 *(serving size: about ½ cup)*
CALORIES 199; **FAT** 10.8g (sat 2.4g, mono 5.4g, poly 2.4g); **PROTEIN** 6g; **CARB** 20g; **FIBER** 3g; **SUGARS** 1g (est. added sugars 0g); **CHOL** 56mg; **IRON** 1mg; **SODIUM** 345mg; **CALC** 74mg

BREADS

As I developed the recipes for this chapter, I discovered that my dog loves the smell of bread baking in the oven—he would sniff and lick the air! And he would always be pushed aside by my children, who, once they got a whiff, would loiter until allowed a sample. I get it: There is just something intoxicating and magical about homemade bread.

WHOLE-GRAIN CORN BREAD

There are two distinct corn bread camps: those who sweeten it and those who wouldn't be caught dead doing so. As a good Southerner, I'm vehemently in the latter camp; sweet corn bread is, as chef Hugh Acheson says, "cake." Now, that's not to say that a drizzle of honey over my kind of corn bread isn't a mighty fine thing—especially with split and toasted leftovers. I prefer medium to fine-ground cornmeal, but you can use a coarser grind for a heftier texture.

HANDS-ON TIME: 15 MINUTES TOTAL TIME: 40 MINUTES

7.5 ounces whole-grain yellow cornmeal (about 1½ cups)

4.75 ounces white whole-wheat flour (about 1 cup)

1 teaspoon baking powder

1 teaspoon kosher salt

½ teaspoon baking soda

1½ cups nonfat buttermilk

¼ cup canola oil

2 large eggs, lightly beaten

3 tablespoons unsalted butter

1. Place a 10-inch cast-iron skillet in oven. Preheat oven to 450°F (leave pan in oven).

2. Weigh or lightly spoon cornmeal and flour into dry measuring cups; level with a knife. Combine cornmeal, flour, baking powder, salt, and baking soda in a large bowl, stirring with a whisk.

3. Combine buttermilk, oil, and eggs, stirring with a whisk. Add to cornmeal mixture; stir just until combined.

4. Cut butter into pieces. Carefully place butter in hot pan in oven; bake at 450°F for 1 to 2 minutes or until butter melts and begins to brown. Carefully remove pan from oven, and pour butter into batter; stir just until combined. Immediately pour batter into pan. Bake at 450°F for 20 minutes or until browned on edges and lightly browned on top. Cool 5 minutes before slicing; serve warm.

SERVES 12 *(serving size: 1 piece)*
CALORIES 185; **FAT** 9.1g (sat 2.5g, mono 4.2g, poly 1.8g); **PROTEIN** 5g; **CARB** 22g; **FIBER** 2g; **SUGARS** 0g (est. added sugars 0g); **CHOL** 39mg; **IRON** 1mg; **SODIUM** 301mg; **CALC** 66mg

PUMPKIN-CHOCOLATE SWIRL BREAD

Nutty teff flour and a rich chocolate swirl are great ways to rev up classic pumpkin bread. Though the recipe uses a cup of sugar, it's not overly sweet—allowing the pumpkin and spice flavors to shine.

HANDS-ON TIME: 20 MINUTES TOTAL TIME: 2 HOURS 30 MINUTES

4.875 ounces teff flour (about 1 cup)

4.5 ounces unbleached all-purpose flour (about 1 cup)

1 teaspoon baking soda

1 teaspoon ground cinnamon

½ teaspoon salt

¼ teaspoon ground nutmeg

¼ teaspoon ground allspice

¼ teaspoon ground cloves

1 cup sugar

1 cup canned unsweetened pumpkin

⅓ cup canola oil

½ cup nonfat buttermilk

1 teaspoon vanilla extract

2 large eggs

½ cup semisweet chocolate chips

1 tablespoon unsweetened cocoa

1. Preheat oven to 350°F.

2. Weigh or lightly spoon flours into dry measuring cups; level with a knife. Combine flours and next 6 ingredients (through cloves), stirring with a whisk.

3. Place sugar, pumpkin, and oil in a large bowl; beat with a mixer at medium speed until well blended. Add buttermilk, vanilla, and eggs; beat until well combined. Add flour mixture; beat at low speed just until combined.

4. Place chocolate chips in a medium, microwave-safe bowl. Microwave at HIGH 45 seconds or until chocolate melts, stirring after 30 seconds. Add 1 cup batter and cocoa to melted chocolate; stir well to combine.

5. Spoon half of pumpkin batter into a 9 x 5–inch loaf pan lined with parchment paper; dollop half of chocolate batter on top. Spoon remaining pumpkin batter over chocolate batter; dollop with remaining chocolate batter. Swirl batters together using a knife. Bake at 350°F for 1 hour or until a wooden pick inserted in center of loaf comes out almost clean. Cool 10 minutes in pan on a wire rack. Remove loaf from pan; cool on rack.

SERVES 16 *(serving size: 1 slice)*
CALORIES 191; **FAT** 7.3g (sat 1.5g, mono 3.7g, poly 1.5g); **PROTEIN** 3g; **CARB** 30g; **FIBER** 2g; **SUGARS** 16g (est. added sugars 15g); **CHOL** 23mg; **IRON** 2mg; **SODIUM** 172mg; **CALC** 35mg

BANANA BREAD WITH PECAN STREUSEL

Millet flour has a lightly sweet flavor and holds moisture well, making it ideal for this 100% whole-grain quick bread. Don't worry—it's just as moist and tender as classic banana breads. Quick tip: If your bananas aren't as ripe as you'd like, toss them (in their peels) in the oven as it preheats, until their skins darken; they'll soften and become sweeter.

HANDS-ON TIME: 20 MINUTES TOTAL TIME: 1 HOUR 30 MINUTES

Bread:

4.25 ounces millet flour (about 1 cup)

4.75 ounces white whole-wheat flour (about 1 cup)

1 teaspoon baking soda

½ teaspoon salt

1½ cups mashed ripe banana (about 3 bananas)

¾ cup granulated sugar

¼ cup canola oil

1½ teaspoons vanilla extract

2 large eggs

Cooking spray

Streusel:

3 tablespoons old-fashioned rolled oats

3 tablespoons brown sugar

1 tablespoon white whole-wheat flour

¼ teaspoon ground cinnamon

Dash of salt

2 tablespoons butter, melted

2 tablespoons chopped pecans

1. Preheat oven to 350°F.

2. To prepare bread, weigh or lightly spoon flours into dry measuring cups; level with a knife. Combine flours, baking soda, and ½ teaspoon salt in a large bowl, stirring with a whisk.

3. Place banana and next 4 ingredients (through eggs) in a large bowl; stir with a whisk until well blended. Add to flour mixture, stirring until just blended. Spoon batter into a 9 x 5–inch loaf pan coated with cooking spray.

4. To prepare streusel, combine oats and next 4 ingredients (through dash of salt) in a small bowl. Drizzle butter over oats mixture; toss well to combine. Stir in pecans. Sprinkle mixture over batter. Bake at 350°F for 1 hour or until a wooden pick inserted in center comes out with a few moist crumbs clinging. Cool bread in pan 10 minutes on a wire rack; remove from pan, and cool on wire rack.

MAKE IT FASTER

Sometimes, you just want banana bread now. To speed things along, scoop batter into mini muffin cups, and bake at 350°F for 10 to 13 minutes. You'll end up with about 36 banana bread bites.

SERVES 16 (serving size: 1 slice)
CALORIES 183; **FAT** 6.7g (sat 1.5g, mono 3.3g, poly 1.6g); **PROTEIN** 3g; **CARB** 28g; **FIBER** 2g; **SUGARS** 15g (est. added sugars 12g); **CHOL** 27mg; **IRON** 1mg; **SODIUM** 185mg; **CALC** 15mg

WHOLE-WHEAT, OATMEAL, AND RAISIN MUFFINS

With whole-grain flour and oats, plus wheat germ, wheat bran, and three dried fruits, these muffins make for one heckuva healthy start to your day. Adding boiling water to the batter and allowing it to sit for 15 minutes before baking allows the hearty oats, wheat germ, and bran to soak up the liquid for a more tender muffin.

HANDS-ON TIME: 17 MINUTES TOTAL TIME: 52 MINUTES

4.75 ounces whole-wheat flour (about 1 cup)
¼ cup granulated sugar
¼ cup packed brown sugar
2 tablespoons untoasted wheat germ
2 tablespoons wheat bran
1½ teaspoons baking soda
1 teaspoon ground cinnamon
½ teaspoon salt
1½ cups quick-cooking oats
⅓ cup chopped pitted dates
⅓ cup raisins
⅓ cup dried cranberries
1 cup low-fat buttermilk
¼ cup canola oil
1 teaspoon vanilla extract
1 large egg, lightly beaten
½ cup boiling water
Cooking spray

1. Lightly spoon flour into a dry measuring cup; level with a knife. Combine flour and next 7 ingredients (through salt) in a large bowl, stirring with a whisk. Stir in oats, dates, raisins, and cranberries. Make a well in center of mixture. Combine buttermilk, oil, vanilla, and egg; add to flour mixture, stirring just until moist. Stir in ½ cup boiling water. Let batter stand 15 minutes.

2. Preheat oven to 375°F.

3. Spoon batter into 12 muffin cups coated with cooking spray. Bake at 375°F for 20 minutes or until muffins spring back when touched lightly in center. Remove muffins from pans immediately; place on a wire rack.

SERVES 12 *(serving size: 1 muffin)*
CALORIES 204; **FAT** 6.4g (sat 0.8g, mono 3.2g, poly 1.8g); **PROTEIN** 5g; **CARB** 35g; **FIBER** 3g; **SUGARS** 17g (est. added sugars 10g); **CHOL** 19mg; **IRON** 1mg; **SODIUM** 288mg; **CALC** 43mg

MILLET MUFFINS WITH HONEY-PECAN BUTTER

Little bits of millet add a fun crunchy element to these sweet, tender muffins. If you don't have a spice grinder, pulse the millet in a mini food processor or blender, or use a mortar and pestle.

HANDS-ON TIME: 20 MINUTES TOTAL TIME: 48 MINUTES

Muffins:
- ⅔ cup uncooked millet
- ¾ cup packed brown sugar
- 1 large egg
- ¾ cup nonfat buttermilk
- ¼ cup canola oil
- 6 ounces whole-wheat pastry flour (about 1½ cups)
- 1 teaspoon baking powder
- ⅜ teaspoon salt
- ¼ teaspoon baking soda
- Cooking spray

Butter:
- 3 tablespoons butter, softened
- 3 tablespoons finely chopped pecans, toasted and cooled
- 1½ tablespoons honey

1. Preheat oven to 375°F.

2. To prepare muffins, place millet in a spice or coffee grinder; pulse 6 times or until lightly crushed. Set aside.

3. Place sugar and egg in a large bowl; beat with a mixer at medium speed until well combined. Stir in millet, buttermilk, and oil.

4. Weigh or lightly spoon flour into dry measuring cups; level with a knife. Combine flour, baking powder, salt, and baking soda, stirring with a whisk. Make a well in center of mixture. Add buttermilk mixture; stir just until moist. Let batter stand 5 minutes.

5. Line 12 muffin cups with paper liners; coat liners lightly with cooking spray. Spoon batter into prepared muffin cups. Bake at 375°F for 18 minutes or until muffins spring back when touched lightly in center. Cool in pan 5 minutes on a wire rack. Remove muffins from pan; place on wire rack.

6. To prepare butter, combine butter, pecans, and honey, stirring well to combine. Serve with muffins.

CHANGE IT UP

Quinoa would work just as well as millet here, with one word of caution: Red or tri-color quinoa will look a bit discolored; best to stick with standard quinoa.

SERVES 12 *(serving size: 1 muffin and about 1½ teaspoons butter)*
CALORIES 249; **FAT** 9.9g (sat 2.5g, mono 4.6g, poly 2.1g); **PROTEIN** 4g; **CARB** 37g; **FIBER** 3g; **SUGARS** 16g (est. added sugars 16g); **CHOL** 23mg; **IRON** 1mg; **SODIUM** 189mg; **CALC** 72mg

APPLE STREUSEL MUFFINS WITH MAPLE DRIZZLE

What I love about these muffins is that they're not too sweet—just a bit of brown sugar goodness in the batter and maple richness in the glaze. For tender apple bits, cut into a small dice; if you'd like a little crunch, go with larger pieces.

HANDS-ON TIME: 25 MINUTES TOTAL TIME: 46 MINUTES

Streusel:

- 2 tablespoons old-fashioned rolled oats
- 2 tablespoons spelt flour
- 1 tablespoon brown sugar
- 1 tablespoon butter, melted
- ½ teaspoon ground cinnamon

Muffins:

- 5 ounces spelt flour (about 1 cup)
- 2.5 ounces whole-wheat pastry flour (about ½ cup)
- 2 teaspoons ground cinnamon
- 1½ teaspoons baking powder
- ½ teaspoon baking soda
- ¼ teaspoon kosher salt
- ¾ cup low-fat buttermilk
- ½ cup brown sugar
- 2 tablespoons canola oil
- 1 tablespoon butter, melted
- 1 large egg, lightly beaten
- 1 Granny Smith apple, diced (about 1¼ cups)
- ½ cup powdered sugar
- 2 tablespoons maple syrup
- ½ teaspoon water

1. Preheat oven to 400°F.

2. To prepare streusel, combine first 5 ingredients in a bowl; set aside.

3. To prepare muffins, weigh or lightly spoon 5 ounces spelt flour and whole-wheat pastry flour into dry measuring cups; level with a knife. Combine flours, cinnamon, baking powder, baking soda, and salt in a medium bowl.

4. Combine buttermilk, ½ cup sugar, oil, 1 tablespoon melted butter, and egg in a bowl. Add buttermilk mixture to flour mixture, stirring just until combined. Fold in apple. Divide batter among 12 paper-lined muffin cups; top with streusel. Bake at 400°F for 16 minutes or until a wooden pick inserted in the center comes out with moist crumbs clinging. Cool in pan 5 minutes. Remove from pan; cool completely.

5. Combine powdered sugar, syrup, and ½ teaspoon water in a bowl; stir until smooth. Drizzle over muffins.

SERVES 12 (*serving size: 1 muffin*)
CALORIES 194; **FAT** 5.2g (sat 1.6g, mono 2.2g, poly 0.8g); **PROTEIN** 4g; **CARB** 35g; **FIBER** 2g; **SUGARS** 20g (est. added sugars 17g); **CHOL** 21mg; **IRON** 1mg; **SODIUM** 196mg; **CALC** 77mg

SOUR CREAM COFFEE CAKE

This slimmed-down iteration of the classic coffee cake is moist and oh-so satisfying. A combination of flours mixed with oats anchors the batter, while just the right amount of butter, light sour cream, and sugars ensures the best texture and flavor for the fewest calories and saturated fat. A slice, with a hot cuppa, is a great way to start incorporating more whole grains into your diet. Mix the dry ingredients with the wet until just combined (don't overstir) for the best result. This is tastiest warm from the oven, but leftovers are also delicious.

HANDS-ON TIME: 25 MINUTES TOTAL TIME: 1 HOUR 45 MINUTES

¾ cup old-fashioned rolled oats (about 2.5 ounces), divided

Cooking spray

4.5 ounces unbleached all-purpose flour (about 1 cup)

1 ounce whole-wheat flour (about ¼ cup)

1 teaspoon baking powder

½ teaspoon baking soda

¼ teaspoon salt

½ cup granulated sugar

½ cup packed brown sugar, divided

⅓ cup butter, softened

2 large eggs

1 teaspoon vanilla extract

1 (8-ounce) carton light sour cream (such as Daisy)

2 tablespoons finely chopped walnuts, toasted

½ teaspoon ground cinnamon

1 tablespoon chilled butter, cut into small pieces

1. Preheat oven to 350°F.

2. Spread oats in a single layer on a baking sheet. Bake at 350°F for 6 minutes or until oats are barely fragrant and light brown.

3. Coat a 9-inch springform pan with cooking spray; set aside.

4. Reserve ¼ cup oats; set aside. Place remaining oats in a food processor; process 4 seconds or until finely ground. Weigh or lightly spoon flours into dry measuring cups; level with a knife. Combine processed oats, flours, baking powder, baking soda, and salt; stir with a whisk.

5. Place granulated sugar, ¼ cup brown sugar, and ⅓ cup butter in a large bowl. Beat with a mixer at medium speed 3 minutes or until light and fluffy. Add eggs, 1 at a time, beating well after each addition. Beat in vanilla. Add flour mixture to sugar mixture alternately with sour cream, beginning and ending with flour mixture. (Batter will be slightly lumpy because of oats.) Spoon batter into prepared pan; spread evenly.

6. Combine reserved ¼ cup oats, ¼ cup brown sugar, nuts, and cinnamon in a bowl. Cut in 1 tablespoon butter with a pastry blender or 2 knives until well blended. Sprinkle top of batter evenly with nut mixture. Bake at 350°F for 38 minutes or until a wooden pick inserted in center comes out clean, top is golden, and cake begins to pull away from sides of pan. Cool cake in pan 10 minutes; remove from pan.

SERVES 10 *(serving size: 1 piece)*
CALORIES 276; **FAT** 11.5g (sat 6.5g, mono 2.5g, poly 1.2g); **PROTEIN** 6g; **CARB** 39g; **FIBER** 1g; **SUGARS** 23g (est. added sugars 21g); **CHOL** 61mg; **IRON** 2mg; **SODIUM** 247mg; **CALC** 59mg

MULTIGRAIN NECTARINE KUCHEN

Think of kuchen as a coffee cake made with yeast. It takes longer to make than a cake leavened with baking powder, but the flavor payoff is huge—that sweet, yeasted taste that makes this feel like a pastry. Vital wheat gluten is important here, giving the heavy, 100% whole-grain dough some much-needed lift; look for it with the flours at natural food stores and some large supermarkets. Reheat any leftovers in the microwave for a few seconds to recreate the tender, moist texture of the freshly baked cake.

HANDS-ON TIME: 20 MINUTES   TOTAL TIME: 2 HOURS 55 MINUTES

Cake:
- ⅔ cup warm 1% low-fat milk (100° to 110°F)
- ⅓ cup sugar
- 1 package dry yeast (about 2¼ teaspoons)
- ¼ cup butter, melted
- 1 teaspoon vanilla extract
- 1 large egg, lightly beaten
- 4.75 ounces spelt flour (about 1¼ cups)
- 6 ounces Kamut flour (about 1¼ cups)
- 2 tablespoons vital wheat gluten
- ½ teaspoon salt
- Cooking spray
- 2 nectarines, pitted and thinly sliced

Streusel:
- 1.625 ounces Kamut flour (about ⅓ cup)
- ⅓ cup sugar
- ½ teaspoon ground cinnamon
- ¼ teaspoon salt
- ¼ teaspoon ground ginger
- 1 tablespoon butter, melted
- 1 tablespoon canola oil
- ⅛ teaspoon vanilla extract

1. To prepare cake, combine milk, ⅓ cup sugar, and yeast in the bowl of a stand mixer; let stand 10 minutes. Stir in ¼ cup butter, 1 teaspoon vanilla, and egg.

2. Weigh or lightly spoon spelt flour and 6 ounces Kamut flour into dry measuring cups; level with a knife. Combine flours, gluten, and salt. Add to milk mixture; beat on low speed with dough hook just until combined. Beat on medium-low speed 5 minutes (dough will be quite wet and sticky, but do not add additional flour). Scrape dough into a large bowl coated with cooking spray; coat top of dough with cooking spray. Cover and let rise in a warm place (85°F), free from drafts, 1 hour or until almost doubled in size.

3. Turn dough out into an 11 x 7–inch glass or ceramic baking dish coated with cooking spray (do not punch dough down). Pat dough evenly into bottom of dish; top with nectarines. Cover and let rise 1 hour or until doubled in size.

4. Preheat oven to 350°F.

5. To prepare streusel, weigh or lightly spoon 1.625 ounces Kamut flour into a dry measuring cup; level with a knife. Combine flour, ⅓ cup sugar, cinnamon, ¼ teaspoon salt, and ginger in a small bowl. Drizzle with 1 tablespoon butter, oil, and ⅛ teaspoon vanilla; toss well to combine. Uncover dough; sprinkle evenly with streusel. Bake at 350°F for 30 to 35 minutes or until golden brown and a wooden pick inserted in center comes out clean.

SERVES 10 *(serving size: 1 piece)*
CALORIES 261; **FAT** 8.5g (sat 4g, mono 2.6g, poly 0.7g); **PROTEIN** 7g; **CARB** 42g; **FIBER** 4g; **SUGARS** 17g (est. added sugars 13g); **CHOL** 35mg; **IRON** 1mg; **SODIUM** 243mg; **CALC** 29mg

STRAWBERRY SCONES WITH LEMON GLAZE

Crisp on the outside, moist inside, and fruity all throughout—these scones give you a tasty reason to rise and shine. Freeze-dried strawberries have a super-concentrated berry flavor; they work great here because, unlike fresh fruit, they don't let off any moisture as they cook. They can be rather expensive at specialty markets, but I have discovered that Target now carries them at a much lower price; look for their Simply Balanced line with the dried fruit.

HANDS-ON TIME: 15 MINUTES TOTAL TIME: 35 MINUTES

7   ounces whole-wheat pastry flour (about 1¾ cups)
¼   cup granulated sugar
1   tablespoon baking powder
⅜   teaspoon salt
5   tablespoons chilled butter, cut into small pieces
1   ounce freeze-dried strawberries
⅔   cup nonfat buttermilk
¾   teaspoon vanilla extract
½   cup powdered sugar
2½   to 3 teaspoons fresh lemon juice

1. Preheat oven to 400°F.

2. Weigh or lightly spoon flour into dry measuring cups; level with a knife. Combine flour, granulated sugar, baking powder, and salt in a large bowl, stirring with a whisk. Cut in butter with a pastry blender or 2 knives (or your fingers) until mixture resembles coarse meal. Add strawberries; toss to combine. Combine buttermilk and vanilla; drizzle over flour mixture. Toss with a fork until dough comes together; knead lightly in bowl to bring dough together.

3. Turn dough out onto a lightly floured surface; pat dough out into a 7-inch circle. Cut dough into 8 equal wedges. Arrange dough wedges on a parchment-lined baking sheet. Bake at 400°F for 15 minutes or until lightly browned. Cool slightly.

4. Combine powdered sugar and lemon juice, stirring until thick and smooth; drizzle over scones.

SERVES 8 *(serving size: 1 scone)*
CALORIES 235; **FAT** 7.8g (sat 4.6g, mono 1.9g, poly 0.3g); **PROTEIN** 4g; **CARB** 38g; **FIBER** 4g; **SUGARS** 16g (est. added sugars 14g); **CHOL** 19mg; **IRON** 1mg; **SODIUM** 345mg; **CALC** 140mg

WHOLE-WHEAT CINNAMON ROLLS WITH MAPLE GLAZE

With cinnamon rolls, I say go big or go home—so there's a lot of spice here that's matched with an irresistible buttery maple glaze. Rapid-rise yeast shaves off about 40% of the usual rising time. The dough is quite soft and sticky; don't be tempted to add extra flour—that would just toughen it. A stand mixer is crucial; the dough is so soft, it's pretty much impossible to knead by hand. (NOTE: I tried doing an overnight proof, but the dough just got tough; it's best to make and bake.)

HANDS-ON TIME: 21 MINUTES TOTAL TIME: 2 HOURS 26 MINUTES

Rolls:
- 1 cup warm 2% reduced-fat milk (100° to 110°F)
- 5 tablespoons granulated sugar, divided
- 1 package rapid-rise yeast (about 2¼ teaspoons)
- ¼ cup melted butter, divided
- 1 large egg, lightly beaten
- 14 ounces whole-wheat pastry flour (about 3½ cups)
- ½ teaspoon salt
- Cooking spray
- ⅔ cup packed light brown sugar
- 1½ tablespoons ground cinnamon

Glaze:
- 1 cup powdered sugar
- ¼ cup maple syrup
- 1 tablespoon melted butter
- ¼ teaspoon salt

1. To prepare rolls, combine milk, 1 tablespoon granulated sugar, and yeast in the bowl of a stand mixer, stirring with a whisk. Let stand 5 minutes. Stir in 2 tablespoons butter, ¼ cup granulated sugar, and egg. Weigh or lightly spoon flour into dry measuring cups; level with a knife. Add flour and salt to yeast mixture. Mix on low speed with dough hook just until combined; mix on medium-low speed 6 minutes. Scrape dough into a large bowl coated with cooking spray (dough will be very soft and sticky). Coat top of dough with cooking spray; cover and let rise in a warm place (85°F), free from drafts, 45 minutes or until doubled in size. (Press two fingers into dough; if indentation remains, dough has risen enough.)

2. Punch dough down; turn out onto a well-floured work surface. Roll dough into a 15 x 11–inch rectangle. Brush dough with 2 tablespoons butter. Combine brown sugar and cinnamon; sprinkle mixture evenly over dough, spreading all the way to edges. Gently roll up dough jelly-roll style, starting with a long end. Cut dough into 15 (1-inch) slices using a sharp serrated knife. Arrange slices in a 13 x 9–inch glass or ceramic baking dish coated with cooking spray. Cover and let rise 40 minutes.

3. Preheat oven to 350°F.

4. Uncover dough. Bake at 350°F for 22 to 25 minutes or until lightly browned. Cool slightly.

5. To prepare glaze, combine powdered sugar, syrup, 1 tablespoon melted butter, and ¼ teaspoon salt, stirring until smooth. Spread glaze evenly over warm rolls. Serve warm.

SERVES 15 *(serving size: 1 roll)*
CALORIES 252; **FAT** 5g (sat 2.8g, mono 1.2g, poly 0.2g); **PROTEIN** 4g; **CARB** 48g; **FIBER** 4g; **SUGARS** 26g (est. added sugars 25g); **CHOL** 24mg; **IRON** 2mg; **SODIUM** 168mg; **CALC** 63mg

◄ WHEAT MINI NAAN

These Indian flatbreads are usually much larger, but I made small ones so they would be easier to manage—and so each person gets a whole one. The traditional shape is that of a tear, easy to achieve if you just lightly pull one end of the dough oval. Though in India they're baked in a tandoori oven, this simple stovetop method works beautifully.

HANDS-ON TIME: 45 MINUTES TOTAL TIME: 2 HOURS 15 MINUTES

8.33 ounces white whole-wheat flour (about 1¾ cups)

2.25 ounces unbleached white all-purpose flour (about ½ cup)

½ cup whole-milk yogurt (not Greek yogurt)

5 tablespoons water

1½ teaspoons dry yeast

¾ teaspoon salt

1 large egg, lightly beaten

Cooking spray

1 tablespoon butter, melted

1. Weigh or lightly spoon flours into dry measuring cups; level with a knife. Place flours and next 5 ingredients (through egg) in the bowl of a stand mixer. Mix on low speed with dough hook just until combined; mix at medium speed 6 minutes. Spoon dough into a large bowl coated with cooking spray, turning to coat top. Cover and let rise in a warm place (85°F), free from drafts, 1½ hours.

2. Uncover dough; turn dough out onto a lightly floured surface. (No need to punch dough down.) Divide dough into 8 equal pieces. Roll each piece into a 6 x 4–inch oval; gently pull one end of each oval to form, roughly, a tear shape.

3. Heat a large cast-iron skillet—or two, if you have them—over medium heat. Add two dough ovals to pan in a single layer; cook 1½ to 2 minutes or until bubbles form on surface and underside is lightly browned; turn dough over, and cook 1½ to 2 minutes. Repeat procedure with remaining dough ovals. Brush flatbreads evenly with butter; serve warm.

SERVES 8 *(serving size: 1 naan)*
CALORIES 149; **FAT** 3.1g (sat 1.5g, mono 0.8g, poly 0.2g); **PROTEIN** 6g; **CARB** 23g; **FIBER** 3g; **SUGARS** 1g (est. added sugars 0g); **CHOL** 29mg; **IRON** 2mg; **SODIUM** 250mg; **CALC** 41mg

WHITE-WHEAT TORTILLAS

Have a hankering for a quesadilla, but don't have tortillas on hand? No problem! With this quick recipe, it's seriously easy enough to whip up a batch of fresh, warm, homemade tortillas that you may just always make your own. (And honestly, these are more flavorful than store-bought.)

HANDS-ON TIME: 46 MINUTES TOTAL TIME: 46 MINUTES

9.5 ounces white whole-wheat flour (about 2 cups)

½ teaspoon salt

¾ cup warm water

2 tablespoons canola oil

1. Weigh or lightly spoon flour into dry measuring cups; level with a knife. Combine flour and salt in a medium bowl. Combine water and oil; add to flour mixture. Stir until a soft dough begins to form; knead in bowl 1 minute or until dough comes together.

(CONTINUED)

2. Divide dough into 10 equal portions. Working with 1 portion at a time (cover remaining dough to keep from drying), roll each dough portion between sheets of plastic wrap into a 7½-inch-wide circle. (Very lightly dust plastic wrap with flour if dough sticks.)

3. Heat a large nonstick skillet over medium heat. Add 1 dough circle; cook 1 minute on each side or until lightly browned in spots. Repeat procedure with remaining dough circles.

SERVES 10 *(serving size: 1 tortilla)*
CALORIES 105; **FAT** 3.2g (sat 0.2g, mono 1.8g, poly 0.8g); **PROTEIN** 3g; **CARB** 14g; **FIBER** 2g; **SUGARS** 0g (est. added sugars 0g); **CHOL** 0mg; **IRON** 1mg; **SODIUM** 118mg; **CALC** 16mg

SUPERFAST INJERA ⒼⒻ ▶

The traditional version of this spongy Ethiopian flatbread takes a few days to make; teff flour is mixed with water and allowed to ferment, creating a wonderful tangy flavor à la sourdough. Since I don't have that kind of time to dedicate, I give you a speedy version made with buttermilk and vinegar for tang. These were such a hit with my family that they've gone into the regular dinner rotation. We like to make a meal out of them by serving with chutney, pickled vegetables, lentils, and/or smashed potatoes.

HANDS-ON TIME: 19 MINUTES TOTAL TIME: 19 MINUTES

4.75 ounces teff flour (about 1 cup)
 ¾ teaspoon baking soda
 ¼ teaspoon salt
 1 cup club soda
 ½ cup nonfat buttermilk
 2 tablespoons white vinegar
 1 tablespoon butter, melted
 2 teaspoons canola oil

1. Weigh or lightly spoon flour into dry measuring cups; level with a knife. Combine flour, baking soda, and salt in a medium bowl, stirring with a whisk. Combine club soda, buttermilk, vinegar, and butter; add to flour mixture, stirring with a whisk until smooth (batter will be thin).

2. Heat a nonstick skillet over medium heat. Add about ¼ teaspoon oil to pan; wipe with a paper towel to create a thin film. Pour about ¼ cup batter onto pan in a spiral, starting in the center, to form a thin layer; cook 45 seconds. Cover pan, and cook 30 seconds or until set and injera can be easily removed. Repeat procedure with remaining oil and batter to form 8 flatbreads.

SERVES 8 *(serving size: 1 flatbread)*
CALORIES 85; **FAT** 3.1g (sat 1g, mono 1.1g, poly 0.4g); **PROTEIN** 3g; **CARB** 12g; **FIBER** 2g; **SUGARS** 0g (est. added sugars 0g); **CHOL** 4mg; **IRON** 1mg; **SODIUM** 228mg; **CALC** 46mg

GRAPE AND OLIVE SPELT FOCACCIA

A beautiful combo of sweet and tangy, salty and meaty, burgundy and green—this flatbread is wow-worthy. Serve with a cheese board, or as an accompaniment to a pasta dinner.

HANDS-ON TIME: 22 MINUTES TOTAL TIME: 3 HOURS 32 MINUTES

1½　cups warm water
　　　(100° to 110°F)
1½　teaspoons sugar
　1　package dry yeast (about
　　　2¼ teaspoons)
3½　tablespoons extra-virgin olive
　　　oil, divided
16.67 ounces spelt flour (about
　　　3½ cups)
1½　tablespoons chopped
　　　fresh rosemary
1½　teaspoons salt
　　　Cooking spray
　6　ounces red seedless
　　　grapes, halved
　3　ounces pitted Castelvetrano
　　　olives, halved
　½　teaspoon freshly ground
　　　black pepper

1. Combine 1½ cups water, sugar, and yeast in the bowl of a stand mixer, stirring with a whisk; let stand 10 minutes. Stir in 2 tablespoons oil.

2. Weigh or lightly spoon flour into dry measuring cups; level with a knife. Combine flour, rosemary, and salt. Add flour mixture to yeast mixture. Mix on low speed with dough hook just until dough comes together; mix on medium speed 6 minutes. Scrape dough into a large bowl coated with cooking spray (dough will be soft and sticky); coat top of dough with cooking spray. Cover and let rise in a warm place (85°F), free from drafts, 1½ hours or until doubled in size.

3. Punch dough down. Spoon dough onto a parchment paper–lined jelly-roll pan. Pat dough out into a 14 x 10–inch rectangle by dimpling dough with fingertips. Cover and let rise 1 hour. (Tip: Another jelly-roll pan, upside down, makes a great cover.)

4. Preheat oven to 425°F.

5. Uncover dough. Drizzle with 1½ tablespoons oil. Scatter grapes and olives over dough, barely pressing into dough. Sprinkle with pepper. Bake at 425°F for 30 minutes or until lightly browned on bottom. Cool on a wire rack.

CHANGE IT UP

Have fun with a variety of focaccia toppings. In place of grapes and olives, try roasted garlic cloves and halved grape tomatoes, shaved butternut squash ribbons and blue cheese, or thinly sliced Bosc pear and caramelized onions.

SERVES 20 *(serving size: 1 piece)*
CALORIES 107; **FAT** 3.5g (sat 0.3g, mono 1.7g, poly 0.3g); **PROTEIN** 3g; **CARB** 17g; **FIBER** 2g; **SUGARS** 2g (est. added sugars 0g); **CHOL** 0mg; **IRON** 1mg; **SODIUM** 263mg; **CALC** 2mg

OATMEAL KNOTS

Pass a basket of these at your next holiday feast, and watch your family's happy faces as they savor your homemade rolls. The recipe makes two dozen—plenty for the meal, plus for turkey or ham sliders the next day.

HANDS-ON TIME: 35 MINUTES TOTAL TIME: 3 HOURS 10 MINUTES

1 cup old-fashioned rolled oats
½ cup honey
2 tablespoons butter
1½ teaspoons salt
2 cups boiling water
1 package dry yeast (about 2 ¼ teaspoons)
⅓ cup warm water (100° to 110°F)
¼ cup flaxseed meal
14.5 ounces whole-wheat flour (about 3 cups)
6.75 ounces unbleached all-purpose flour (about 1½ cups), divided
Cooking spray
1 teaspoon water
1 large egg
1 tablespoon old-fashioned rolled oats
1 tablespoon poppy seeds
1 tablespoon sesame seeds

1. Combine first 4 ingredients in a large bowl; add 2 cups boiling water, stirring until well blended. Cool to room temperature.

2. Dissolve yeast in ⅓ cup warm water in a small bowl; let stand 5 minutes. Add yeast mixture to oats mixture; stir well. Stir in flaxseed meal.

3. Lightly spoon flours into dry measuring cups; level with a knife. Gradually add 3 cups whole-wheat flour and 1 cup all-purpose flour to oats mixture; stir until a soft dough forms. Turn dough out onto a lightly floured surface. Knead until smooth and elastic (about 8 minutes); add enough of remaining all-purpose flour, 1 tablespoon at a time, to prevent dough from sticking to hands (dough will feel tacky).

4. Place dough in a large bowl coated with cooking spray, turning to coat top. Cover and let rise in a warm place (85°F), free from drafts, 1 hour or until doubled in size. (Press two fingers into the dough. If indentation remains, the dough has risen enough.) Punch dough down, and let rest 5 minutes.

5. Divide dough in half; cut each half into 12 equal portions. Working with 1 portion at a time (cover remaining dough to prevent from drying), shape each portion into an 8-inch rope. Tie each rope into a single knot; tuck top end of rope under bottom edge of roll. Place each roll on a baking sheet coated with cooking spray. Cover with plastic wrap coated with cooking spray; let rise in a warm place (85°F), free from drafts, 30 minutes or until doubled in size.

6. Preheat oven to 400°F.

7. Combine 1 teaspoon water and egg in a small bowl; brush egg mixture over rolls. Combine 1 tablespoon oats, poppy seeds, and sesame seeds; sprinkle evenly over rolls. Bake at 400°F for 15 minutes or until golden. Cool on wire racks.

SERVES 24 *(serving size: 1 roll)*
CALORIES 138; **FAT** 2.7g (sat 0.9g, mono 0.7g, poly 0.9g); **PROTEIN** 4g; **CARB** 26g; **FIBER** 3g; **SUGARS** 6g (est. added sugars 5g); **CHOL** 13mg; **IRON** 1mg; **SODIUM** 160mg; **CALC** 22mg

CLOVERLEAF ROLLS

These soft, pillowy rolls are enriched with evaporated milk, butter, and egg. Freeze any leftovers up to 2 months; reheat in foil for 10 minutes at 350°F.

HANDS-ON TIME: 31 MINUTES TOTAL TIME: 2 HOURS 19 MINUTES

½   cup warm water (100° to 110°F)

1   teaspoon sugar

1   package dry yeast (about 2¼ teaspoons)

7.2   ounces white whole-wheat flour (about 1½ cups), divided

⅔   cup warm 2% evaporated milk (100° to 110°F)

3   tablespoons butter, softened

1½   teaspoons kosher salt

1   large egg, lightly beaten

10   ounces all-purpose flour (about 2¼ cups), divided

Cooking spray

1. Combine ½ cup water, sugar, and yeast in a large bowl. Let stand 5 minutes or until mixture is bubbly. Weigh or lightly spoon white whole-wheat flour into dry measuring cups; level with a knife. Stir 1 cup white whole-wheat flour, milk, butter, salt, and egg into yeast mixture. Weigh or lightly spoon all-purpose flour into dry measuring cups; level with a knife. Gradually add ½ cup white whole-wheat flour and 2 cups all-purpose flour to yeast mixture, stirring until a soft dough forms.

2. Sprinkle 2 tablespoons all-purpose flour on a work surface. Turn dough out onto surface; knead until flour is incorporated. Knead in 2 tablespoons all-purpose flour until dough is smooth and elastic (about 10 minutes). Place dough in a large bowl coated with cooking spray, turning to coat. Cover and let rise in a warm place (85°F), free from drafts, 1 hour or until doubled in size.

3. Preheat oven to 400°F.

4. Coat 18 muffin cups with cooking spray. Punch dough down; turn out onto a lightly floured surface. Cover and let rest 15 minutes. Divide dough into 18 pieces. Roll each piece into a 1-inch-thick rope; divide each into 3 pieces. Roll each piece into a ball. Place 3 balls into each of the prepared muffin cups; cover and let rise 30 minutes or until doubled in size. Bake at 400°F for 18 minutes or until golden brown.

SERVES 18 *(serving size: 1 roll)*
CALORIES 126; **FAT** 2.7g (sat 1.3g, mono 0.6g, poly 0.2g); **PROTEIN** 4g; **CARB** 20g; **FIBER** 2g; **SUGARS** 1g (est. added sugars 0g); **CHOL** 17mg; **IRON** 1mg; **SODIUM** 175mg; **CALC** 36mg

SMOKY BLACK PEPPER GRISSINI

These crunchy breadsticks get their flavor inspiration from beef jerky—pepper-spicy and smoky and downright addictive. You'll need to smoke (yes, smoke!) the flour first, which is easier to do than you might think.

HANDS-ON TIME: 37 MINUTES TOTAL TIME: 2 HOURS

6.3 ounces whole-wheat flour (about 1⅓ cups)

⅓ cup apple or cherry wood chips

1¼ teaspoons dry yeast

1 teaspoon sugar

⅓ cup plus 3 tablespoons warm water (100° to 110°F)

3 tablespoons extra-virgin olive oil

1½ teaspoons freshly ground black pepper

1 teaspoon kosher salt

Cooking spray

1. Weigh or lightly spoon flour into dry measuring cups; level with a knife. Pierce 10 holes on one side of the bottom of a 13 x 9–inch heavy-duty disposable aluminum foil pan. Arrange wood chips over holes inside pan. Spread flour onto far opposite side of pan. Place hole side of pan over stovetop burner. Turn burner on high. When wood chips start to smoke, carefully cover pan with foil. Turn burner on medium-high; cook 2 minutes. Remove pan from heat; uncover pan, reserving foil. Carefully remove wood chips with tongs; place on foil. Wipe any wood fragments out with a damp paper towel.

2. Dissolve yeast and sugar in ⅓ cup plus 3 tablespoons warm water in the bowl of a stand mixer; let stand 10 minutes. Stir in oil. Add smoked flour, pepper, and salt; mix on low speed with dough hook until just combined. Beat on medium-low speed with dough hook 5 minutes. Place dough in a bowl coated with cooking spray, turning to coat top. Cover and let rise in a warm place (85°F), free from drafts, 1 hour or until doubled in size.

3. Preheat oven to 350°F.

4. Punch dough down; divide into 16 equal pieces. Working with one piece at a time (cover remaining dough to prevent drying), roll into a 14- to 15-inch rope (should not need floured surface for this); place on a large baking sheet lined with parchment paper. Repeat with remaining dough pieces. Bake at 350°F for 27 to 28 minutes or until lightly browned and crisp. Cool completely on a wire rack.

IN PRAISE OF SMOKE

I adore this smoking technique and call for it a few times in this book. Why? First, because it's fast and easy. More importantly, smoking is my go-to when I want to create big, intense flavor without adding a single calorie, fat gram, or speck of sodium. It should be a tool in every healthy cook's arsenal.

SERVES 16 *(serving size: 1 breadstick)*
CALORIES 59; **FAT** 2.9g (sat 0.4g, mono 1.9g, poly 0.4g); **PROTEIN** 1g; **CARB** 8g; **FIBER** 1g; **SUGARS** 0g (est. added sugars 0g); **CHOL** 0mg; **IRON** 0mg; **SODIUM** 120mg; **CALC** 4mg

DESSERTS

Nearly all these desserts are 100% whole grain, and I do believe they stand up to or are better than refined-grain versions. My husband has a theory about this: He says white flour is bland, so it absorbs and dilutes flavor. But whole-grain flours amplify buttery, nutty, and toasty notes—you know, the flavors you want in a dessert.

OATMEAL CREAM PIES

My kids love the commercial version of these hefty sandwich cookies, but I always felt guilty about serving them because of that rather long ingredient list on the package (which includes partially hydrogenated oil—trans fat). Dare I say these homemade versions are way better? I do: They are! Whip up a batch; they stay fresh in an airtight container at room temperature for up to 1 week. Use any leftover filling, which also will keep for about a week, as a topping for brownies, cupcakes, or even ice cream.

HANDS-ON TIME: 38 MINUTES TOTAL TIME: 1 HOUR 14 MINUTES

Cookies:
- 1½ cups old-fashioned rolled oats
- 5⅞ ounces whole-wheat pastry flour (about 1½ cups)
- 1 teaspoon baking powder
- 1 teaspoon ground cinnamon
- ½ teaspoon salt
- ½ teaspoon baking soda
- 6 tablespoons canola oil
- ¼ cup butter, softened
- 1 cup packed dark brown sugar
- 2 tablespoons molasses
- 2 teaspoons vanilla extract
- 1 large egg

Filling:
- 9 tablespoons granulated sugar
- ⅓ cup light-colored corn syrup
- 3 tablespoons water
- ⅛ teaspoon salt
- ¼ teaspoon cream of tartar
- 2 large egg whites
- ½ teaspoon vanilla extract

1. Preheat oven to 350°F.

2. To prepare cookies, spread oats onto a jelly-roll pan. Bake at 350°F for 10 to 12 minutes or until lightly browned, stirring every 3 minutes. Remove from oven (do not turn oven off); cool slightly.

3. Place oats in a mini or full-sized food processor; pulse 5 times or until finely chopped but not ground. Place oats in a large bowl. Weigh or lightly spoon flour into dry measuring cups; level with a knife. Add flour and next 4 ingredients (through baking soda) to oats, stirring with a whisk.

4. Place oil, butter, brown sugar, and molasses in a large bowl; beat with a mixer at medium speed until well blended (3 minutes). Add 2 teaspoons vanilla and 1 egg; beat until well combined. Beat in oats mixture at low speed.

5. Spoon dough by scant tablespoonfuls, 2 inches apart, onto baking sheets lined with parchment paper to yield 40 cookies. Bake at 350°F for 9 minutes or until puffed and just set. (Do not overbake or cookies will get too hard.) Cool on pans 2 minutes; cool completely on a wire rack.

6. To prepare filling, combine granulated sugar, corn syrup, 3 tablespoons water, and ⅛ teaspoon salt in a small saucepan over medium-high heat; bring to a boil, stirring just until sugar dissolves. Cook, without stirring, until a candy thermometer registers 240°F. Place cream of tartar and egg whites in a large bowl; beat with a mixer at high speed until soft peaks form. Gradually pour hot sugar syrup into egg white mixture, beating first at medium speed and then at high speed; beat in ½ teaspoon vanilla. Beat at high speed 5 minutes or until mixture is the texture of marshmallow fluff. Spoon about 1 tablespoon filling onto flat side of each of 20 cookies; top each with 1 cookie.

SERVES 20 *(serving size: 1 cream pie)*
CALORIES 201; **FAT** 7.4g (sat 1.9g, mono 3.5g, poly 1.5g); **PROTEIN** 2g; **CARB** 32g; **FIBER** 2g; **SUGARS** 18g (est. added sugars 18g); **CHOL** 15mg; **IRON** 1mg; **SODIUM** 159mg; **CALC** 27mg

CRUNCHY-CHEWY SALTED CHOCOLATE CHUNK COOKIES

This has been my "house" cookie for years—when I say I'm making cookies, it's these guys. They're crisp around the edges and chewy in the middle; that soft center comes from using all brown sugar (no granulated) and a touch of honey.

HANDS-ON TIME: 9 MINUTES TOTAL TIME: 36 MINUTES

1 cup packed dark brown sugar
6 tablespoons canola oil
6 tablespoons butter, softened
2 tablespoons honey
1½ teaspoons vanilla extract
1 large egg
9.5 ounces whole-wheat flour (about 2 cups)
1 teaspoon baking soda
⅜ teaspoon salt
4 ounces premium semisweet chocolate, chopped
⅜ teaspoon fleur de sel or other sea salt

1. Preheat oven to 375°F.

2. Place first 3 ingredients in a large bowl; beat with a mixer at medium speed until well blended. Add honey, vanilla, and egg; beat until well combined.

3. Weigh or lightly spoon flour into dry measuring cups; level with a knife. Combine flour, baking soda, and salt, stirring with a whisk. Add flour mixture to sugar mixture; beat at low speed until almost combined. Add chocolate; beat at low speed until just combined.

4. Spoon dough by rounded tablespoonfuls onto parchment-lined baking sheets (12 cookies per baking sheet); sprinkle ⅛ teaspoon sea salt over each batch of 12, pressing gently to adhere. Bake in batches at 375°F for 8 to 10 minutes or until barely browned around edges. Cool cookies on pan 3 minutes; place on a wire rack to cool.

CHANGE IT UP

Use this recipe as a customizable template. I tested it with several different flours, including a couple of gluten-free ones, and found that they all worked well. I also baked a batch with refined all-purpose flour and had 15 or so people taste. Unanimously, the cookies made with refined flour were the least favorite because they tasted flat and bland.

Brown rice flour (8.8 ounces/2 cups): Cookies flattened out but were very crispy and nutty; they tasted as if they had peanut butter in them.

Buckwheat flour (9 ounces/2 cups): Batter is sandy, but cookies cook up beautifully, resembling dark molasses crinkle cookies. Buckwheat's slight bitterness makes the cookies taste as if they're made with deep, dark chocolate.

White whole-wheat flour (9.5 ounces/2 cups): Cookies are slightly puffy and pretty, with more upfront sweetness than the other versions.

Whole-wheat pastry flour (8.5 ounces/2 cups + 2 tablespoons): Crispier, crunchier texture; flavor is mild, buttery, and sweet.

SERVES 36 *(serving size: 1 cookie)*
CALORIES 105; **FAT** 5.7g (sat 2.1g, mono 2g, poly 0.8g); **PROTEIN** 1g; **CARB** 14g; **FIBER** 1g; **SUGARS** 8g (est. added sugars 8g); **CHOL** 10mg; **IRON** 0mg; **SODIUM** 104mg; **CALC** 9mg

PEANUT BUTTER AND JELLY THUMBPRINT COOKIES (GF)

Superfine teff flour works nicely for this cookie that riffs off the classic combo. To get the best shape for the cookies, use a cookie scoop for rounded dough mounds, or roll dough into balls (dough will feel oily). Make the thumbprint hollow after the cookies have baked, while they're still hot; use the handle of a wooden spoon to save your thumbs from the heat. Use any kind of jelly or preserves you like; strawberry is always a favorite in my house.

HANDS-ON TIME: 15 MINUTES TOTAL TIME: 45 MINUTES

7.05 ounces teff flour (about 1⅓ cups)
1 teaspoon baking soda
½ teaspoon salt
1 cup packed brown sugar
1 cup creamy peanut butter
3 tablespoons canola oil
3 tablespoons 2% reduced-fat milk
1½ teaspoons vanilla extract
1 large egg
20 teaspoons strawberry, grape, or apple jelly

1. Preheat oven to 350°F.

2. Weigh or lightly spoon flour into dry measuring cups; level with a knife. Combine flour, baking soda, and salt, stirring with a whisk; set aside.

3. Place brown sugar, peanut butter, and oil in the bowl of a stand mixer. Cream together with paddle attachment until fully incorporated (about 1 minute). Add milk, vanilla, and egg; mix on medium-low speed another 1 minute or until emulsified. Add flour mixture, and mix on low speed until just combined (about 15 seconds). Using a rubber spatula, make sure there are no rogue streaks of peanut butter.

4. Scoop dough with a 1-tablespoon cookie scoop 2 inches apart onto baking sheets lined with parchment paper (or roll tablespoonfuls of dough into balls and arrange on baking sheets). Bake at 350°F for 10 minutes. Remove from oven; immediately make a "thumbprint" impression with the handle of a wooden spoon (tamp down 2 or 3 times for a nickel-sized indentation). Place cookies on a wire rack; cool completely. Spoon ½ teaspoon jelly into indentation of each cookie.

SERVES 40 *(serving size: 1 cookie)*
CALORIES 94; **FAT** 4.6g (sat 0.8g, mono 2.3g, poly 1.2g); **PROTEIN** 2g; **CARB** 12g; **FIBER** 1g; **SUGARS** 8g (est. added sugars 8g); **CHOL** 5mg; **IRON** 0mg; **SODIUM** 95mg; **CALC** 16mg

DOUBLE-SORGHUM SPICE COOKIES (GF)

Sweet sorghum flour and tangy sorghum syrup give these addictive goodies the same appeal as old-fashioned molasses cookies, but with a wonderfully coarse texture, similar to a cornmeal cookie. If you can't find sorghum syrup (often sold at farmers' markets or natural foods stores), substitute molasses.

HANDS-ON TIME: 20 MINUTES TOTAL TIME: 1 HOUR 30 MINUTES

9 ounces sweet sorghum flour (about 2 cups)
1 teaspoon ground cinnamon
½ teaspoon baking powder
½ teaspoon baking soda
½ teaspoon ground ginger
¼ teaspoon salt
⅛ teaspoon ground cloves
½ cup packed brown sugar
6 tablespoons granulated sugar, divided
6 tablespoons butter, softened
3 tablespoons canola oil
¼ cup sorghum syrup
1 large egg

1. Weigh or lightly spoon flour into dry measuring cups; level with a knife. Combine flour and next 6 ingredients (through cloves), stirring with a whisk.

2. Place brown sugar, 3 tablespoons granulated sugar, butter, and oil in a large bowl; beat with a mixer at medium speed until light and fluffy (about 2 minutes). Add syrup; beat until well combined. Beat in egg. Add flour mixture; beat at low speed just until combined. Cover and chill dough 1 hour.

3. Preheat oven to 350°F.

4. Shape dough into 28 balls (about 1 tablespoon each). Roll dough balls in 3 tablespoons granulated sugar. Place 2 inches apart on baking sheets lined with parchment paper. Bake at 350°F for 14 minutes or until barely browned on edges and set. Cool on pans 3 minutes; place on a wire rack to cool.

SERVES 28 *(serving size: 1 cookie)*
CALORIES 106; **FAT** 4.4g (sat 1.7g, mono 1.7g, poly 0.6g); **PROTEIN** 1g; **CARB** 16g; **FIBER** 1g; **SUGARS** 9g (est. added sugars 9g); **CHOL** 13mg; **IRON** 1mg; **SODIUM** 76mg; **CALC** 15mg

Sea Salt–
Caramel Ice
Cream, page 298

SEA SALT–CARAMEL ICE CREAM (GF)

Whole-grain ice cream? Yep, that's right! This is not a gimmick recipe that inserts whole grains where they have no place; there's a real purpose here. Thick, mild-flavored Millet Cream serves as the "thickener," providing a rich, creamy texture without any actual saturated fat–heavy cream. You must be sure to get the Millet Cream as smooth as possible. If you have a high-powered blender, this is the place for it. I use an individual smoothie blender (geared toward pulverizing ice), finding it does a better job than my full-sized blender; I just whir the Millet Cream in batches.

HANDS-ON TIME: 17 MINUTES TOTAL TIME: 6 HOURS 47 MINUTES

1 cup sugar

¼ cup water

2 tablespoons butter

1 (12-ounce) can evaporated whole milk

1½ teaspoons vanilla extract

¾ teaspoon coarse sea salt (such as sel gris)

2 cups Millet Cream (page 36)

1. Combine sugar and ¼ cup water in a medium, heavy saucepan over medium-high heat; cook until sugar dissolves, stirring gently as needed to dissolve sugar evenly (about 3 minutes). Continue cooking, without stirring, 8 to 10 minutes or until mixture is light amber in color. Remove from heat; carefully stir in butter and evaporated milk (caramelized sugar will harden and stick to spoon, and mixture will bubble vigorously). Place pan over medium-high heat until caramelized sugar melts. Remove from heat; stir in vanilla and salt. Place pan in a large ice water–filled bowl; let stand 10 minutes or until cooled, stirring occasionally.

2. Combine caramel mixture and Millet Cream in a large bowl; refrigerate until well chilled.

3. Pour mixture into the freezer can of an ice-cream freezer; freeze according to manufacturer's instructions. Spoon ice cream into a freezer-safe container; cover and freeze 2 hours or until firm.

SERVES 8 (serving size: about ⅔ cup)
CALORIES 229; **FAT** 6.9g (sat 4.1g, mono 1.9g, poly 0.4g); **PROTEIN** 5g; **CARB** 37g; **FIBER** 1g; **SUGARS** 31g (est. added sugars 25g); **CHOL** 22mg; **IRON** 0mg; **SODIUM** 296mg; **CALC** 140mg

WHOLE-WHEAT SHORTBREAD

As I worked on these, I worried that a 100% whole-wheat shortbread wouldn't have the distinctive buttery, crumbly texture you expect from this type of cookie. Well, thanks to whole-wheat pastry flour, there's no need to worry. This shortbread is so good, you'll turn to this recipe again and again. To keep saturated fat to reasonable levels, canola oil steps in for some of the butter called for in traditional recipes.

HANDS-ON TIME: 15 MINUTES TOTAL TIME: 1 HOUR 22 MINUTES

9 ounces whole-wheat pastry flour (about 2 cups)
½ cup powdered sugar
¼ cup cornstarch
½ teaspoon salt
½ cup butter, softened
½ cup canola oil
¼ cup granulated sugar
1 teaspoon vanilla extract

1. Preheat oven to 325°F.

2. Weigh or lightly spoon flour into dry measuring cups; level with a knife. Combine flour, powdered sugar, cornstarch, and salt, stirring with a whisk.

3. Place butter, oil, granulated sugar, and vanilla in a large bowl; beat with a mixer at medium speed until well blended. Add flour mixture; beat just until combined.

4. Turn dough out onto a baking sheet lined with parchment paper. Pat dough out into a 10 x 8–inch rectangle. Pierce entire surface liberally with a fork. Bake at 325°F for 35 minutes or until set and lightly browned around edges. Remove from oven; immediately cut hot dough into 36 pieces. (A pizza wheel works nicely.) Cool on pan 2 minutes on a wire rack. Remove cookies from pan; cool completely on wire rack.

SERVES 36 *(serving size: 1 cookie)*
CALORIES 93; **FAT** 5.8g (sat 1.9g, mono 2.6g, poly 1g); **PROTEIN** 1g; **CARB** 10g; **FIBER** 1g; **SUGARS** 3g (est. added sugars 3g); **CHOL** 7mg; **IRON** 0mg; **SODIUM** 55mg; **CALC** 6mg

SUPER-FUDGY TEFF BROWNIES (GF)

These rich treats are such a game-changer that I will never go back to traditional brownies again. Why would I, when they deliver exactly what I'm looking for: dense texture, incredibly fudgy interior, amazing sugar crust on top. It's that superfine teff flour that makes the magic happen; it becomes slightly gelatinous when cooked—which makes for a moist and fudgy brownie. These decadent sweets are 100% whole grain, no refined flour in sight. Did I mention that they're gluten free, too?

HANDS-ON TIME: 10 MINUTES   TOTAL TIME: 1 HOUR 40 MINUTES

3.5 ounces teff flour (about ¾ cup)
  1 cup granulated sugar
  ¾ cup unsweetened cocoa
  ½ cup packed light brown sugar
  ½ teaspoon baking powder
  ⅓ teaspoon salt
  4 ounces bittersweet chocolate, chopped
  ¼ cup butter, cut into pieces
  ⅓ cup 1% low-fat milk
  2 tablespoons canola oil
  1 teaspoon vanilla extract
  2 large eggs, lightly beaten
Cooking spray

1. Preheat oven to 350°F.

2. Weigh or lightly spoon flour into dry measuring cups; level with a knife. Combine flour and next 5 ingredients (through salt) in a medium bowl, stirring with a whisk.

3. Place chocolate and butter in a medium, microwave-safe bowl. Microwave at HIGH 1 minute or until melted, stirring every 20 seconds. Stir in milk, oil, vanilla, and eggs. Add chocolate mixture to flour mixture; stir to combine.

4. Spoon batter into an 8-inch square light-colored metal baking pan coated with cooking spray. Bake at 350°F for 40 minutes or until mixture feels set, slightly springs back when touched in middle, and a wooden pick inserted near edges comes out with moist crumbs clinging. (A wooden pick in center will never test clean.) Cool in pan on a wire rack. Cut into 16 pieces using a damp knife.

SERVES 16 *(serving size: 1 brownie)*
CALORIES 193; **FAT** 9g (sat 4g, mono 2.3g, poly 0.7g); **PROTEIN** 3g; **CARB** 30g; **FIBER** 2g; **SUGARS** 22g (est. added sugars 22g); **CHOL** 31mg; **IRON** 1mg; **SODIUM** 108mg; **CALC** 38mg

BLUEBERRY STREUSEL BARS

A little lemon rind and juice in the blueberry filling offer a lovely flavor boost—the rind contributing floral perfume and the juice a tangy hit.

HANDS-ON TIME: 13 MINUTES TOTAL TIME: 65 MINUTES

2 cups fresh blueberries
¼ cup granulated sugar
1 tablespoon cornstarch
2 tablespoons water
1 teaspoon grated lemon rind
1 tablespoon fresh lemon juice
4 ounces whole-wheat pastry flour (about 1 cup)
1 cup old-fashioned rolled oats
⅔ cup packed brown sugar
½ teaspoon salt
5 tablespoons chilled butter, cut into small pieces
3 tablespoons canola oil
½ teaspoon vanilla extract
Cooking spray

1. Preheat oven to 350°F.

2. Combine first 4 ingredients in a small saucepan; bring to a boil. Reduce heat to medium-low; cook 6 minutes or until thick, stirring frequently. Remove from heat; stir in rind and juice.

3. Weigh or lightly spoon flour into a dry measuring cup; level with a knife. Place flour, oats, brown sugar, and salt in a food processor; pulse 2 times to combine. Add butter; pulse 5 times or until mixture resembles coarse meal. Combine oil and vanilla; drizzle over flour mixture. Pulse 4 times or until moist.

4. Reserve ⅔ cup flour mixture. Pour remaining flour mixture into a parchment-lined 8-inch square light-colored metal baking pan coated with cooking spray; pat into an even layer in bottom of pan. Spread blueberry mixture on top all the way to edges. Sprinkle evenly with reserved ⅔ cup flour mixture. Bake at 350°F for 45 minutes or until topping is lightly browned and filling is bubbly and almost set on edges. Cool completely in pan on a wire rack. Cut into 16 bars.

SERVES 16 *(serving size: 1 bar)*
CALORIES 162; **FAT** 6.8g (sat 2.5g, mono 2.7g, poly 1g); **PROTEIN** 2g; **CARB** 25g; **FIBER** 2g; **SUGARS** 14g (est. added sugars 12g); **CHOL** 10mg; **IRON** 1mg; **SODIUM** 108mg; **CALC** 15mg

CRISPY RICE BARS FOUR WAYS

Marshmallow-and-crispy-rice squares remain one of the great, simple treats, loved by kids of all ages. And they can be a whole-grain, gluten-free treat if you just choose a crispy brown rice cereal.

LEMON—WHITE CHOCOLATE CHEWY CRISPY BARS (GF)

A white chocolate drizzle elevates the classic dessert, while grated citrus rind adds a soft (not tart) lemon lift.

HANDS-ON TIME: 12 MINUTES TOTAL TIME: 27 MINUTES

- 2 tablespoons butter
- 10 ounces marshmallows
- 1 tablespoon grated lemon rind
- 6 cups crispy brown rice cereal
- Cooking spray
- 4 ounces chopped premium white chocolate

1. Melt butter and marshmallows over medium-low heat in a Dutch oven. Stir lemon rind into melted marshmallows. Add cereal; toss well to combine. Press cereal mixture into a 13 x 9–inch pan coated with cooking spray. Place white chocolate in a microwave-safe bowl. Microwave at HIGH 1½ minutes or until melted, stirring every 20 seconds; drizzle over cereal mixture. Refrigerate 15 minutes before slicing.

SERVES 20 *(serving size: 1 bar)*
CALORIES 121; **FAT** 3.3g (sat 1.9g, mono 0.9g, poly 0.2g); **PROTEIN** 1g; **CARB** 23g; **FIBER** 1g; **SUGARS** 12g (est. added sugars 12g); **CHOL** 4mg; **IRON** 0mg; **SODIUM** 28mg; **CALC** 15mg

ESPRESSO-TOFFEE CHEWY CRISPY BARS (GF)

These bars make the transition from kid treat to grown-up fare thanks to the addition of espresso powder.

HANDS-ON TIME: 10 MINUTES TOTAL TIME: 10 MINUTES

- 2 tablespoons butter
- 1 tablespoon espresso powder
- 10 ounces marshmallows
- 1 cup toffee bits
- 6 cups crispy brown rice cereal
- Cooking spray

1. Melt butter over medium-low heat in a Dutch oven. Stir in espresso powder before adding marshmallows. Add toffee bits and cereal; toss well to combine. Press cereal mixture into a 13 x 9–inch pan coated with cooking spray.

SERVES 20 *(serving size: 1 bar)*
CALORIES 155; **FAT** 5.5g (sat 2.8g, mono 0.4g, poly 0.2g); **PROTEIN** 1g; **CARB** 27g; **FIBER** 1g; **SUGARS** 16g (est. added sugars 15g); **CHOL** 7mg; **IRON** 0mg; **SODIUM** 83mg; **CALC** 4mg

S'MORES CHEWY CRISPY BARS

Why not combine two childhood favorites into one delectable treat? Broiled marshmallows give these bars authentic campfire flavor.

HANDS-ON TIME: 10 MINUTES TOTAL TIME: 10 MINUTES

10 ounces marshmallows
Cooking spray
2 tablespoons butter
½ cup graham cracker crumbs
½ cup semisweet chocolate minichips
6 cups crispy brown rice cereal

1. Preheat broiler to high.

2. Arrange marshmallows on a foil-lined baking sheet coated with cooking spray; broil 2 minutes or until charred. Melt marshmallows and butter over medium-low heat in a Dutch oven. Stir graham cracker crumbs and chocolate minichips into melted marshmallows. Add cereal; toss well to combine. Press cereal mixture into a 13 x 9–inch pan coated with cooking spray.

SERVES 20 *(serving size: 1 bar)*
CALORIES 120; **FAT** 3g (sat 1.6g, mono 0.9g, poly 0.3g); **PROTEIN** 1g; **CARB** 24g; **FIBER** 1g; **SUGARS** 12g (est. added sugars 11g); **CHOL** 3mg; **IRON** 0mg; **SODIUM** 33mg; **CALC** 5mg

CHOCOLATE-BUTTERSCOTCH CHEWY CRISPY BARS GF

You'll love the flavor and fancy swirl topping with these easy sweets; for a nutty flavor twist, use peanut butter chips in place of butterscotch.

HANDS-ON TIME: 12 MINUTES TOTAL TIME: 27 MINUTES

2 tablespoons butter
10 ounce marshmallows
6 cups crispy brown rice cereal
Cooking spray
1 cup chocolate chips
½ cup butterscotch chips
2 teaspoons fat-free milk

1. Melt butter and marshmallows over medium-low heat in a Dutch oven. Add cereal; toss well to combine. Press cereal mixture into a 13 x 9–inch pan coated with cooking spray. Place chocolate chips in a microwave-safe bowl. Microwave at HIGH 1 minute, stirring every 20 seconds. Spread over cereal mixture. Place ½ cup butterscotch chips and 2 teaspoons fat-free milk in a microwave-safe bowl. Microwave at HIGH 30 seconds; stir once. Dollop butterscotch mixture over chocolate; swirl with a knife. Chill until set.

SERVES 20 *(serving size: 1 bar)*
CALORIES 154; **FAT** 5.3g (sat 3.3g, mono 1.3g, poly 0.3g); **PROTEIN** 1g; **CARB** 28g; **FIBER** 1g; **SUGARS** 16g (est. added sugars 16g); **CHOL** 3mg; **IRON** 0mg; **SODIUM** 27mg; **CALC** 8mg

POPCORN BALLS SIX WAYS

Putting these popcorn balls on a skewer makes them even more irresistible.

OLD-FASHIONED POPCORN BALLS (GF)

HANDS-ON TIME: 35 MINUTES TOTAL TIME: 45 MINUTES

1 tablespoon canola oil
⅓ cup unpopped popcorn
1 cup sugar
½ cup light-colored agave nectar
¼ cup water
1 tablespoon butter
½ teaspoon salt
Cooking spray
1 teaspoon vanilla extract

1. Heat a Dutch oven over medium-high heat. Add oil to pan; swirl to coat. Add popcorn; cover and cook 3 minutes or until kernels pop, shaking pan frequently. When popping slows down, remove pan from heat. Let stand 1 minute.

2. Combine sugar and next 4 ingredients (through salt) in a heavy saucepan coated with cooking spray. Cook over medium-high heat until a candy thermometer registers 300°F. Remove from heat; stir in vanilla. Immediately pour over popcorn; toss well using a silicone spatula coated with cooking spray. Cool slightly. Carefully form mixture into 12 balls, being careful not to compact too tightly; place a skewer into each ball, if desired.

SERVES 12 *(serving size: 1 popcorn ball)*
CALORIES 146; **FAT** 2.5g (sat 0.7g, mono 1.2g, poly 0.5g); **PROTEIN** 1g; **CARB** 31g; **FIBER** 1g; **SUGARS** 28g (est. added sugars 27g); **CHOL** 3mg; **IRON** 0mg; **SODIUM** 107mg; **CALC** 1mg

TROPICAL POPCORN BALLS (GF)

HANDS-ON TIME: 35 MINUTES TOTAL TIME: 45 MINUTES

1 tablespoon canola oil
⅓ cup unpopped popcorn
1 cup sugar
½ cup light-colored agave nectar
¼ cup water
1 tablespoon butter
½ teaspoon salt
Cooking spray
1 teaspoon vanilla extract
½ cup diced dried mango
⅓ cup chopped macadamia nuts
⅓ cup toasted flaked coconut

1. Heat a Dutch oven over medium-high heat. Add oil to pan; swirl to coat. Add popcorn; cover and cook 3 minutes or until kernels pop, shaking pan frequently. When popping slows down, remove pan from heat. Let stand 1 minute.

2. Combine sugar and next 4 ingredients (through salt) in a medium, heavy saucepan coated with cooking spray. Cook over medium-high heat until a candy thermometer registers 300°F. Remove from heat; stir in vanilla. Add mango, macadamia nuts, and coconut to popcorn. Immediately pour hot syrup over popcorn mixture; toss well to coat using a silicone spatula coated with cooking spray. Cool slightly (about 1 to 2 minutes). Carefully form mixture into 12 balls, being careful not to compact too tightly; place a skewer into each ball, if desired.

SERVES 12 *(serving size: 1 popcorn ball)*
CALORIES 208; **FAT** 7g (sat 2.6g, mono 3.3g, poly 0.6g); **PROTEIN** 1g; **CARB** 37g; **FIBER** 1g; **SUGARS** 31g (est. added sugars 27g); **CHOL** 3mg; **IRON** 0mg; **SODIUM** 110mg; **CALC** 14mg

CANDIED APPLE POPCORN BALLS (GF)

HANDS-ON TIME: 35 MINUTES TOTAL TIME: 45 MINUTES

1 tablespoon canola oil
⅓ cup unpopped popcorn
1 ounce lightly crushed apple chips
1 cup sugar
½ cup cinnamon hard candies (about 21 candies)
¼ cup water
1 tablespoon butter
½ teaspoon salt
Cooking spray
1 teaspoon vanilla extract

1. Heat a Dutch oven over medium-high heat. Add oil to pan; swirl to coat. Add popcorn; cover and cook 3 minutes or until kernels pop, shaking pan frequently. When popping slows down, remove pan from heat. Let stand 1 minute or until popping stops. Stir in apple chips.

2. Combine sugar and next 4 ingredients (through salt) in a medium, heavy saucepan coated with cooking spray. Cook over medium-high heat until a candy thermometer registers 300°F. Remove from heat; stir in vanilla. Immediately pour hot syrup over popcorn; toss well to coat using a silicone spatula coated with cooking spray. Cool slightly (about 1 to 2 minutes). Carefully form mixture into 12 balls, being careful not to compact too tightly; place a skewer into each ball, if desired.

SERVES 12 *(serving size: 1 popcorn ball)*
CALORIES 116; **FAT** 2.5g (sat 0.7g, mono 1.2g, poly 0.5g); **PROTEIN** 1g; **CARB** 23g; **FIBER** 1g; **SUGARS** 19g (est. added sugars 17g); **CHOL** 3mg; **IRON** 0mg; **SODIUM** 110mg; **CALC** 1mg

WHITE CHOCOLATE—CHERRY POPCORN BALLS (GF)

HANDS-ON TIME: 35 MINUTES TOTAL TIME: 45 MINUTES

1 tablespoon canola oil
⅓ cup unpopped popcorn
1 cup sugar
½ cup light-colored agave nectar
¼ cup water
1 tablespoon butter
½ teaspoon salt
Cooking spray
1 teaspoon vanilla extract
⅔ cup coarsely chopped dried cherries
⅓ cup white chocolate chips

1. Heat a Dutch oven over medium-high heat. Add oil to pan; swirl to coat. Add popcorn; cover and cook 3 minutes or until kernels pop, shaking pan frequently. When popping slows down, remove pan from heat. Let stand 1 minute or until popping stops.

2. Combine sugar and next 4 ingredients (through salt) in a medium, heavy saucepan coated with cooking spray. Cook over medium-high heat until a candy thermometer registers 300°F. Remove from heat; stir in vanilla. Add cherries and white chocolate to popcorn. Immediately pour hot syrup over popcorn; toss well to coat using a silicone spatula coated with cooking spray. Cool slightly (about 1 to 2 minutes). Carefully form mixture into 12 balls, being careful not to compact too tightly; place a skewer into each ball, if desired.

SERVES 12 *(serving size: 1 popcorn ball)*
CALORIES 194; **FAT** 4g (sat 1.7g, mono 1.6g, poly 0.6g); **PROTEIN** 1g; **CARB** 40g; **FIBER** 3g; **SUGARS** 33g (est. added sugars 30g); **CHOL** 4mg; **IRON** 0mg; **SODIUM** 111mg; **CALC** 13mg

ROCKY ROAD POPCORN BALLS (GF)

HANDS-ON TIME: 35 MINUTES TOTAL TIME: 45 MINUTES

1 tablespoon canola oil
⅓ cup unpopped popcorn
1 cup sugar
½ cup light-colored agave nectar
¼ cup water
1 tablespoon butter
½ teaspoon salt
Cooking spray
1 teaspoon vanilla extract
1 cup mini marshmallows
⅔ cup chocolate chips

1. Heat a Dutch oven over medium-high heat. Add oil to pan; swirl to coat. Add popcorn; cover and cook 3 minutes or until kernels pop, shaking pan frequently. When popping slows down, remove pan from heat. Let stand 1 minute or until popping stops.

2. Combine sugar and next 4 ingredients (through salt) in a medium, heavy saucepan coated with cooking spray. Cook over medium-high heat until a candy thermometer registers 300°F. Remove from heat; stir in vanilla. Add mini marshmallows and chocolate chips to popcorn. Immediately pour hot syrup over popcorn mixture; toss well to coat using a silicone spatula coated with cooking spray. Cool slightly (about 1 to 2 minutes). Carefully form mixture into 12 balls, being careful not to compact too tightly; place a skewer into each ball, if desired.

SERVES 12 (serving size: 1 popcorn ball)
CALORIES 204; **FAT** 5.3g (sat 2.4g, mono 2.1g, poly 0.6g); **PROTEIN** 1g; **CARB** 41g; **FIBER** 1g; **SUGARS** 35g (est. added sugars 35g); **CHOL** 3mg; **IRON** 0mg; **SODIUM** 111mg; **CALC** 4mg

SALTY MAPLE-PECAN POPCORN BALLS (GF)

HANDS-ON TIME: 35 MINUTES TOTAL TIME: 45 MINUTES

1 tablespoon canola oil
⅓ cup unpopped popcorn
1 cup sugar
½ cup maple syrup
¼ cup water
1 tablespoon butter
1 teaspoon sea salt
Cooking spray
1 teaspoon vanilla extract
⅔ cup chopped toasted pecans

1. Heat a Dutch oven over medium-high heat. Add oil to pan; swirl to coat. Add popcorn; cover and cook 3 minutes or until kernels pop, shaking pan frequently. When popping slows down, remove pan from heat. Let stand 1 minute or until popping stops.

2. Combine sugar and next 4 ingredients (through salt) in a medium, heavy saucepan coated with cooking spray. Cook over medium-high heat until a candy thermometer registers 275°F. Remove from heat; stir in vanilla. Add pecans to popcorn. Immediately pour hot syrup over popcorn; toss well to coat using a silicone spatula coated with cooking spray. Cool slightly (about 1 to 2 minutes). Carefully form mixture into 12 balls, being careful not to compact too tightly; place a skewer into each ball, if desired.

SERVES 12 (serving size: 1 popcorn ball)
CALORIES 182; **FAT** 6.9g (sat 1.1g, mono 3.6g, poly 1.9g); **PROTEIN** 1g; **CARB** 30g; **FIBER** 1g; **SUGARS** 26g (est. added sugars 26g); **CHOL** 3mg; **IRON** 2mg; **SODIUM** 170mg; **CALC** 19mg

MIXED GRAIN AND NUT BRITTLE

When I began experimenting with fried grains, I just knew that their satisfying crunch would work just as well as nuts in ice cream sundaes, casseroles, and, well, candy! Popped amaranth adds a playful textural twist to the chocolate coating.

HANDS-ON TIME: 26 MINUTES TOTAL TIME: 35 MINUTES

1½ cups sugar
½ cup water
¼ teaspoon salt
½ cup sliced almonds, toasted
½ cup Crunchy Fried Farro (page 32)
¾ cup semisweet chocolate chips
2 tablespoons Popped Amaranth (page 30)
1½ tablespoons finely chopped pistachios

1. Line a jelly-roll pan with parchment paper.

2. Combine first 3 ingredients in a medium, heavy saucepan. Stir gently over high heat just until sugar dissolves (do not stir beyond this point). Cook sugar mixture over medium-high heat until light golden brown (about 8 to 10 minutes). Remove pan from heat; gently stir in almonds and Crunchy Fried Farro. Immediately pour mixture onto prepared pan. Spread into a 10 x 10–inch square. Let stand 4 minutes or until cool enough to handle (do not allow to cool completely before cutting).

Cut in half crosswise using a pizza wheel or large heavy knife for 2 (5 x 10–inch pieces). Cut each piece lengthwise into 8 pieces. Cool completely.

3. Place chocolate chips in a small microwave-safe bowl; microwave at HIGH 1 minute or until chocolate melts, stirring every 20 seconds. Dip about 2 inches of one end of each brittle strip into chocolate, allowing excess to drip off. Place on parchment paper. Sprinkle chocolate evenly with amaranth and pistachios. Refrigerate until chocolate sets.

SERVES 16 *(serving size: 1 piece)*
CALORIES 185; **FAT** 6.7g (sat 2g, mono 3.2g, poly 1.2g); **PROTEIN** 2g; **CARB** 32g; **FIBER** 2g; **SUGARS** 27g (est. added sugars 26g); **CHOL** 0mg; **IRON** 1mg; **SODIUM** 44mg; **CALC** 17mg

CARDAMOM-QUINOA "TAPIOCA" PUDDING (GF)

Slightly overcooked quinoa becomes almost tapioca-like, little spheres that burst when you bite them. And that inspired this new spin on tapioca pudding. Rinsing the quinoa extra-well, and then toasting it in butter helps remove some of its bitter-grassy flavor. Enjoy the pudding on its own, or top with berries or pomegranate arils.

HANDS-ON TIME: 20 MINUTES TOTAL TIME: 60 MINUTES

½   cup uncooked quinoa
2   tablespoons butter, divided
1½   cups water
½   teaspoon salt, divided
3   cardamom pods
2½   cups 2% reduced-fat milk
¾   cup sugar
3½   tablespoons cornstarch
2   large eggs, lightly beaten
1½   teaspoons vanilla extract

1. Rinse quinoa in cold water, rubbing grains between fingers to agitate; drain well. Melt 1 tablespoon butter in a large saucepan over medium-high heat. Add quinoa; sauté 5 minutes or until toasted and fragrant. Add 1½ cups water, ¼ teaspoon salt, and cardamom; bring to a boil. Cover, reduce heat, and simmer 20 minutes. Remove from heat; let stand 10 minutes or until all water is absorbed.

2. Combine milk, sugar, cornstarch, and ¼ teaspoon salt, stirring well with a whisk. Stir milk mixture into quinoa mixture; bring to a simmer over medium heat, stirring frequently. Place eggs in a medium bowl. Gradually add about 1 cup hot milk mixture, 2 tablespoons at a time, to eggs, stirring constantly. Stir egg mixture into pan; cook over low heat 2 minutes or until bubbly and thick. Remove from heat; stir in 1 tablespoon butter and vanilla. Discard cardamom pods.

3. Spoon mixture into a large bowl or a shallow dish; cool slightly. Cover with plastic wrap, pressing wrap directly on surface of pudding. Chill.

SERVES 6 *(serving size: about ¾ cup)*
CALORIES 279; **FAT** 8.3g (sat 4.3g, mono 2.4g, poly 1g); **PROTEIN** 8g; **CARB** 44g; **FIBER** 1g; **SUGARS** 31g (est. added sugars 25g); **CHOL** 80mg; **IRON** 1mg; **SODIUM** 303mg; **CALC** 140mg

POMEGRANATE-ORANGE TART WITH PISTACHIO SHORTBREAD CRUST

Confession: I adore meringue—I even prefer it to whipped cream! To me, it's just yummier, more marshmallowy-wonderful, texture-wise. And guess how much saturated fat it contains? Zilch. Whipped cream, however? An innocent 2-tablespoon dollop packs in about 4 grams sat fat. That may not seem like much, but what are you putting that dollop on? Chances are it's something like pie, which already has butter in the crust. I like to stick with my meringue and deploy the fat where it has the biggest impact, the crust.

HANDS-ON TIME: 25 MINUTES TOTAL TIME: 3 HOURS 35 MINUTES

¼ cup minced dry-roasted, unsalted pistachios

4 ounces whole-wheat pastry flour (about 1 cup)

¼ cup powdered sugar

¼ teaspoon salt

5 tablespoons chilled butter, cut into small pieces

2 tablespoons canola oil

Baking spray with flour

½ cup fresh or frozen blueberries, thawed

2 cups pomegranate juice

⅓ cup granulated sugar

3 tablespoons cornstarch

2 large egg yolks

1 teaspoon grated orange rind

3 large egg whites

½ teaspoon vanilla extract

¼ teaspoon cream of tartar

⅛ teaspoon salt

¾ cup granulated sugar

⅓ cup water

Pomegranate arils (optional)

1. Preheat oven to 350°F.

2. Place pistachios in a food processor; process until almost ground. Weigh or lightly spoon flour into a dry measuring cup; level with a knife. Add flour, powdered sugar, and ¼ teaspoon salt to processor; pulse to combine. Add butter; drizzle with oil. Pulse until mixture resembles coarse meal. (It will be dry and slightly sandy.) Press mixture into bottom and up sides of a 9-inch removable-bottom tart pan coated with baking spray. Bake at 350°F for 25 to 30 minutes or until golden. Cool completely.

3. Place blueberries in a medium saucepan; mash with a potato masher. Add juice, ⅓ cup sugar, and cornstarch, stirring with a whisk. Bring to a low boil over medium-high heat, stirring frequently. Reduce heat; simmer 1 minute or until thick, stirring constantly. Place egg yolks in a medium bowl; add ½ cup hot juice mixture to yolks, stirring with a whisk. Pour egg mixture into pan; bring to a boil over medium-low heat. Cook 1 minute or until bubbly and thick, stirring constantly. Remove from heat. Strain through a sieve into a bowl; stir in rind. Place bowl in a larger ice-filled bowl for 20 minutes or until cooled, stirring occasionally. Pour mixture into crust. Cover and chill 3 hours or until set.

4. Place egg whites in a large bowl. Add vanilla, cream of tartar, and ⅛ teaspoon salt; beat with a mixer at high speed until soft peaks form. Combine ¾ cup sugar and ⅓ cup water in a saucepan; bring to a boil. Cook, without stirring, until a candy thermometer registers 250°F. Gradually pour hot sugar syrup in a thin stream over egg whites, beating at medium-low speed, and then at high speed until stiff peaks form. Spread meringue over tart. Garnish with pomegranate arils, if desired.

SERVES 10 *(serving size: 1 slice)*
CALORIES 287; **FAT** 11.1g (sat 4.4g, mono 4.4g, poly 1.6g); **PROTEIN** 4g; **CARB** 44g; **FIBER** 2g; **SUGARS** 32g (est. added sugars 25g); **CHOL** 52mg; **IRON** 1mg; **SODIUM** 164mg; **CALC** 27mg

MAKE AHEAD

The tart holds well overnight, so make it the day before, and serve chilled right from the refrigerator.

STRAWBERRY TART WITH QUINOA-ALMOND CRUST (GF)

The key to the crunchy quinoa crust is to lightly pat it into the pan; if you press too firmly and compact it, the crust will be tough and hard to cut.

HANDS-ON TIME: 40 MINUTES TOTAL TIME: 5 HOURS 7 MINUTES

Crust:

- 1 cup uncooked quinoa, rinsed and drained
- 1.75 ounces almond flour (about ½ cup)
- 2 tablespoons brown sugar
- ¼ teaspoon salt
- 1 large egg, lightly beaten
- Cooking spray

Almond cream:

- 1 cup 2% reduced-fat milk
- 2½ ounces almond paste, crumbled
- 3 tablespoons cornstarch
- 1 tablespoon granulated sugar
- 1 large egg
- 1 large egg yolk
- ⅛ teaspoon salt
- 2 teaspoons unsalted butter

Crema:

- 2½ ounces ⅓-less-fat cream cheese
- 1 tablespoon granulated sugar
- 3 tablespoons heavy whipping cream
- 2 teaspoons grated lemon rind, divided
- 2 teaspoons fresh lemon juice
- 1½ teaspoons thyme leaves, divided
- 12 ounces strawberries, hulled and sliced lengthwise
- 1 tablespoon seedless strawberry jam

1. Preheat oven to 350°F.

2. To prepare crust, spread quinoa and almond flour evenly on a foil-lined baking sheet. Bake at 350°F for 9 minutes or until lightly browned, rotating pan after 5 minutes. Cool completely on pan. Place mixture in a food processor; process 1½ minutes or until almost finely ground, scraping bowl after 1 minute. Add brown sugar and ¼ teaspoon salt; pulse to combine. Add egg; pulse 3 to 4 times or until mixture begins to clump (mixture will be moist). Lightly press mixture into the bottom and up sides of a 9-inch removable-bottom tart pan coated with cooking spray. Bake at 350°F for 18 minutes or until lightly browned, rotating pan after 10 minutes. Cool completely on a wire rack. (Do not remove sides of pan.)

3. To prepare almond cream, combine milk and almond paste in a medium saucepan over medium heat; bring to a simmer. Cook 2 minutes or until almond paste melts, stirring frequently with a whisk. Combine cornstarch, 1 tablespoon granulated sugar, 1 egg, 1 egg yolk, and ⅛ teaspoon salt in a medium bowl, stirring with a whisk until smooth. Drizzle hot milk mixture into egg mixture, stirring constantly with a whisk. Return mixture to pan. Bring to a boil over medium heat, stirring constantly with a whisk; cook 1 minute or until thick, whisking vigorously. Remove pan from heat; add butter, stirring with a whisk until butter melts. Place pan in a large ice water–filled bowl; cool to room temperature, stirring occasionally.

4. To prepare crema, beat cream cheese and 1 tablespoon sugar at medium speed until smooth. Add whipping cream, 1 teaspoon rind, and juice, beating until mixture thickens (about 30 seconds). Stir in 1 teaspoon thyme leaves.

5. Place sliced strawberries and jam in a bowl; toss gently to coat.

6. Spread almond cream in bottom of cooled crust. Gently spread crema on top of almond cream. Arrange strawberries over top of crema. Sprinkle 1 teaspoon rind and ½ teaspoon thyme over top of strawberries. Chill 4 hours.

SERVES 8 *(serving size: 1 wedge)*
CALORIES 305; **FAT** 14.8g (sat 4.7g, mono 6.5g, poly 2.5g); **PROTEIN** 9g; **CARB** 35g; **FIBER** 4g; **SUGARS** 16g (est. added sugars 10g); **CHOL** 89mg; **IRON** 2mg; **SODIUM** 178mg; **CALCIUM** 112mg

CHERRY-ALMOND HAND PIES

The crust here is a variation on a genius recipe from Cooking Light's *sister publication* Southern Living—*it uses almond paste in place of some of the butter. My adaptation uses far less butter and no refined flour, with great results. The vodka in the dough helps it stay moist and pliable as you work with it, but it evaporates as the pies bake; you'll taste nothing boozy.*

HANDS-ON TIME: 23 MINUTES TOTAL TIME: 2 HOURS 1 MINUTE

¼ cup almond paste, cut into small pieces

¼ cup chilled butter, cut into small pieces

7 ounces whole-wheat pastry flour (about 1¾ cups)

1 tablespoon granulated sugar

½ teaspoon salt

½ teaspoon baking powder

3 tablespoons ice-cold vodka

3 tablespoons ice-cold water

1 cup cherry juice or black cherry juice (not tart cherry juice)

1 (5-ounce) package dried sweet cherries

1 large egg, lightly beaten

2 tablespoons turbinado sugar or 1 tablespoon granulated sugar

1. Place almond paste and butter in freezer for 5 minutes.

2. Weigh or lightly spoon flour into dry measuring cups; level with a knife. Place flour, sugar, salt, and baking powder in a food processor; pulse 2 times to combine. Add almond paste and butter; pulse 5 times or until mixture resembles coarse meal. Gradually add vodka and water through food chute while pulsing; pulse just until combined. Gather dough together; knead gently 1 to 2 times to bring dough together. Divide dough into 8 equal portions. Working with 1 dough portion at a time, press dough into a 2-inch circle; roll to a 5-inch circle between plastic wrap. Stack dough circles between plastic wrap or wax paper; chill 1 hour.

3. While dough chills, combine juice and cherries in a small saucepan; bring to a boil over medium-high heat. Reduce heat, and simmer, uncovered, 25 minutes or until most of liquid evaporates. Remove from heat; cool to room temperature.

4. Preheat oven to 425°F.

5. Working with 1 dough circle at a time, spoon 1 rounded tablespoon cherry mixture into center of each circle. Lightly brush edges of dough circles with beaten egg. Carefully fold dough over filling; press edges together with a fork to seal. Place pies on a baking sheet lined with parchment paper. Lightly brush egg over pies; sprinkle evenly with turbinado sugar. Cut 2 diagonal slits across top of each pie. Bake at 425°F for 18 minutes or until golden brown; cool on a wire rack.

SERVES 8 *(serving size: 1 pie)*
CALORIES 300; **FAT** 8.8g (sat 4g, mono 3g, poly 0.8g); **PROTEIN** 5g; **CARB** 47g; **FIBER** 6g; **SUGARS** 27g (est. added sugars 7g); **CHOL** 39mg; **IRON** 2mg; **SODIUM** 237mg; **CALC** 73mg

APPLE PIE WITH CHEDDAR CRUST

Instead of the same old slice of cheese with your apple pie, bake the cheddar right into the crust. The dough is sticky at first but firms up in the fridge. When rolling out, be patient and roll gradually, starting in the center and rolling out to the edges.

HANDS-ON TIME: 20 MINUTES TOTAL TIME: 2 HOURS 50 MINUTES

7 ounces whole-wheat pastry flour (about 1¾ cups)

½ teaspoon salt, divided

3 ounces sharp white cheddar cheese, shredded (about ¾ cup)

⅓ cup plus 1 tablespoon canola oil

⅓ cup 2% reduced-fat milk

2 pounds Honeycrisp apples, peeled, cored, and thinly sliced

2 tablespoons cider vinegar

½ cup granulated sugar

1½ tablespoons cornstarch

1 teaspoon ground cinnamon

1 large egg yolk, lightly beaten

1 tablespoon turbinado sugar

1. Weigh or lightly spoon pastry flour into dry measuring cups; level with a knife. Combine pastry flour, ¼ teaspoon salt, and cheese in a large bowl, stirring well to combine. Add oil and milk; stir until a moist dough forms. Divide dough in half; press each half into a 4-inch disk. Wrap dough in plastic wrap; refrigerate 30 minutes.

2. Preheat oven to 400°F.

3. Combine apples and vinegar in a large bowl; toss well to coat. Combine granulated sugar, cornstarch, cinnamon, and ¼ teaspoon salt, stirring until well combined. Pour sugar mixture over apple mixture; toss well to coat. Set aside.

4. Remove dough from refrigerator. Roll 1 dough piece between plastic wrap into a 10½-inch circle. Remove top piece of plastic wrap; fit dough, plastic wrap side up, into a 9-inch pie plate. Remove remaining plastic wrap. Spoon apple mixture into dough. Roll remaining dough piece between plastic wrap into an 11½-inch circle. Remove top piece of plastic wrap; top pie with dough, plastic wrap side up. Remove remaining plastic wrap. Press edges of dough together; fold edges under, and flute. Cut slits in top of dough to allow steam to escape.

5. Carefully brush egg yolk over dough; sprinkle with turbinado sugar. Bake at 400°F for 10 minutes. Reduce oven temperature to 350°F (do not remove pie from oven). Bake at 350°F for 50 minutes or until crust is browned and filling is bubbly. Cool on a wire rack 1 hour before slicing into wedges.

CHANGE IT UP

For a more fragrant filling, swap out half the apples for pears; or go all in with pears for a sweeter treat. Anjou and Bartlett varieties work best for pies.

SERVES 10 *(serving size: 1 wedge)*
CALORIES 294; **FAT** 12.8g (sat 2.7g, mono 6.7g, poly 2.7g); **PROTEIN** 5g; **CARB** 41g; **FIBER** 4g; **SUGARS** 21g (est. added sugars 11g); **CHOL** 28mg; **IRON** 1mg; **SODIUM** 176mg; **CALC** 95mg

BROWNED BUTTER PEACH CRISP

The change that comes over butter when you brown it is amazing: It goes caramel-sweet and wonderfully nutty, a perfect match for sweet, juicy peaches.

HANDS-ON TIME: 20 MINUTES TOTAL TIME: 1 HOUR 15 MINUTES

Topping:
- 5 tablespoons butter
- 2 tablespoons canola oil
- ¼ teaspoon vanilla extract
- 2.67 ounces whole-wheat pastry flour (about ⅔ cup)
- 1 cup old-fashioned rolled oats
- ½ cup packed light brown sugar
- ¼ teaspoon salt

Filling:
- 3 pounds peaches, sliced (about 6 cups)
- ⅓ cup packed light brown sugar
- 1½ tablespoons cornstarch
- Cooking spray

1. Preheat oven to 375°F.

2. To prepare topping, place butter in a small saucepan; cook over medium heat 3 minutes or until browned and very toasty-fragrant. Remove from heat; stir in oil and vanilla. Cool slightly.

3. Weigh or lightly spoon flour into a dry measuring cup; level with a knife. Combine flour, oats, ½ cup sugar, and salt in a medium bowl; drizzle with butter mixture. Toss well to completely incorporate so there are no floury bits left.

4. To prepare filling, place peaches in a large bowl. Combine ⅓ cup sugar and cornstarch, stirring well; sprinkle over peaches. Toss well to combine. Spoon peach mixture into a 2-quart glass or ceramic baking dish coated with cooking spray. Top with topping. Bake at 375°F for 40 minutes or until topping is lightly browned and filling is bubbly. Serve warm.

SERVES 9
CALORIES 284; **FAT** 10.7g (sat 4.4g, mono 3.9g, poly 1.5g); **PROTEIN** 3g; **CARB** 47g; **FIBER** 4g; **SUGARS** 31g (est. added sugars 20g); **CHOL** 17mg; **IRON** 1mg; **SODIUM** 128mg; **CALC** 33mg

PLUM-BASIL GALETTE

Plums and basil are a beautiful pairing, brought together here with a quick jam that enlivens the whole freeform pie. A little cornmeal funs-up the crust with some crunch.

HANDS-ON TIME: 35 MINUTES TOTAL TIME: 1 HOUR 30 MINUTES

6 tablespoons sugar, divided
1 ounce package basil sprigs
6 plums, divided (about 1⅔ pounds)
4 teaspoons cornstarch, divided
3.6 ounces white whole-wheat flour (about ¾ cup)
1.65 ounces whole-grain cornmeal (about ⅓ cup)
½ teaspoon salt
5 tablespoons chilled butter, cut into small pieces
2 to 3 tablespoons ice water
Basil leaves (optional)

1. Preheat oven to 375°F.

2. Muddle 3 tablespoons sugar and basil sprigs together vigorously in a small saucepan. Peel, pit, and chop 2 plums; add chopped plums and 1 teaspoon cornstarch to pan. Bring mixture to a boil; reduce heat, and simmer 6 minutes or until plums are very tender. Cool slightly; discard basil. Place plum mixture in a mini food processor; process until smooth.

3. Weigh or lightly spoon flour and cornmeal into dry measuring cups; level with a knife. Place flour, cornmeal, 2 tablespoons sugar, and salt in a food processor. Add butter; pulse until mixture resembles coarse meal. Drizzle 2 to 3 tablespoons ice water through food chute, pulsing until moist (mixture will not form a ball). Turn mixture out onto a work surface; knead lightly to bring dough together. Flatten dough into a 4-inch disk. Place on a large sheet of parchment paper; cover with plastic wrap. Roll dough into a 12-inch circle. Slide dough (on parchment) onto a baking sheet; place in freezer 5 minutes or until plastic wrap can be easily removed.

4. Combine 1 tablespoon sugar and 1 tablespoon cornstarch; sprinkle over dough, leaving a 2-inch border. Pit and thinly slice 4 plums; toss with pureed plum mixture. Spoon plum mixture over cornstarch mixture, leaving a 2-inch border. Fold dough border over plums, pressing gently to seal; use a bench scraper to lift dough off parchment paper, if necessary. Bake at 375°F for 35 minutes or until dough is lightly browned and juices are bubbly. Remove from oven; cool at least 10 minutes before slicing into wedges. Sprinkle with basil leaves, if desired.

SERVES 8 *(serving size: 1 wedge)*
CALORIES 184; **FAT** 7.7g (sat 4.6g, mono 2g, poly 0.4g); **PROTEIN** 2g; **CARB** 27g; **FIBER** 2g; **SUGARS** 14g (est. added sugars 9g); **CHOL** 19mg; **IRON** 1mg; **SODIUM** 213mg; **CALC** 14mg

ORANGE, ALMOND, AND OLIVE OIL CAKE

Not too sweet, this is a grown-up dessert that's perfect with a cup of afternoon tea. Kamut flour, cornmeal, and ground almonds give it a rustic texture.

HANDS-ON TIME: 20 MINUTES TOTAL TIME: 1 HOUR 55 MINUTES

Cake:
- ⅔ cup slivered almonds, toasted
- 7.25 ounces Kamut flour (about 1½ cups)
- ½ cup whole-grain cornmeal
- 1 teaspoon baking powder
- ½ teaspoon salt
- ½ teaspoon baking soda
- ¾ cup plus 2 tablespoons packed brown sugar
- 1½ tablespoons grated orange rind
- ¾ cup fresh orange juice
- ½ cup extra-virgin olive oil
- ¼ cup nonfat buttermilk
- 1 teaspoon vanilla extract
- 2 large eggs
- Baking spray with flour

Orange slices:
- 1 whole navel orange
- 1¼ cups water
- ½ cup granulated sugar
- Cooking spray

1. Preheat oven to 375°F.

2. To prepare cake, place almonds in a mini food processor; pulse until finely ground (do not go so far as to make nut butter). Weigh or lightly spoon flour into dry measuring cups; level with a knife. Combine flour, almonds, cornmeal, baking powder, salt, and baking soda, stirring with a whisk.

3. Place brown sugar and next 6 ingredients (through eggs) in a large bowl; beat with a mixer at low and then medium speed until well blended (about 1 minute). Add flour mixture; beat at low speed 1 minute or until well combined. Pour batter into a 9-inch springform pan coated with baking spray. Bake at 375°F for 35 minutes or until a wooden pick inserted in center comes out clean. Cool in pan on a wire rack 10 minutes. Run a thin knife around edge of pan; remove sides and bottom of pan. Cool cake on rack.

4. Meanwhile, to prepare orange slices, cut orange in half lengthwise; cut into ¼-inch-thick slices. (You will only need 12 for the final cake, but it's good to have extras.) Bring 1¼ cups water and granulated sugar to a boil in a medium skillet. Add orange slices. Reduce heat to medium, and cook 20 minutes or until slices are translucent and liquid is syrupy and reduced to about 2 or 3 tablespoons. Turn slices occasionally as they cook. Carefully remove slices from syrup; cool on a wire rack coated with cooking spray. Reserve syrup.

5. Brush warm cake with syrup. Arrange 12 orange slices on top of cake.

SERVES 12 *(serving size: 1 slice)*
CALORIES 302; **FAT** 13.3g (sat 1.8g, mono 8.8g, poly 1.9g); **PROTEIN** 5g; **CARB** 44g; **FIBER** 3g; **SUGARS** 27g (est. added sugars 24g); **CHOL** 31mg; **IRON** 1mg; **SODIUM** 208mg; **CALC** 68mg

BOURBON—BROWN SUGAR POUND CAKE

Patrick, my husband, offered the best praise ever when he suggested that I bring this cake to the next family reunion, where the great Southern cooks are known for their excellent pound cakes. Steeping a vanilla bean in canola oil, a secret I learned from our nutrition editor, Sidney Fry, turns the bland oil into something sweet and almost creamy—a great trick for boosting flavor while reducing sat fat. The bourbon in the glaze cooks for a bit, so the flavor is soft and more vanilla-forward, not alcohol-hot.

HANDS-ON TIME: 35 MINUTES TOTAL TIME: 1 HOUR 40 MINUTES

6 tablespoons canola oil
1 vanilla bean, split lengthwise
1¾ cups packed brown sugar
½ cup butter, softened
2 large eggs
11 ounces whole-wheat pastry flour (about 2¾ cups)
2 tablespoons baking powder
½ teaspoon salt
¾ cup evaporated fat-free milk
Baking spray with flour
¼ cup granulated sugar
¼ cup bourbon

1. Preheat oven to 350°F.

2. Heat oil and vanilla bean in a small saucepan until bean begins to bubble. Remove from heat; let stand 10 minutes or until mixture reaches room temperature. Scrape seeds from vanilla bean; add to oil. Discard bean.

3. Place brown sugar, butter, and vanilla oil in a large bowl; beat with a mixer at medium speed until well blended (about 5 minutes). Add eggs, 1 at a time, beating well after each addition.

4. Weigh or lightly spoon flour into dry measuring cups; level with a knife. Combine flour, baking powder, and salt, stirring with a whisk. Beating at low speed, add flour mixture and milk alternately to sugar mixture; beat until blended. Pour mixture into a 10-cup Bundt pan coated with baking spray. Bake at 350°F for 48 minutes or until a wooden pick inserted in center comes out clean. Cool in pan on a wire rack 10 minutes; remove cake from pan. Invert onto wire rack.

5. While cake bakes, bring granulated sugar and bourbon to a simmer in a small saucepan; cook 2 minutes or until sugar dissolves, stirring occasionally. Cool slightly. Brush bourbon mixture over warm cake until all is absorbed. Cool cake completely.

SERVES 16 *(serving size: 1 slice)*
CALORIES 303; **FAT** 12g (sat 4.2g, mono 5.1g, poly 1.8g); **PROTEIN** 4g; **CARB** 44g; **FIBER** 3g; **SUGARS** 28g (est. added sugars 27g); **CHOL** 39mg; **IRON** 1mg; **SODIUM** 216mg; **CALC** 111mg

CARROT CAKE CUPCAKES

These cupcakes are incredibly moist, and the spelt flour gives them a subtle nuttiness that's terrific with the spices and carrots. Macerating the carrots in a little sugar at the beginning is a trick I picked up from Cooking Light's dessert goddess, Deb Wise; this step starts breaking down the carrot's fibers so that each bite of the cupcake is tender.

HANDS-ON TIME: 20 MINUTES TOTAL TIME: 1 HOUR 14 MINUTES

Cupcakes:
- 1½ cups finely shredded carrot
- ¾ cup granulated sugar, divided
- Cooking spray
- 4⅞ ounces spelt flour (about 1¼ cups)
- 1 teaspoon baking soda
- 1 teaspoon ground cinnamon
- ½ teaspoon salt
- ½ teaspoon baking powder
- ½ teaspoon ground ginger
- ½ cup canola oil
- 1 teaspoon vanilla extract
- 2 large eggs

Frosting:
- 4 ounces ⅓-less-fat cream cheese, softened (about ½ cup)
- 2 tablespoons butter, softened
- ¼ teaspoon vanilla extract
- ⅛ teaspoon salt
- 1 cup powdered sugar

1. To prepare cupcakes, combine carrot and 2 tablespoons granulated sugar; toss well to coat. Let stand 10 minutes.

2. Preheat oven to 350°F. Line 12 muffin cups with cupcake liners; coat liners with cooking spray.

3. Weigh or lightly spoon flour into dry measuring cups; level with a knife. Combine flour and next 5 ingredients (through ginger), stirring with a whisk.

4. Place 10 tablespoons sugar, oil, 1 teaspoon vanilla, and eggs in a large bowl. Beat with a mixer at medium speed until well blended (about 2 minutes). Beat in carrot mixture. Add flour mixture; beat at low speed just until combined.

5. Divide batter among prepared muffin cups. Bake at 350°F for 20 minutes or until a wooden pick inserted in center comes out clean. Remove cupcakes from pan; cool completely on a wire rack.

6. To prepare frosting, place cream cheese and butter in a medium bowl; beat with a mixer at medium speed until well blended (about 1 minute). Beat in ¼ teaspoon vanilla and ⅛ teaspoon salt. Add powdered sugar; beat at low speed just until combined (do not overbeat). Spread about 1 tablespoon frosting over each cupcake.

A NOTE ABOUT CANOLA OIL

You'll notice that I call for canola oil a good bit. I do so because it's a versatile oil with a high smoke point and neutral flavor—and because it has the lowest saturated fat content of all the fats, plus a higher beneficial omega-3 fatty acid content than most cooking oils. The majority of canola oil you'll find in supermarkets (about 93%) is made from GMO canola, but there are other options if you'd rather avoid this while reaping the same health benefits. Just look for products with the non-GMO verified stamp, or buy organic canola oil.

SERVES 12 *(serving size: 1 cupcake)*
CALORIES 264; **FAT** 14.4g (sat 3.4g, mono 7.3g, poly 3g); **PROTEIN** 3g; **CARB** 32g; **FIBER** 1g; **SUGARS** 24g (est. added sugars 22g); **CHOL** 43mg; **IRON** 0mg; **SODIUM** 315mg; **CALC** 33mg

CHOCOLATE MOLTEN LAVA CAKES

Quite possibly the sexiest item on the dessert menu, chocolate lava cake is all about decadence. A dense batter of chocolate, butter, sugar, and eggs is slightly underbaked to create a gooey, liquid center. This spectacular version preserves all the indulgence, while dramatically cutting the calories. The whole-wheat pastry flour adds a bit of structure to preserve texture. Canola oil subs in for some of the butter, tenderizing the cake with less saturated fat.

As the cakes bake, the reserved melted-chocolate mixture sinks into the middle, providing a molten flow when you fork into the finished cakes. If you prefer a more soufflé-like cake, add all the chocolate into the egg mixture during step 3.

HANDS-ON TIME: 20 MINUTES TOTAL TIME: 2 HOURS

3 ounces high-quality dark or bittersweet chocolate (60% to 70% cacao), chopped

3 tablespoons unsalted butter

2 tablespoons canola oil

3 ounces whole-wheat pastry flour (about ⅔ cup)

½ cup unsweetened cocoa

1½ teaspoons baking powder

¼ teaspoon kosher salt

½ cup granulated sugar

½ cup packed brown sugar

½ teaspoon vanilla extract

3 large eggs

Baking spray with flour

Powdered sugar (optional)

1. Combine chooclate, butter, and oil in the top of a double boiler. Cook over simmering water until chocolate almost fully melts, stirring gently with a spatula. Remove top of double boiler; stir until chocolate fully melts.

2. Weigh or lightly spoon flour into dry measuring cups; level with a knife. Combine flour, cocoa, baking powder, and salt in a bowl; stir well with a whisk.

3. Place granulated sugar, brown sugar, vanilla, and eggs in a large bowl; beat with a mixer at medium speed until light and fluffy (about 2 minutes). Set aside 2½ tablespoons chocolate mixture. Gradually pour remaining chocolate mixture in a thin stream over egg mixture, beating at medium speed. Gently fold flour mixture into egg mixture. Divide batter evenly among 10 (5-ounce) ramekins coated with baking spray. Working with 1 ramekin at a time, spoon ¾ teaspoon reserved chocolate mixture into center, pushing teaspoon toward center of batter. Repeat with remaining ramekins and chocolate mixture. Arrange ramekins on a jelly-roll pan. Cover and refrigerate 1 hour.

4. Preheat oven to 400°F.

5. Let ramekins stand at room temperature 15 minutes. Uncover and bake at 400°F for 13 minutes or until cakes are puffy and slightly crusty on top (centers will not be set). Place a dessert plate on top of each ramekin. Using a dry kitchen towel to hold ramekin, invert each cake onto plate. Garnish with powdered sugar, if desired. Serve immediately.

SERVES 10 (*serving size: 1 cake*)
CALORIES 249; **FAT** 11.8g (sat 5.1g, mono 4.4g, poly 1.3g); **PROTEIN** 4g; **CARB** 35g; **FIBER** 3g; **SUGARS** 24g (est. added sugars 24g); **CHOL** 65mg; **IRON** 2mg; **SODIUM** 135mg; **CALC** 71mg

CHOCOLATE-BERRY LAYER CAKE

I set out to prove that you can make a luscious showstopper dessert with 100% whole grains, no refined flour. After a few attempts, this stunning layer cake, made with finely milled whole-wheat pastry flour, came together. Buttermilk and canola oil keep the cake moist, a layer of yogurt cream (whipped cream stretched and lightened with Greek yogurt) adds richness, and the chocolate glaze on top takes this into uh-mah-gah territory. My husband said he likes it better than any other chocolate cake he's tried— that the whole wheat actually forwards the chocolate flavor in a way that white flour doesn't. And so now this is what I bake for his birthday. We love this dessert, and if you make it, you'll see why.

HANDS-ON TIME: 40 MINUTES TOTAL TIME: 1 HOUR 40 MINUTES

Cake:

   Cooking spray

7.33 ounces whole-wheat pastry flour (about 1¾ cups)

 ¾ cup unsweetened cocoa

1½ teaspoons baking powder

 ½ teaspoon salt

 ½ teaspoon baking soda

1½ cups granulated sugar

 ½ cup canola oil

 2 large eggs

 1 cup nonfat buttermilk

 ⅓ cup warm water

1½ teaspoons vanilla extract

Glaze:

 ½ cup powdered sugar

 ¼ cup unsweetened cocoa

 2 tablespoons 2% reduced-fat milk

 1 ounce semisweet chocolate chips

 1 tablespoon butter

   Dash of salt

Yogurt cream:

 ½ cup heavy whipping cream

 ⅓ cup powdered sugar

 ½ cup plain 2% reduced-fat Greek yogurt

 ¼ teaspoon vanilla extract

Remaining ingredients:

 1 cup fresh blackberries

 1 (6-ounce) container fresh raspberries

 1 cup fresh cherries

1. Preheat oven to 350°F.

2. To prepare cake, coat 2 (9-inch) round cake pans with cooking spray; line bottoms of pans with parchment or wax paper. Coat paper with cooking spray; set aside.

3. Weigh or lightly spoon flour into dry measuring cups; level with a knife. Combine flour and next 4 ingredients (through baking soda), stirring with a whisk.

4. Place granulated sugar, oil, and eggs in a large bowl; beat with a mixer at medium speed until well blended (about 2 minutes). Beat in buttermilk, ⅓ cup warm water, and 1½ teaspoons vanilla. Add flour mixture; beat on low speed until just combined, and then beat on medium speed 1 minute.

(CONTINUED)

5. Divide batter between prepared pans. Bake at 350°F for 23 to 25 minutes or until a wooden pick inserted in center comes out clean. Cool in pans on a wire rack 10 minutes. Remove from pans; carefully remove paper. Cool completely.

6. To prepare glaze, combine ½ cup powdered sugar and next 5 ingredients (through dash of salt) in a small saucepan over low heat. Cook 3 minutes or until butter and chocolate melt, stirring constantly. Cool slightly.

7. To prepare yogurt cream, place cream and ⅓ cup powdered sugar in a large bowl; beat with a mixer at high speed until stiff peaks form (about 1½ minutes). Add yogurt and ¼ teaspoon vanilla; beat at high speed until well combined.

8. Place 1 cake layer on a cake stand or plate; top evenly with yogurt cream, leaving a ½-inch border. Top with remaining cake layer; carefully pour chocolate glaze over top of cake, spreading to edges. Top with berries; arrange cherries on top.

SERVES 16 (serving size: 1 slice)
CALORIES 296; **FAT** 12.7g (sat 3.4g, mono 5.9g, poly 2.3g); **PROTEIN** 5g; **CARB** 45g; **FIBER** 5g; **SUGARS** 29g (est. added sugars 26g); **CHOL** 36mg; **IRON** 1mg; **SODIUM** 197mg; **CALC** 74mg

NUTRITIONAL INFORMATION

HOW TO USE IT AND WHY

At *Cooking Light*, our team of food editors, experienced cooks, and registered dietitians builds recipes with whole foods and whole grains, and bigger portions of plants and seafood than meat. We emphasize oil-based fats more than saturated, and we promote a balanced diet low in processed foods and added sugars (those added during processing or preparation).

Not only do we focus on quality ingredients, but we also adhere to a rigorous set of nutrition guidelines that govern calories, saturated fat, sodium, and sugar based on various recipe categories. The numbers in each category are derived from the most recent set of USDA Dietary Guidelines for Americans, as shown in the following chart. As you look through our numbers, remember that the nutrition stats included with each recipe are for a single serving. When we build recipes, we look at each dish in context of the role it plays in an average day: A one-dish meal that fills a plate with protein, starch, and vegetables will weigh more heavily in calories, saturated fat, and sodium than a recipe for roasted chicken thighs. Similarly, a bowl of ice cream may contain more than half of your daily added sugar recommendation, but balances out when the numbers are folded into a day's worth of healthy food prepared at home.

When reading the chart, remember that recommendations vary by gender and age; other factors, including lifestyle, weight, and your own health—for example, if you're pregnant or breast-feeding or if you have genetic factors such as risk for hypertension—all need consideration. Go to choosemyplate.gov for your own individualized plan.

IN OUR NUTRITIONAL ANALYSIS, WE USE THESE ABBREVIATIONS

sat	saturated fat	CARB	carbohydrates	g	gram
mono	monosaturated fat	CHOL	cholesterol	mg	milligram
poly	polyunsaturated fat	CALC	calcium	est.	estimated (added sugars)

DAILY NUTRITION GUIDE

	Women ages 25 to 50	Women over 50	Men ages 25 to 50	Men over 50
Calories	2,000	2,000*	2,700	2,500
Protein	50 g	50 g	63 g	60 g
Fat	65 g*	65 g*	88 g*	83 g*
Saturated Fat	20 g*	20 g*	27 g*	25 g*
Carbohydrates	304 g	304 g	410 g	375 g
Fiber	25 g to 35 g	25 g to 35 g	25 g to 35 g	25 g to 35 g
Added Sugars	38 g	38 g	38 g	38 g
Cholesterol	300 mg*	300 mg*	300 mg*	300 mg*
Iron	18 mg	8 mg	8 mg	8 mg
Sodium	2,300 mg*	1,500 mg*	2,300 mg*	1,500 mg*
Calcium	1,000 mg	1,200 mg	1,000 mg	1,000 mg

*Or less, for optimum health

Nutritional values used in our calculations either come from The Food Processor, Version 10.4 (ESHA Research), or are provided by food manufacturers.

METRIC EQUIVALENTS

COOKING/OVEN TEMPERATURES

	Fahrenheit	Celsius	Gas Mark
Freeze Water	32° F	0° C	
Room Temp.	68° F	20° C	
Boil Water	212° F	100° C	
Bake	325° F	160° C	3
	350° F	180° C	4
	375° F	190° C	5
	400° F	200° C	6
	425° F	220° C	7
	450° F	230° C	8
Broil			Grill

LIQUID INGREDIENTS BY VOLUME

¼ tsp					=	1 ml	
½ tsp					=	2 ml	
1 tsp					=	5 ml	
3 tsp	=	1 Tbsp	=	½ fl oz		15 ml	
2 Tbsp	=	⅛ cup	=	1 fl oz	=	30 ml	
4 Tbsp	=	¼ cup	=	2 fl oz	=	60 ml	
5⅓ Tbsp	=	⅓ cup	=	3 fl oz	=	80 ml	
8 Tbsp	=	½ cup	=	4 fl oz	=	120 ml	
10⅔ Tbsp	=	⅔ cup	=	5 fl oz	=	160 ml	
12 Tbsp	=	¾ cup	=	6 fl oz	=	180 ml	
16 Tbsp	=	1 cup	=	8 fl oz	=	240 ml	
1 pt	=	2 cups	=	16 fl oz	=	480 ml	
1 qt	=	4 cups	=	32 fl oz	=	960 ml	
				33 fl oz	=	1000 ml	= 1 l

DRY INGREDIENTS BY WEIGHT

(To convert ounces to grams, multiply the number of ounces by 30.)

1 oz	=	¹⁄₁₆ lb	=	30 g
4 oz	=	¼ lb	=	120 g
8 oz	=	½ lb	=	240 g
12 oz	=	¾ lb	=	360 g
16 oz	=	1 lb	=	480 g

LENGTH

(To convert inches to centimeters, multiply inches by 2.5.)

1 in					=	2.5 cm	
12 in	=	1 ft			=	30 cm	
36 in	=	3 ft	=	1 yd	=	90 cm	
40 in	=					100 cm	= 1 m

EQUIVALENTS FOR DIFFERENT TYPES OF INGREDIENTS

Standard Cup	Fine Powder (ex. flour)	Grain (ex. rice)	Granular (ex. sugar)	Liquid Solids (ex. butter)	Liquid (ex. milk)
1	140 g	150 g	190 g	200 g	240 ml
¾	105 g	113 g	143 g	150 g	180 ml
⅔	93 g	100 g	125 g	133 g	160 ml
½	70 g	75 g	95 g	100 g	120 ml
⅓	47 g	50 g	63 g	67 g	80 ml
¼	35 g	38 g	48 g	50 g	60 ml
⅛	18 g	19 g	24 g	25 g	30 ml

RESOURCES

Now you can find many whole grains at your local grocery, big-box store, or natural foods market. This is a short list of sources and manufacturers to explore when purchasing for your whole grain pantry.

Anson Mills
www.ansonmills.com
Grits, farro, oats, and some whole-grain flours

Arrowhead Mills
www.arrowheadmills.com
Brown rice, steel-cut oatmeal, whole-grain flours

Bionaturae
www.bionaturae.com
Whole-grain pasta

Bob's Red Mill
www.bobsredmill.com
Almost every whole grain and many whole-grain flours

Freekeh Foods
www.freekeh-foods.com
Organic cracked freekeh

Hodgson Mill
www.hodgsonmill.com
Steel-cut oatmeal, whole-grain pasta

Jovial Foods
www.jovialfoods.com
Brown rice pasta, einkorn berries, einkorn flour

King Arthur Flour
www.kingarthurflour.com
Barley, whole-grain flours

Shiloh Farm
www.shilohfarms.com
Amaranth, barley, brown rice flours, buckwheat groats, bulgur, Kamut, teff

Lundberg Family Farms
www.lundberg.com
Brown rice, brown rice pasta

Near East
www.neareast.com
Quinoa

Wild Oats Marketplace
www.wildoats.com
Whole-grain pasta

ACKNOWLEDGMENTS

I am fortunate to have the support of wonderful people whose talent and generosity helped bring this book to life. You have my deepest gratitude; please know that I raise a glass of bourbon in your honor.

I would be nothing, would have nothing of value, without my family. I married the funniest man on the planet, and for that I am grateful every day. Patrick, thank you for turning your sharp wit on the chaos of recipe development and for helping me laugh at myself whenever I tried too hard. Without that humor, we might have all lost our minds. Thanks, too, for building me the beautiful new kitchen cart to hold the mountains of ingredients required to create these recipes; I love that you knew to call my bluff, that you understood my agonizing over more kitchen storage was just a way for me to procrastinate. For your patience, encouragement, and belief in me, I thank you. To our twin boys, Connor and Daniel, thank you for your honest, insightful feedback, and for the adventurous spirit with which you tried everything. To my parents, Dan and Suzie, thank you for teaching me that good food is worth the effort, even driving four hours each way for one memorable meal. I am lucky to have a best friend/sister-in-law who nurtures and takes care of me: Becky, thank you for always being there. And to my brother, Tim, thanks for helping me remember that I should never take myself too seriously.

To my dear friend and former boss, Scott Mowbray, thanks for volunteering me for this project in the first place. You knew it scared the hell out of me and that it was the best thing for me at the time. I am humbled by your unmatched wisdom and indebted to you for your advice and encouragement. Thanks for getting excited about my recipe ideas and for inspiring many new ones. And thanks for always pushing me to try new things; you have never steered me wrong.

To Keith Schroeder, I am deeply grateful for your unwavering faith in me. I have no idea what I did to deserve it and am still not convinced I do.

I am beholden to the entire *Cooking Light* staff for inspiring me with their passion and talent; so many great ideas are born here every day. Special thanks to Hunter Lewis for your expert guidance and counsel, and to Rachel Lasserre for your keen eye. Sidney Fry, thank you for your enthusiasm and your help; I could not have gotten through this without you.

Sincerest thanks to the Oxmoor House team for their partnership in this project. To my editor, Betty Wong, thank you for your patience and for helping turn my half-baked ideas into fully cooked ones. Callie Nash, Karen Rankin, and Julia Levy, I appreciate the great care you took with these recipes in the Test Kitchen; I so value your expertise and advice. Iain Bagwell and Hélène Dujardin, I am in awe of your talent; the photography is stunning. Heartfelt thanks to Victoria E. Cox and Nathan Carrabba for the beautiful food styling, and to Kay Clarke for the lovely prop styling. A million thanks for making this book so pretty!

To Ashley Sherrick and the folks at Bob's Red Mill, thank you for the boxes of grains and flours you sent me to play with. You truly do great work.

And Hugh Acheson, thanks so much for your support. You're definitely one of the good guys.

If I could, I would have all of you over together for dinner at my little house, where I'd fret over you, and we'd all laugh and tell stories while my dogs (and maybe my children) annoy you in a somewhat charming way. Short of that impossibility, I've gathered you here together on this page to raise a virtual toast. Thank you, thank you, from the bottom of my heart—*thank you*.

INDEX